# Restorative Justice Recalibrated

a trauma-informed approach to rebuilding
the web of relationships harmed by crime

By Alexis Franklin Osborn

*Restorative Justice Recalibrated: A Trauma-Informed Approach to Rebuilding the Web of Relationships Harmed by Crime*

Copyright © 2024. Alexis Franklin Osborn

All Rights Reserved. No part of this publication may be reproduced, distributed, or transmitted in any form or by any means, including photocopying, recording, or other electronic or mechanical methods, or by any information storage and retrieval system without the prior written permission of the publisher, except in the case of very brief quotations embodied in critical reviews and certain other noncommercial uses permitted by copyright law.

ISBN: 978-1-964638-00-3

First printing edition May 5, 2024.

www.resilienceprisonproject.com

a trauma-informed approach to rebuilding the web of relationships harmed by crime

# Contents

| | |
|---|---:|
| **Foreword** | 1 |
| **Preface** | 3 |
| **It was The End...** | 7 |
| **What is Restorative Justice Recalibrated?** | 12 |
|     History Proves the Wisdom of Restorative Justice | 14 |
|     A Childhood Experience as a Microcosm of Ancient Wisdom | 21 |
|     Departure from Ancient Wisdom | 22 |
| **What's Wrong With Me? No, What Happened to Me?** | 31 |
| **Resilience: Pygmalion's Influence and Trauma** | 41 |
|     Pygmalion Origins and Background | 41 |
|     Golem Effect and ACEs | 43 |
|     How Authority Influences Rehabilitation | 44 |
|     Applying the Principle for Yourself | 46 |
| **Hope Rising: The Bridge to Resilience** | 50 |
|     Three Phases of HOPE | 51 |
|     Bridging Hope and Resilience | 54 |
|     Cultivating Hope in Practice | 55 |
| **Building Community Resilience** | 59 |
|     Adverse Childhood Experiences in Context of Restorative Justice | 62 |
|     KISS Framework for Community Resilience | 67 |
|     NEAR Sciences | 70 |
|     Brain Networks and Their Needs | 82 |
|     The Individual Experience | 87 |
|     Know Your ROLES with Trauma | 91 |

| | |
|---|---:|
| Supportive Environments for Healing | 106 |
| Healing Networks Beyond Punishment | 107 |
| Resilience Inside Corrections | 108 |
| **Flow: Finding Balance and Resilience** | **112** |
| Flow in Context of Trauma and Resilience | 113 |
| Flow Map: Optimizing Skill and Challenge | 114 |
| Reframing Threat Responses and Applying Flow | 125 |
| **ACEs, Crime, and Empathy Deficits** | **128** |
| The Resilience Prescription | 132 |
| Rat Park Experiment | 134 |
| In-grouping, Out-Grouping, and the Retributive Justice Paradox | 139 |
| Empathy and Social Exclusion | 145 |
| Empathy's Role in Human Connection | 148 |
| Empathic Failure and Crime | 151 |
| PERMA Model and Well Being | 152 |
| **Holistic Transformation in Correctional Education** | **157** |
| Transformative Learning | 158 |
| Integrated Framework of Resilience Prison Project | 164 |
| **Restorative Justice: A Needs Centered Approach** | **169** |
| Understanding Your Needs | 173 |
| Meeting Your Needs via Restorative Justice | 176 |
| Holistic Spectrum of Needs | 179 |
| **Unlocking Healing Through Restorative Dialogue** | **182** |
| Critical Components of Restorative Dialogue | 184 |
| Facilitating Restorative Role Play | 185 |
| The Transformative Potential of Dialogue | 186 |
| Unlocking Your Journey with Nonviolent Communication | 186 |

## Mindfulness in Restorative Justice — **191**
   Foundations of Mindfulness — 193
   Recalibrating Toward Mindfulness in Restorative Justice — 195
   Mindfulness Exercises for Restorative Justice Participants — 197
      Breath Awareness Exercise — 197
      Body Scan Meditation — 198
      Observation of Surroundings — 200
      Gratitude Journaling — 201
      Mindful Listening — 203
      Walking Meditation — 205
      Sensory Awareness Exercise — 207
      Mindful Reflection — 209
   Emotional Regulation Strategies and Framework — 212
   Mindfulness in Restorative Dialogue — 216

## Integrating Restorative Justice into Daily Life — **219**

## Stories of Transformation — **222**
   Jeremy: From Victimhood to Victory — 222
   Louise: How Being Believed In Helps Us Reclaim Our Power — 224
   Devan: Finding the Faith that Leads to First Hand Knowledge — 230

## Facilitation Guidelines for Mock Parole Hearing — **235**
   Overview of Purpose — 235
   Introduce the Approaches — 236
   Set the Stage — 237
   Roles, Briefings, Expectations — 240
   NVC Preparations — 241
   ACEs and a Resilience Perspective — 243
   Mock Parole Hearing Structure — 245
   RPP Participant's Questionnaire — 257

| | |
|---|---|
| **Facilitation Guidelines for Restorative Dialogues** | 258 |
| Introductions | 259 |
| Building Connections | 260 |
| Moving Beyond | 271 |
| **Resilience Prison Project Participant Questionnaire** | 278 |
| **ACEs Quiz** | 285 |
| **42 Resilience Building Blocks** | 288 |
| **Acknowledgements** | 290 |
| **Glossary** | 292 |
| **References** | 299 |
| **About the Author** | 307 |

## Dedication

*To Austin, my son, who I wasn't able to be the father I had dreamed of being, but who I am more proud of than any father you could have had instead of me. I offer this book to you, buddy, as my gift. It is a testament to the life I have lived without you while holding onto you with my whole heart. I humbly pray that I have a place in yours as well.*

\*\*\*

a trauma-informed approach to rebuilding the web of relationships harmed by crime

*"We are all travelers in the wilderness of this world, and the best we can find in our travels is an honest friend."*

~Robert Louis Stevenson

# Foreword

As someone who has spent a lot of time working in trauma-informed care and restorative justice, I was very interested in reading Alexis Franklin Osborn's book *Restorative Justice Recalibrated*. I know Alexis personally because we share a deep commitment to helping people change for the better, and this connection makes me see his work in a special light. However, I believe that even people who don't know Alexis will be deeply touched and interested by the concepts and ideas in this book.

*Restorative Justice Recalibrated* is more than just a book. It's a source of hope and a genuine call for a kinder, more effective way of dealing with rehabilitation, written by someone whose life has been deeply affected by the justice system he wants to improve. Alexis's story is one of deep reflection and constant effort to better himself and society, and it gives us a fresh perspective on crime, punishment, and making things right again. His experience and honest writing style make this book educational and genuinely inspiring.

For those who have a personal connection to the criminal justice system, this book will resonate deeply. It doesn't just provide understanding, it offers tangible ways to support and heal. Alexis's voice, a blend of vulnerability and strength, illuminates a space often shrouded in despair, making this book a personal journey for each reader.

This book does more than just teach; it sparks a fire in us to challenge our own views and motivates us to make a difference in our communities. While achieving "World Peace" might seem far-fetched, the real stories in this book push us closer to that dream, one person at a time.

Let Alexis's journey serve as a catalyst, his insights as a compass, and the wisdom within these pages as a driving force. By taking action, we not only foster the potential for change in others, but also contribute to the creation of a more compassionate and just world. A world where the ripple effects of restorative justice bring us closer to the peace we all yearn for.

Rick Griffin
*Community Resilience Initiative*
*Executive Director*

***

*"If you treat an individual as he is, he will remain how he is. But if you treat him as if he were what he ought to be and could be, he will become what he ought to be and could be."*

~Johannes Wolfgang von Goethe

# Preface

Dear Reader,

As we set out on this journey together, I extend my right hand of friendship while offering gleanings from a life lived behind bars—a challenging yet positive transformational journey of over 26 years. I am intimately familiar with the hope for change within a system that I have called home for a longer time than my life before incarceration. What follows is a response to the echoes of longing I hear as a collective cry for change.

I have felt the gaps, witnessed the flaws, and yearned for a more humane approach to justice. This work acknowledges my imperfections and the system under scrutiny.

Much of my adult life has been spent exploring, examining, and finding ways to remove the stick from my eye so I can help others remove the sticks from theirs. I hope my writing reflects this.

What follows in this book is my attempt to contribute meaningfully to a world that I realize often silences voices like mine that speak out from behind bars. The content is the result of study, introspection, and lived experience—in what, for me at times, has been an imagined monastery, laboratory, and college, all the while acknowledging the cold embrace of concrete walls and razor-wire fences.

This plea for change also reaches out to and speaks on behalf of the countless hearts of those harmed by crime–who, without proper guidance–have been directed by cultural conditioning and the current criminal justice system to find fulfillment via retribution.

Before going further, I want to depart from the narrative briefly and sincerely acknowledge the harm my actions have created for so many people. Somebody lost a life because of something I did. This life was precious, had value, and left this earth way too soon. No amount of restitution could ever make up for the tremendous pain and loss that has resulted from the unskilled acts that led to that death.

I am genuinely sorry for what I have done, what I failed to do, and the pain and suffering I caused for the family, friends, and members of our larger community. I, like countless others I have met along the way, yearn for a way to help heal these wounds. My life has become oriented toward that goal despite my inability to connect directly with those most hurt by my actions or make adequate restitution for the harm I have caused.

My longing for change and dissatisfaction with the criminal justice system is in no way a reflection of my lack of care for those harmed or a lack of accountability for what I have done. What follows is also not an attempt to minimize my guilt or my responsibility to make restitution for my actions. Instead, it serves as a painful recognition of the inadequacies within a system that often fails to address the root causes of harm or offer meaningful pathways for the rehabilitation of all parties.

Trauma and its impacts have affected all those involved in criminal justice. For true healing to occur, we must acknowledge this.

Dear reader, will you join me on this quest to recalibrate restorative justice? It's a worthy cause that can transform lives and create peaceful, thriving communities. It is my sincere hope that what follows encourages insights and transformative growth. It is focused particularly on those in custody. It may also serve facilitators, practitioners, and those involved with the criminal justice system who wish to imagine what it is like to walk a mile in the shoes of those in custody.

May it inspire a renewed commitment to empathy, understanding, and connection for all who participate. Pure authentic love expressed empathically is undoubtedly the only force capable of truly healing our individual and collective trauma.

We will examine restorative justice within the integrated framework of the Resilience Prison Project. It is an approach echoing larger societal aspirations. We hope to be the change we want to see in the world.

I hope you may use this book as a guide for your restorative justice journey and can appreciate its relevance in reshaping lives within the correctional environment and contributing to a more compassionate and just society. This value is equally true for those among us who may never see the other side of these razor-wire fences.

As restorative justice agents, some may help transform our culture from the inside out. Your way of paying it forward is to reshape the lives you touch inside the prisons that have become your home.

Finally, rest assured, brothers, sisters, friends, innovators, and advocates: the day will come when the times we live through now may be seen as barbaric. A refined humanity purified by travails born of our mistakes will look back with curiosity at how today's humanity immersed ourselves so far into such a materialistic era.

They will marvel at how we could both create harm as you and I have created and respond in the way that so many involved in our justice system have responded to it. They will feel gratitude for the shifts that occurred through efforts like ours that laid the foundation for a different world. In the meantime, let us hew the path toward those folks looking back with the choices that will make such a future possible.

Sincerely,

Alexis Franklin Osborn

***

a trauma-informed approach to rebuilding the web of relationships harmed by crime

*"What we call the beginning is often the end. And to make an end is to make a beginning. The end is where we start from."*

~T.S. Elliot

# It was *The End...*

Long ago, in a place where people once lived together in harmony, humanity lost its intimate connection with nature and became increasingly divided.

Forces of separation pierced human hearts. It led them to forget their true divine nature. They were collectively falling asleep.

What used to be a tight-knit community built upon foundations of safety and connection increasingly turned into one of strangers trapped in their worlds.

Less-than-nurturing experiences awakened deep fears of losing control. Trauma magnified itself and made neighbors seem like potential enemies.

Rising threats led the society, initially governed by wise councils and communal bonds, to distance themselves through authoritative rulership. They adopted laws that estranged relationships when harm was committed. Punishment was favored over dialogue and understanding.

Isolated barren land ringed with high fences was built to ensure no return for those expelled. If the "Powers that Be" didn't have to witness the effects of their systems directly, they would be easier to perpetuate.

In this isolation, these ousted unknowns started getting to know one another. Banishment forced upon them by structures of domination eventually led them to reach out to each other. Over time, these exiles tried to regain a sense of belonging.

Being wired for connection, they started living as friends. Quite naturally, they combined what little they had. Without as many artificial distractions, they slowly began to experience glimpses of being awake again, i.e., awake from their slumber of disconnection.

Over time, more exiles joined the growing community of outcasts. Yet haunting shadows from the past society still followed. The learned behaviors caused some to perpetuate the same trauma responses that led to their banishment. These individuals, too, created places of exile within their newfound community, constructing walls that could further separate those deemed as bad people.

In some sections, exiles became worse instead of better as the increasingly fear-based struggle to survive exploited the ugliest from the newfound societies.

And so, it went on until there were many outcasts within exile who each sought protection from danger in the community on the one hand while still being responsible for isolating others just like themselves on the other. Fleeing from the consequences of their actions but inadvertently rebuilding the worst of what they had left behind into their new culture. The hurt among them hurt others.

Among all those who had continued to conform to the culture of sleepers, a wise, reflective person came forth from within this expanding society of exiles.

He sought to draw from the best of the culture he had been removed from. Having significantly suffered himself, he had both observed and experienced various instances of injustice, giving birth to a wisdom of travail and a resilience of adversity.

He questioned the system's effectiveness, which seemed to create the opposite of what was intended, and instead drew out the best in the people around him. The memories living among them about when forgiveness and connection prevailed returned to their minds, as did the longing for an alternative path back to it.

This visionary worked his way around the people in exile, offering love and compassion to those harmed and those creating harm. Instead of expelling anyone out of their midst, they fostered dialogue, advocating that reconciliation would be a complicated but worthy process for lasting change.

Those who had committed harm were challenged to mourn the harmful behavior of those they hurt correctly. They were taught to clearly understand the consequences of their actions and get actively involved in making up for it.

The people who had been harmed were encouraged to experience healing, which meant cleansing the wounds properly and facing the people who had hurt them. With support, they would help restore the person who had harmed them back into the larger community.

It wasn't condoning the harmful acts, but it was accepting the people who acted harmfully. In doing so, they transformed their perspectives so that threat responses could return to safety. Natural giving became a common experience among these folks as empathy nurtured the depths of connection.

As this vision was embraced by the awakened in the society, many changes began to occur. The collective trauma began to transform into community resilience.

Educators emerged among these reformed individuals who taught others and helped end unnatural lifestyles that came at such an expense to others. What followed was that vengeance evaporated from human hearts. The healed among the harmed also began to support others still infected with a desire for revenge and punishment.

Many strategies were implemented by the community that helped support the growth of safety, connection, and learning. They offered knowledge and insight about methods that could help restore relationships, reshape society, and reawaken what had fallen asleep in people.

Once lonely and desolate, this place of exile became a beacon of how humanity can transform fear and separation into understanding, forgiveness, and cooperation. Those who used to come from the society that banished the exiles to offer help now came to get insights they could take back to the world to help it.

And then, actual progress quickened. Ironically, the outcasts among humankind became an example of how love and empathy can improve everything. The once despised among society grew to become those capable of guiding humanity back to its true nature. Wherever people were forced by utter necessity to rediscover their true nature, wisdom, i.e., crystallized pain, etched itself into awakened souls.

Experience obtained from directly facing harm became a wise legacy passed over from those who no longer slept to those who seemed to be on the verge of waking. By reconciling and restoring justice, they shattered the chains linked from fear. The fences that formerly separated exiles from society were pulled down, and banishment became another memory.

Once again, a fire blazed in the heart of humanity, capable of warding off the infection from the gross materialism into which they had fallen. Echoes of this transformation reverberated throughout the world.

And it came to pass, as a testimony of forgiveness, reconciliation, and resilience, that humanity found once more that we could choose healing and unity over brokenness and banishment. The path toward peaceful, thriving communities was paved and was now illuminated by love radiating from human hearts.

The many journeys traveled upon such pathways for life would create innumerable chapters of hope and celebration. This, dear reader, is our story. From this day forward, may it also become our legacy.

And now, *The Beginning*.

***

*"In seeking justice, remember that the true measure lies not in punishment but in the restoration of humanity."*

~Howard Zehr

## What is Restorative Justice Recalibrated?

And what exactly do I mean by recalibrated?

Perhaps it would be best to use a metaphor that almost everyone can understand. In today's world, our technology moves so fast that a software update is almost always around the corner. Even on the inside, our issued tablets undergo updates regularly.

Imagine if, for argument's sake, your phone went offline. You could access what was on your actual phone but remained disconnected from everything else. A year passes, and you regain connectivity. To properly function again, the software has to undergo an update to accommodate the changes that happened over the previous year. In essence, the entire system must be recalibrated, i.e. adapted, to the new advances in the technology related to your device.

Similarly, Restorative Justice was introduced to our modern world and was trending for a time. It captivated us. Our societies have even adapted in some ways. Today, there are small pockets of enthusiasts and advocates who wave the flag and reiterate salient points of restorative justice, especially when it comes to those who have created harm and understanding the impact their actions had on those harmed. Still, only the writings and practices gathered from pioneers who introduced it so long ago seem to quietly reverberate through halls of justice presently silent to its call.

Meanwhile, many discoveries have been made. We know so much now from science, psychology, and the criminal justice system that, if applied to the restorative justice field, it would make it even more applicable and relevant today.

This vision to "recalibrate" restorative justice requires an update to its application. For restorative justice to truly thrive alongside a world that continues to evolve, it must incorporate what follows in some way. Otherwise, it may continue to deteriorate into forms special interest groups use to call attention to the trauma they have experienced but inadequately dealt with. Instead of packing restorative justice with more and more nutrients like an enriched smoothie, it will end up requiring a diet version just to keep an already unhealthy society still interested.

I hope for the sake of everything restorative justice stands for that what follows might help improve things so that it can be brought back online as an effective remedy for a system growing increasingly incapable of restoring justice. This is said with it in mind that like the rest of us, I look out into the world with limited insight.

For all I know, others like me feel this same call and are acting accordingly. If so, may we come together and strengthen the bridge to the world we envision so that others may find safe passage.

## History Proves the Wisdom of Restorative Justice

To acquaint ourselves with restorative justice, we first examine how the Indigenous practiced restorative justice. These are a few examples of how life was before we began compromising human values for so-called "progress."

Perhaps, like me, you also can look back at your own life and remember someone who lived by some of these principles. If not, it's never too late to become that person for someone else!

Long ago in our ancient history, human beings dwelled within, not without, nature. Our innate sense of justice was inspired by how this harmony with nature reflected in our way of life. The artificial constructs of today that seem to alienate us from each other were not present then.

Indigenous people thrived unfettered by such constraints. Today, we seem to be slowly returning to the principles of restorative justice even though we appear to have lost the relationship with nature that helped bring it about. Embarking on the journey into restorative justice, we uncover a transformative philosophy born from such times.

Today, many brave souls find themselves daring to challenge conventional norms. Some support adults in custody who have been offered little to no help in learning how to express ownership or offer voluntary restitution for what they've done.

Awakened to their authentic selves, they are like tuning forks struck and brought into proximity with others potentially keyed to the same pitch. They hope that by resonance, adults in custody might feel within themselves something beautiful arising from who they really are.

Consider this your invitation to explore and experience the foundational principles where deep roots intertwine with a fresh perspective on healing, accountability, and fostering communal harmony. It is genuinely about returning to who and what we were born to be and giving ourselves the freedom to pursue it.

## Reconnecting with Indigenous Wisdom

When we begin combing through history, we find that the ancient wisdom of Indigenous people outshines our current best attempts at justice. There appears to be an intrinsic understanding across many cultures that a community-level response was required to restore order and harmony among the people when the harm occurred.

The Resilience Prison Project (RPP) calls attention to the vital nature of indigenous justice in one of our "Remembrances" drawn from Jack Kornfield's book *The Art of Forgiveness, Loving, Kindness, and Peace*. He describes the Babemba tribe of South Africa's Forgiveness Ritual, which is reminiscent of the wisdom we will be referring to, as shown in the following excerpt:

> *"In the Babemba tribe of South Africa when a person acts irresponsibly or unjustly, he is placed in the center of the village, alone and unfettered. All work ceases, and every man, woman, and child in the village gathers in a large circle around the accused individual.*
>
> *Then, each person in the tribe speaks to the accused, one at a time, each recalling the good things the person in the center of the circle has done in his lifetime. Every incident, every experience that can be recalled with any detail and accuracy, is recounted.*
>
> *All his positive attributes, good deeds, strengths, and kindnesses are recited carefully and at length. This tribal ceremony often lasts for several*

> *days. In the end, the tribal circle is broken, a joyous celebration occurs, and the person is symbolically and literally welcomed back into the tribe."*

Far different from the courtrooms you and I entered following the harms we created, these tribal circles represented both an acknowledgment of their roles in shaping the lives of those who erred as well as the roles in restoring them to their authentic selves.

To restore justice today, we must gather again in communal circles led by those in touch with the element needing restoration in those creating harm and those receiving it. Join us on a journey of self-discovery, transformation, and renewal. Let us recalibrate our hearts toward restoration that justice may follow.

## Maori People and Peacemaking Circles

"Whanaungatanga" is about a sense of family connection and belonging to the Maori people of New Zealand. This concept emphasizes the kind of communal living that makes peacemaking circles among the restorative practices that address harm within their communities. Such traditional practices date back centuries to their indigenous ancestors.

Exploring the Maori people's broader history and encounters with European settlers is essential. The following table breaks down the evolutionary phases crucial to understanding the historical significance of Maori Peacemaking Circles.

---

✔ **Pre-Colonial Maori Society**. Before the arrival of European colonizers in the late 18th century, the Maori lived in tribal communities with a rich oral tradition, solid communal ties, and well-defined social structures. Conflict resolution within these communities often relied on traditional practices grounded in collective decision-making and a deep sense of interconnectedness.

✔ **European Colonization.** The colonization of New Zealand by Europeans, starting with Captain James Cook's arrival in 1769, marked a significant shift in Maori society. The introduction of European legal systems and land ownership models disrupted traditional Maori structures, leading to conflicts over resources, territory, and cultural differences.

✔ **Maori Social Structures' Impact.** The imposition of European laws and land alienation policies contributed to social upheaval within Maori communities. Traditional methods of conflict resolution faced challenges in the face of changing power dynamics and external pressures.

✔ **Adaptation and Resilience.** The Maori people demonstrated resilience and adaptability despite these challenges. Elements of their cultural practices, including "whanaungatanga" (building relationships), persisted as a vital aspect of Maori identity and community cohesion.

✔ **Revival of Traditional Practices.** In the latter half of the 20th century and into the 21st century, interest in reviving and preserving Maori cultural practices has been resurgent. This cultural renaissance has included a renewed emphasis on traditional conflict resolution methods, such as Peacemaking Circles, to address contemporary challenges while staying true to cultural values.

---

The European colonization of New Zealand brought profound changes to Maori culture. Thus, the modern resurgence of these peacemaking circles represents a deliberate attempt to revive and integrate traditional practices into their modern-day pursuit of justice and overall thriving.

## Iroquois Confederacy's Consensus Decision-Making

The Iroquois Confederacy, known for its commitment to consensus decision-making, believed in resolving conflicts through open talks and reaching out to agreement instead of isolating individuals through punitive measures. According to B.E. Johansen, the Iroquois Confederacy is the oldest living participatory democracy on earth. A league of nations was formed under the leadership of the "Great Peacemaker," who believed all people could live together as one great nation.

The governance structure of the Iroquois Confederacy reflects centuries' worth of indigenous wisdom that predates European contact and demonstrates how adaptable native peoples were. In the 18th century, figures like Benjamin Franklin found inspiration from this political system. Franklin investigated the Iroquois Confederacy constitution and way of life, which influenced the design of the United States Constitution and molded governance during a period of transformational history.

In 1988, the US Senate gave its respects in a resolution that said,

> *"The confederation of the original 13 colonies into one republic was influenced by the political system developed by the Iroquois Confederacy, as were many of the democratic principles incorporated into the Constitution itself."* ~1988, US Senate

Embedded within the Iroquois heritage is a deep-seated commitment to consensus-based decision-making that stresses inclusiveness.

In other words, all community members must be able to identify with decisions made under this system: the Iroquois practice involved open dialogues where different perspectives led to transparency and mutual understanding. In the Iroquois approach, each of the five tribes had representative Chiefs elected by the eldest mothers who would sit and witness the grand council of fifty who decided matters for the people.

Consensus decision-making has been central to ensuring long-term stability within the Iroquois Confederacy by promoting shared responsibility and unity among its members. By its communal nature, this process goes beyond governance structures, making it possible to withstand the test of time, hence creating sustainable confederacies.

The common folk had ways to make their voices heard. Consensus decision-making runs deep into every thread woven into their society's cultural fabric. It shows respect for nature, interconnectedness, and community input as an enduring testament to a culture rich with indigenous wisdom.

## Ubuntu in African Tradition

In different African cultures, the philosophy of "Ubuntu" is a commonality that highlights interdependence and communal responsibility. It is a profound belief that there are intricate connections among people in any society such that no individual can exist without others; translated, "I am because we are."

We enter the world with our brains unfinished. In essence, we learn how to be truly human only because there are other human beings there to show us, to mirror this, to provide the ideal human template. Thus, we are truly bound together in communion with each other.

The harmony within Ubuntu extends beyond a theoretical framework. It recognizes that one person's welfare cannot be separated from the well-being of others, hence creating a shared existence within its framework. Therefore, this interconnectedness philosophy becomes a guiding principle through which communities view their relationships with each other.

Ubuntu is inherently restorative rather than punitive. In cases where harm was done within communities or families, Ubuntu focuses on healing wounds and rebuilding trust among all parties involved. In other words, addressing the root causes of conflict while respecting the dignity of everyone affected, thus promoting understanding and empathy.

Communal responsibility, as championed by Ubuntu, remains dynamic towards resolution. During disputes, what matters most is not who started it but how best both parties could engage themselves again to rebuild what was broken among them. Thus, to foster restoration throughout this process, it must involve more than just two individuals and include a broader community while strengthening communal bonds.

One core principle underpinning the Ubuntu philosophy is the recognition of shared humanity—a communion between the true and authentic within human beings. When somebody suffers harm, it becomes necessary for people involved to see humanity within each other, including those who have been hurt and the people who hurt them. As a result, the focus shifted from isolation or punishment towards a collective journey into understanding, empathy, and healing. The Ubuntu serves as a compass in facing challenges together.

Conflict can be seen as an opportunity for growth, learning, and strengthened relations. That is how the Ubuntu philosophy extends its influence in conflict resolution as a unifying thread underlying African cultures and with unique expressions distinct to the given group.

Various communities infuse it with cultural nuances that reflect the rich diversity of traditions contributing to African philosophy. In addition, the philosophy finds expression in rituals and ceremonies and embodies principles of interconnectedness, communal responsibility, and restoration of balance in everyday life.

Ubuntu in African traditions is a philosophy that goes beyond theoretical considerations. It is a lived experience guiding communities toward healing and growth by recognizing and embracing the shared humanity that binds them together in a rich tapestry of interconnectedness.

## A Childhood Experience as a Microcosm of Ancient Wisdom

As a small boy, the most significant positive childhood role model for me was my Gramma. She lived out this ancient wisdom in her everyday life. She was almost the only adult in my family who did not physically abuse me, and her love helped me through an otherwise difficult childhood.

Once, when I was staying over for the weekend, I remember how she dealt with a neighborhood boy who had broken one of her giant sunflowers off just at the fence line. It was after school, and he was heading home. She caught him just as he walked by. I could see his reluctance and immediate shame.

He knew he had been caught. There was no doubt about that.

When she approached the boy, she knelt so their eyes could meet at the same level. She was smiling and used a gentle tone as she introduced herself. After getting his name, she gracefully coaxed the truth, assuming the best.

As she had surmised, he had taken the sunflower as a gift for his mother. After admitting the act, she helped him understand how much his method hurt her plant and thwarted her efforts to make her front yard beautiful for all to enjoy.

She asked him, "What if I had intended that sunflower for someone else?" It was empathy she sought to cultivate in him rather than shame.

Once he understood the harm he had created, he expressed his remorse and started to cry. She showed affection and assured him it would be ok. The way he could make it up to her would be by asking her permission the next time.

She told him she would love to make his momma happy with her flowers, but they needed to do it together as friends. Her goal was to restore broken trust and create a bond between them to minimize the likeliness of a repeat offense.

He was relieved and helped her pick a few more colorful and fragrant flowers for his momma before he left. She put those in a vase and sent him on his way, now a friend she could call by name.

I spent much time at my Gramma's house in the summers and on weekends. I never heard of her losing any more flowers after that, and when I saw him pass by, he was sure to wave and smile.

> *"A pessimist sees the difficulty in every opportunity; an optimist sees the opportunity in every difficulty."* ~Winston Churchill

I didn't know it then, but my Gramma planted a seed much like an echo of that ancient wisdom in my heart that I later returned to. Her love and kindness have been among my life's beautiful treasures. It has helped reduce the negative impact of family dysfunction and evolve resilience.

## Departure from Ancient Wisdom

The move away from restorative and communal practices is clearly found in both historical and societal changes that have arbitrarily impacted the landscape of justice systems. Western legal systems were imposed during colonization, emphasizing individual rights and punitive measures. As these legal codes got codified and centralized, this imposition marginalized or oppressed indigenous practices, overshadowing traditional communal approaches to justice.

The advent of industrialization and urbanization also reshaped society in new ways. The formal legal systems began to gain prominence due to increased complexity and a disappearing feeling in the community. These installed systems often pushed aside traditional communal approaches towards justice because people were becoming more dispersed and individualistic.

The approach to meeting needs changed as societies evolved within the context of the modern nation-state. This change marked a departure from the initial win/win orientation towards a domination structure, which altered the fundamental principles underpinning justice systems.

This led to an eventual rise in punitive justice systems within such societies. Punitive measures took center stage as tools employed by those in authority to maintain social order. It replaced holistic approaches of justice focused on restoration with one that emphasized punishment and isolation.

As a kind of socioeconomic survival of the fittest, a consciousness of scarcity sprung to the mainstream. Punitive justice arose because of this ideological shift within the modern nation-state aimed at consolidating power and maintaining control.

Consequently, a more divided terrain resulted from moving away from an all-inclusive method that emphasized healing. This resulted in individuals and communities succumbing to punitive measures beyond justice.

When retributive justice came into dominance, reconciliation and communal well-being were no longer essential issues. Instead, punishment often perpetuated cycles of harm rather than promoting healing, thus creating a rigid framework that favored authority over restoration.

Therefore, this shift resulted in intricate systems shaping societal values and norms, with some people benefitting at the expense of others. The trauma stemming from such impacts has been, in large part, responsible for our current criminal justice crisis.

The ideology of reconciliation and communal well-being became secondary to punitive justice. Often, this meant that cycle after cycle continued without any genuine change happening in the system in the community. This led society to prioritize the system itself over restoration.

The individualization of justice has further entrenched the unnatural and artificial nature of punitive alternatives in contemporary legal systems. As a result, restorative measures were ignored, and communities themselves were left isolated from each other as harm-doers found themselves separated from their support groups. At the same time, those who were harmed became alienated from their societies.

> *"The degree of civilization in a society can be judged by entering its prisons."*  ~Fyodor Dostoevsky

Such a break away from collective responsibility reduces chances for shared healing and understanding among those involved and shows how punishment has become an unrealistic societal approach. It is impossible to achieve proper rehabilitation through this method alone.

In pursuing individualized justice, intricate bonds that once wove communities together struggle to hold on. This is because when harm occurs, it isolates both parties involved regarding physical proximity and social interaction, thus disrupting the normal flow of communal life.

In a world where microwave ovens, drive-thru windows, and Amazon delivery reign supreme, is it any wonder that we also choose the easy way out with criminal justice? There are added costs for society but it seems so convenient - today. Interestingly, just as we cannot thrive when fed from drive-thru windows alone, so are societal health concerns arising all around us stemming from our current justice system.

Furthermore, where punitive measures lose touch with the community context, they fail to resolve underlying causes behind conflicts. Due to this approach being artificial and almost experientially blind to the individual experiences behind criminal acts, justice becomes narrow in scope and unable to reach out to everyone affected by an act causing harm.

Complete restoration must include more general considerations about society rather than just offender-government relationships. Significant consequences are currently accruing in record proportions for artificially severing individuals from the rest of society. For example, a child who has a parent who goes to prison is seven times more likely to go to prison than a child whose parents never go to prison.

Restorative justice is a contemporary movement that shows a growing recognition of the limitations of punitive approaches. It seeks to reconnect wisdom in indigenous/traditional practices.

The impact of punitive measures on society has led to renewed interest in restoring harmony, fostering empathy, and rebuilding relationships within a communal context. The journey toward restorative justice also signifies the rediscovery and reclaiming of ancient wisdom, which valued healing over punishment, understanding over isolation, and community over individualization.

## Ancient Wisdom for Healing and Accountability

Restorative justice is, at its core, different from the vindictive nature of conventional justice systems that are based upon "getting even." It is not about punishment. It focuses on healing and repairing the harm done through accountability and empathy.

One of its essential principles calls for creating dialogues and encounters between those harmed and those who created harm. They are designed to facilitate understanding, compassion, empathy, and healing. Again, the centerpiece is relationships rather than laws.

Punitive justice isolates people, whereas restorative justice brings in the broader community. It recognizes that harm affects individuals and the entire social fabric. Thus, communities get actively involved in the process of restoration.

Restorative justice redefines accountability as a dynamic journey where individuals take responsibility for their actions while doing what they can to make restitution for the harm they've created. This shift surpasses retributive measures, instead aiming at transformative change for individuals and communities.

When people who have created harm participate actively in restoring relationships damaged by their actions, they make significant contributions towards mending these social networks and addressing the consequences accruing from such behaviors. As a result, this collaborative involvement fosters shared responsibility and feelings, leading to healing on both sides. The process demonstrates how those who've created harm can be rehabilitated back into society positively instead of indifferently separating them from it and the family and friends relying on them for support.

The traditional punitive system (especially when an individual has a life sentence) often serves little more than confinement purposes. Restorative justice sees long periods spent inside prisons, not necessarily guaranteeing real accountability. It recognizes how lengthy sentences do not translate into positive change merely because of extended periods of incarceration.

Restorative justice promotes active participation in the healing process through understanding each other and offering compensation where possible. It presents a compelling alternative to retribution, which seeks to somehow redeem "offenders" by inflicting pain and deprivation.

In sum, restorative justice holds individuals accountable and enables proper rehabilitation because it aims to reintegrate those who have caused harm into society as responsible and contributing members. As for those harmed, it aims to help free them from the chains of unforgiveness and vengeance so they can truly move on with their lives.

Restorative justice's foundation remains in the needs-centered approach, which is about meeting the needs of victims, those who've created harm, and community stakeholders. This principle resonates with concepts that prove people stay true to their nature when all essential elements required to meet our needs are available.

This broader perspective goes beyond the justice sphere. It resonates universally. It emphasizes that meeting basic needs is key within crime or conflict situations and across various human interactions. These needs must be acknowledged and satisfied to rehabilitate, enabling us to restore equilibrium and proactively prevent harm in every aspect of our interconnected lives.

Restorative justice highly values empathy, thus echoing the belief that crime often results from a lack/ failure of empathy. It seeks to bring back this capacity, recognizing its importance in fostering understanding and connection among others.

## Contemporary Revival with Influence and Impact

Scholars like Howard Zehr played a vital role in giving restorative justice modern traction based on ancient wisdom. Zehr is known as the "grandfather" of this philosophy because he introduced it to mainstream discussions regarding how a justice system could focus more on healing and communal well-being. The profound effect of his work on the current revival can be evidenced by changing societal views and approaches towards justice.

Just before 1980, Zehr worked in criminal justice, dealing with its punitive limitations. Zehr was motivated by his wish for a better system offering humane treatment; thus, he studied restorative justice. One of Zehr's great works, which has had a lot of influence, is his book *Changing Lenses: A New Focus for Crime and Justice,* which seeks to challenge traditional thinking about crime and justice. Published in 1990, *Changing Lenses* exposed its readers to the power of an alternative approach, coined "restorative justice," while highlighting some weaknesses associated with punitive retribution measures.

In addition, Zehr's advocacy efforts helped promote the use of restorative practices in different contexts outside academia through his contribution to ensure that therapeutic principles get implemented by all stakeholders involved, including community members who play an essential role during the restoration process within any given society.

Critical concepts emphasized by Zehr include encounter/dialogue and a journey toward transformational accountability instead of simply retribution. His influence has stretched globally, shaping various cultural perspectives surrounding restorative justice and how to practice it within legal systems across different countries.

Even after retiring from a full-time teaching career at Eastern Mennonite University (EMU), Zehr continues being an active advocate and educator with ongoing efforts to advance this kind of rehabilitation model internationally. He still represents this idea through talks, seminars, and workshops, among others, meant to enhance its implementation understanding through collaborations.

Zehr transformed the field of justice. By advocating for restorative justice principles, he initiated a modern renaissance that went beyond theory to influence practical approaches in real-world contexts, thereby contributing to the continued development of judicial systems around the globe today.

Dr. Barb Toews has also made significant contributions towards restorative justice, building upon Zehr's influential history with restorative justice. As one of the founders of *The Zehr Institute for Restorative Justice*, Toews has been instrumental in advancing restorative practices worldwide, not just based on theories but through her work ensuring that people embrace this form of punishment, specifically when dealing with prisoners.

In prisoner rehabilitation, Toews has played a vital role in extending the principles of restorative justice into correctional settings. Her initiatives focus on fostering dialogue, healing, and rehabilitation among adults in custody, recognizing their potential for personal growth and positive change.

Toews underscores the importance of accountability, understanding, and community reintegration by advocating for the inclusion of adults in custody in the restorative justice process. Through her efforts, she has broadened the application of restorative justice, illustrating its capacity to benefit individuals within the criminal justice system as well as contribute to the well-being of the larger communities in which they are part.

As you explore the foundations of restorative justice, remember that this philosophy is not just an alternative but a visionary shift toward justice that heals, transforms, and fosters a more compassionate and interconnected society. The journey into restorative justice has only just begun, and its roots run deep in the timeless quest for true justice. Let us keep this spirit alive and vibrant by reinforcing its foundation with what we now know about healing harm.

***

*"In the final analysis, the questions of why bad things happen to good people transmute into some very different questions, no longer asking why something happened but asking how we will respond and what we intend to do now that it happened."*

~Pierre Teilhard de Chardin

# What's Wrong With Me? No, What Happened to Me?

Within a week of my birth, after my father was shot in the arm, our family fled to San Miguel, Mexico, where my grandmother worked as a professor at the college. We would stay for the first nine months of my life.

My father was someone who, among other things, killed people for money, had contracts on his head by some underworld crime families, and had the power, without even being present in my life, to get me and my mom killed. Learning this at a very young age shaped how I saw the world. His incarceration for the murder of Kelly Hogan when I was eight years old, and his infamous prison escape with a deputy warden's wife when I was sixteen made him the most enigmatic figure in my life, to say the least.

On the other hand, the fact that he was a gifted painter, sculptor, teacher, marksman, jewelry maker, and pilot who could speak at least three languages fluently and two others partially caused me some confusion.

This man was complicated. I remember, at ten years old, reading a newspaper article about a little girl who was going to die without a liver transplant and him auctioning off a twelve-piece bronze set of sculptures he had crafted for $60,000 to save her life. My mom took me to the Broken Arrow Public Library, where we combed through file after file to discover article after article. I didn't understand how such extremes could exist within one person. That's when I learned that we were living in the same town where the Kelly Hogan murder occurred.

I grew up with Luke Skywalker as my hero without trivializing these facts. I strongly identified with his relationship with his father, Anakin/Darth Vader. And like Luke, I had to choose which side I would ultimately identify with.

I grew up with a mom who would use French accents at random times in public places to camouflage our identity, drive by our house several times before feeling safe enough to actually pull in, and teach me never to trust strangers, law enforcement, or government agents. This didn't do much to promote the idea of love, trust, and safety during those very important developmental years of my life.

Her behavior stemmed from his training, combined with her fears of suffering a fate that she came very close to experiencing.

I learned around age seven that the woman my father married a year or so after my mom left him was found dead in her home after being shot by men looking for him. It happened around the same time that my uncle Glen (who had done some things with my father in connection with the FBI that made some people unhappy) stepped outside his home at 2 am to get his back broken, his throat cut, and his body stabbed over two dozen times and left for dead. Much of this is also confirmed in a book by Charles Sasser titled *At Large: The Life and*

*Crimes of Randolph Dial.*

I remember hiding under the dining room table at my grandparents' house while listening to family talk softly about it all. My uncle had little chance of living, but each day he pulled through. And somehow, thankfully, he lived.

My mom had the man who became my stepdad adopt me and have my name changed to his to protect me from that world. The adoption took place within a year of those events.

But it brought its own complications.

Not long after my stepdad entered my life, he began to try and connect with me in the best way he knew how. He thought it was fun to wrestle me to the ground, climb on top of me, and tickle me while using his weight to crush me, making it difficult for me to breathe.

I must admit that at first, I thought it was funny too because it only lasted a second or two, and I was four years old. But then, over time, the time he spent on top of me grew to the point of me losing all of my air, panicking, and thinking I wasn't going to make it. Once, I got dizzy, blacked out, and saw stars when my vision returned.

It made me avoid situations where that could happen, and I preferred weekends at my grandparents. My mom finally paid attention when it happened, and as I squealed for air and she saw my small arms reaching out from under his massive body, she put an end to it. Even today, he doesn't know the impact of his seemingly innocent attempts at connection, which were traumatic for me. Unfortunately, moments like that led to not only a withdrawal of affection from him but also what seemed like competition for my mom's attention.

During those years, I found myself experiencing a divided sense of loyalty, depending on which parent seemed better than the other. When I witnessed my mom drunk and making out with one of his friends while he was out in the garage entertaining others, I felt emotionally distraught and clung to my stepdad the most. I was 9 years old. My whole understanding of fidelity was shattered. I even had to be the one to go and get him so he could pull my mom off his friend and take her upstairs.

Their drug abuse got so bad that at one point, when I was twelve, my younger sister and I had to be removed from our home. My mom became so mentally unstable that she started seeing tiny little bugs that she swore dove into her skin and laid eggs that would hatch. According to her, they would eat through the window screens and come in through the water as well.

Her appearance became almost anorexic, her skin pasty white, and sores arose all over her body (from her using a sewing needle to pick at the places where the bugs supposedly dug into her). Shortly after, she thought my little sister was getting dive-bombed by those bugs, too. Finally, when my sister started getting those same sores my stepdad sent us to my Aunt Linda's and Uncle Glen's farm for the summer.

While we were gone, my mom blew out their back bedroom window with a 12-gauge shotgun and ultimately had a stroke. She claimed that she left her body as they tried to revive her. Her physical wounds healed, but not the ones that ran much deeper.

Because of the DARE (Drug Abuse Resistance Education) campaign at my school in the fifth grade, I tried to talk to my Gramma about what my parents had been doing one weekend when I was having a sleepover. She promised she wouldn't say anything, but on the ride home, my mom made it clear that my trust had been violated. She said that she would always find out.

When Mom felt most threatened. She would talk about how dangerous life would be for me if I were ever taken away. She would return to reminding me of

Randolph's underworld life and all of the corruption with police and government it involved (especially local).

Mom made me believe that she was the only one I could trust. Ironically, from then on, I was never allowed past my parents' bedroom door again. Their room became off-limits for me. It was the place where my younger sister (their daughter together) and they would spend time together–without me. Sometimes, I stood outside their door or sat with a book, listening to the three playing and carrying on, so that I could somehow be a part of it.

I spent most of my time in my room or on my own, reading books, watching TV, or inventing another world I could enjoy with all of my favorite characters from Star Wars or He-Man.

Twice that I recall, my parents received anonymous phone calls claiming that the unknown voice on the other end of the phone knew who we were, and who I was, i.e., the son of Randolph Dial and that they could reach out and touch us at any time. I was pulled from school for weeks at a time when that would happen. For a brief time, my mom wouldn't let me out of her sight.

Their financial situation was as much a roller coaster as their drug use. Sometimes, the only thing I could find to eat after school was a spoonful of A1 sauce. A few times I remember us going to my aunt's church, where they had huge cupboards of food that we would bag up and take home. Sometimes it was weeks before we could do laundry and Mom had a special set of quarters that would let her get free washers and dryers at the laundromat. Once it got stuck and when I came over to see, she smacked me away not wanting me to know....but I knew.

Once, at 13 years old, during a separation that led to their divorce, my stepdad had come over so they could get high on methamphetamines and have sex. I had just come home from playing a middle school football game and wasn't enthused about his being there.

My Mom went to the store, and I wanted to do something, but he wouldn't say I could or couldn't. My huffy response apparently did not go over so well. Looking back, I recognize now that it was when they had been high on meth that they tended to be the most abusive and/or neglectful.

I could feel all 220 pounds of him walking quickly to my door before throwing it open, grabbing me by the shirt, and throwing my 115-pound frame into the wall. It knocked the wind out of me immediately. My body was like a ragdoll for the next few minutes as it was tossed about.

I remember watching things get thrown across my room as I lay there. The lamp he had bought me when I was eight broke into several pieces. Then he picked me up with his hands around my shirt and neck. He was raging words that I couldn't even follow at that point. When he was done, I fell to the floor, and he stormed out of the room.

I ran away from home that night. My body had carpet burns, scrapes, and what looked like a collage of hickeys scattered across my upper torso, neck, and arms. My mom went looking for me, found me, and told my friend's mom that if I didn't go home with her, she would call the police, and they might take me away. I finally surrendered and returned home with her. I didn't know what else to do or who else to talk to about what happened. I wanted out, but the world my parents had painted for me was not one I could trust.

They were together off and on after that for a few years. Then, my Mom went through one abusive, drug-addicted boyfriend after another.

One of them refused to go away when she said she was done. One day he ran inside with a knife, pushed her down which broke her arm, slit her waterbed, and took off. I chased after him trying to stop him. He backed his truck up and drove it through the chain link fence and into the front deck of our house, throwing me several feet in the process before speeding away.

Just weeks before they got evicted, the three of us lived out at Keystone Lake, which became our makeshift campground with their cars and property. It was summertime, and I got the VW Rabbit as my home. They would wake up, do meth, force breakfast down, and start the day. We used five-gallon buckets filled with water to stand in and bathe. It was tricky, but it got the job done. It was at least a month before my stepdad was arrested for driving under suspension, and they temporarily hijacked his property, filling it with all their belongings. I could not believe what they were doing but stayed to make sure they didn't sell any of his things. I called my stepdad's mom and let her know my stepdad was in jail so she could help him get out.

During this time, my Mom and her boyfriend hooked up with a local con man and somehow organized using my stepdad's property as a drop site for 300 lbs. of smuggled marijuana that the crew paid them $8 per pound for using the space for two days. It was all very professionally done. I was told to manage the cleanup and keep my mouth shut. The tall guy, who seemed to be in charge even though he barely spoke English, pulled me aside and said that if he found out that I talked about anything I saw, he would have everyone in my family killed. I was so scared that I didn't even tell my Mom about the conversation. Simply, that was that and there was no more discussion.

When my stepdad got out of jail, everything turned chaotic very quickly. My Gramma from my stepdad's side showed up, and there was a major family feud. My Mom had no right to do what she did. I was torn about what to do, but I left with my stepdad because of how mad I was at my mom. I felt so bad for him. He seemed to always get the short end of the stick in their relationship. Even after that boyfriend didn't work out, my stepdad was still there to try and pick up the pieces. It just never lasted.

My first experience with alcohol, marijuana, and meth all came from them. In fact, the latter was during a trip with my stepdad to Oklahoma City. As was typical, he was trying to win me over and, this time, offered me meth. I hated how they acted when they did that stuff, but for some reason, it made me feel closer to him to say yes. He handed over a small clear Ziplock bag with tiny yellowish crystals inside. I was around fifteen years old.

It wasn't long after, and perhaps as an attempt to finally build my own life, I met Stacy. Within a few months, we got pregnant and, not long after, married. I was sixteen. This forced me to grow up. I didn't want to be like my parents, so I did what I could to redirect my life toward providing a home for him. I did well on the dad part, but his mom and I proved too young and immature to handle marriage at that age.

Just before coming to prison, I had been working a good job, taking care of my son on my own and offering housing to my mom and sister. I came home one day to find my mom and a guy naked in my bed with aluminum foil drug paraphernalia all over my living room.

Looking back, it's abundantly clear that my parents were the worst thing about my life. I am unable to discuss my next steps because of the legal ramifications and the impact they might have on others. But trauma seemed to invade every aspect of who the people were who brought me into this world and attempted to care for me.

I guess my Mom gave her best attempt at being a mom. She did her best to protect me from the dangerous world she saw through the lens of her own life experience. My stepdad, too, did his best. They had their own adverse childhood experiences (ACEs) as well.

After years of being on the run and close to nine years since I had been incarcerated, my biological father was caught by law enforcement. Not long after his arrest, he was placed in a maximum-security prison, where he learned through one of my old roommates about my conviction and ODOC location. We got permission to write to each other for almost a year before he died.

It was, for me, very much like removing Darth Vader's helmet and seeing the man behind the mask. Complex layers of trauma hid behind that mask, and after almost a year of writing back and forth, so many life confusions and questions were answered; it all made a lot more sense to me.

During my 26 years of incarceration, I was able to connect with my Mom on a deeper level as well. We had some hard but meaningful discussions about the past. Before she died, we resolved all that stood as barriers between us and reconciled on even the most painful parts of our shared experiences.

~~~

It literally took coming to prison, freeing myself from my family's dysfunction and twisted worldview, to help me discover another way of both seeing and experiencing the world.

It has been my journey of acquiring this knowledge and insight that has equipped me to understand how ACEs impacted my decisions and choices and helped me reframe my worldview in harmony with reality. My experience of transformation was deeply spiritual and began with a crisis, much like what is described as transformative learning, but I had no knowledge of Jack Mezirow or his approach at the time.

I have shared the preceding stories as mere glimpses into my upbringing because they were the building blocks of trauma that wired themselves into my brain. It is not exhaustive, nor does it consider positive mitigating factors that were also present. These circumstances directly correlate to my *individual experience* as outlined in this book and have been where I have focused much of my rehabilitative efforts.

Changing our concepts about the world must be the foundation upon which we build another worldview and, therefore, another life. This is critical because the meaning we give the world comprises the concepts we build and our predictions about it.

Our future depends in large part upon our past. Thus, changing our relationship to "How we got here" alters the trajectory of where we end up. A slight adjustment of the ship's sails can change the crew's course entirely. It has been true for me, and it can be true for you as well.

Despite the pain and dysfunction, a golden thread wove itself through all of those experiences to help me grow and become the man I am today. I am ever thankful to my grandparents and the friendships I was able to form during those formative years, which helped me forge an unbreakable bond with Hope and pave an unyielding path to resilience.

Having shared my experiences with ACEs, let us build a bridge together to another life with new possibilities.

***

a trauma-informed approach to rebuilding the web of relationships harmed by crime

*"For me, forgiveness and compassion are always linked: how do we hold people accountable for wrongdoing and yet at the same time remain in touch with their humanity enough to believe in their capacity to be transformed?"*

~Bell Hooks

# Resilience: Pygmalion's Influence and Trauma

Let us explore how you can use the Pygmalion Effect to help shift from trauma to resilience. This is a personal journey, but understanding this psychological theory can give you some practical tools for transformation. First, let's bring you up to speed on the background to guide our exploration better.

## Pygmalion Origins and Background

In Greek mythology, Pygmalion is a sculptor who becomes disillusioned with mortal women because he thinks they have many defects and lack. He dedicated himself to his artwork, constructing a statue of a woman that was so perfect and realistic that he fell in love with it. Pygmalion prayed to the goddess Aphrodite for the statue to come alive out of his total devotion and love for her.

Aphrodite saw how sincere he was and granted him his wish; thus making Galatea become a real human being.

This fable demonstrates belief systems in its fullest sense. His unwavering faith that what he created was perfect led to its transformation into a living thing rather than just an object lying there motionless on the ground. The story shows how our beliefs shape our reality.

The Pygmalion effect, found in psychology, was first demonstrated by Robert Rosenthal and Lenore Jacobson in a 1960s experiment. Their study, "Pygmalion in the Classroom," involved elementary school teachers receiving false information about their students' intellectual capabilities. Specifically, they were informed that some students had been identified as academic 'spurters' expected to show significant intellectual growth over the school year.

These children were selected randomly without any basis for calling them "spurters" other than supplying incorrect facts to educators. At the end of one year's studies, researchers discovered that students branded as spurters made far more intellectual progress than their peers during this term. This phenomenon mainly affected young children regardless of variables such as their initial IQ scores or personal backgrounds.

The main point is that the teachers' attitudes toward pupils influenced what they did with them, shaping students' academic achievement indirectly or directly based on the teacher's perception of their abilities. Teachers who believed that some students could improve academically unwittingly exposed them to more learning experiences, thus making the positive expectations about students come true.

People's beliefs and expectations significantly influence their behavior and performance outcomes, a concept illustrated by the Pygmalion effect in mythological and psychological research. This is an important reminder of each person's capacity for hopeful change and serves as a call to action for creating caring, empowering environments that facilitate growth and development.

## Golem Effect and ACEs

The Pygmalion Effect has a dark twin, the "Golem Effect." While the former is all about hopes leading to positive outcomes, the latter is quite different. It happens when negative beliefs or expectations produce poorer performance or conduct.

What these negative beliefs reflect are those learned from trauma during childhood and other difficult experiences. If a child is raised in an environment characterized by neglect, abuse, or instability, he or she might internalize overwhelmingly pessimistic perceptions of his or her value, worth, and potentiality.

These negative attitudes heavily influence children's development and well-being. In their lives, they may experience challenges such as low self-esteem and difficulty forming healthy relationships, amongst others, in academics, employment, etc.

Additionally, this effect can perpetuate a vicious cycle: A youngster repeatedly informed that they are useless or unable might eventually start believing such comments. Consequently, these negative patterns will be reinforced through decisions and behaviors displayed following these negative beliefs, sustaining adversity's circle.

However, knowledge about the Pygmalion Effect gives individuals the power to use positive beliefs to change their outcomes. Understanding the Golem Effect opens one's eyes to the implications of having inwardly directed thoughts regarding oneself. One can even begin challenging these patterns by realizing that Adverse Childhood Experiences (ACEs discussed at length in upcoming chapters) affect the development of one's values and behavior patterns.

It isn't easy, but with time and effort, people can escape from under the grip of the Golem effect. Therapy and counseling support could offer valuable opportunities for challenging false beliefs and building resilience among those seeking help. At the same time, surrounding oneself with positive influences may be helpful alongside cultivating supportive networks involving friends, family, or mentors who counteract adverse childhood experiences towards a brighter future will go a long way toward recovery.

# How Authority Influences Rehabilitation

In the criminal justice system, Pygmalion/Golem Effects assume a different meaning, especially concerning the role of prison staff in shaping incarcerated individuals' experiences. Just like Rosenthal's teacher belief experiment in which teachers'

views and expectations influence students' academic performance, the attitude and conduct of prison staff affect the rehabilitation and reentry of persons in the criminal justice system. Unfortunately, this is not emphasized enough inside correctional training. Recalibrating restorative justice must include envisioning a different world as Pygmalion did and creating a culture where our true selves are nurtured and reinvigorated when lacking.

Think about a situation where prison wardens, administrators, and security staff with negative stereotypes and biases are dismissive or punitive towards those in custody. These assumptions tend to lower one's esteem, motivation to change for the better, or even imagine any other future beyond serving a jail term.

Eventually, some may shy away from educational programs that could be rehabilitative, quit looking for better personal skills, or simply refuse to dream about their life after release. Part of our recalibration must be how our correctional environments mold and shape the people in their custody.

Conversely, if correctional staff embrace empathy, respect, and aspirations towards positive changes when coming into contact with adults in custody, then an environment conducive to rehabilitation and reintegration is created. Whereas Rosenthal's experiment showed that a teacher's positive beliefs about

students can improve their academic performance, this implies that encouraging attitudes emanating from prison staff can stimulate incarcerated people to engage in steps that will enable them to develop personally.

The effects are far-reaching, given the high levels of recidivism within criminal justice systems worldwide. Other factors leading to recidivism include economic inequality, lack of resources access as well as being unable to come back into society through systemic barriers, among others. However, these cannot overshadow those involving people in the criminal justice system.

Those involved with criminal justice have a crucial role if recidivism rates are to be reduced. We can foster successful reintegration by acknowledging the capacity for change inherent in every individual and promoting an atmosphere characterized by respectful relationships, supportiveness, and empowerment within correctional facilities.

In the same way, Pygmalion believed his statue had possibilities until it came alive, just as correctional staff can believe in their contributions to remolding the lives of incarcerated people. This empowers those in custody to reconstruct their self-narratives and walk the path of resilience and redemption.

## Applying the Principle for Yourself

It is easy to feel stuck when locked away, but everything can change when you understand that your beliefs shape your reality.

So, what is the real value of the Pygmalion Effect? It's about faith in oneself and others. When you believe in your ability to grow and change, you are more inclined to work hard enough to overcome obstacles and attain your goals. Therefore, this self-belief becomes the foundation for a resilient journey.

Imagine this scenario: You have been through hell or high water, much worse than the average person. But something inside tells you that you can achieve more than you've already done.

This is where the Pygmalion inspiration comes in handy. You start seeing beyond your current circumstances once you are surrounded by positive influences—supportive residents, prison staff who understand, rehabilitative programs, etc..

There's also the importance of feedback. Receiving words of encouragement and positive reinforcement from others strengthens self-confidence. You may be learning a new skill or participating in a program. Seeing the progress and hearing some words of motivation are like an energy boost on a journey. It means it still shows you're on track, even if it seems complicated.

But it really should not be all about you alone. The Pygmalion effect goes the extra mile as far as relating with peers is concerned. Believing in the potential of the people around you while supporting them when they need help creates positivity within incarcerated communities. It helps encourage someone away from what may lead them astray inside the prison environment.

It could be assisting someone with his/her studies, including them in your daily exercise program, listening to someone else, or just giving a word of encouragement to another person around. The smallest of deeds and support facilitate resilience and growth culture. Everything builds on everything.

So, how can you apply these principles in your everyday life behind bars? Here are a few examples:

✔ **Have specific goals:** For instance, obtaining a GED, an additional degree(s), or other certifications (if offered), learning a new career or self-improvement objectives, or starting yoga or mindfulness practice. Carpe diem! (translation: "Seize the Day!") on all growth opportunities and experiences.

Write them down and keep them where you will see them daily to remind yourself what you are working towards.

✔ **Reach out for help**: You shouldn't hesitate to ask for assistance when needed. Support groups, participation in religious and/or educational programs, or simply connecting with others to build community are some resources that can help you while on this journey.

✔ **Give back. Offer support to others**: Be there for people who may need it, including those incarcerated with you, by speaking encouraging words to them. Offer support, lend a helping hand, and celebrate each other's successes. Ironically, giving back often gives you the energy you need to persevere and stay focused on your journey. Together, you can create a community that nurtures resilience and growth.

~~~

Remember that the path from trauma to resilience is not easy; however, it is worth it. By believing in oneself, finding a support system, and giving back to others who need it most, one would tap into Pygmalion's power even within the walls of a prison, allowing his/her potential to grow and transform during incarceration, too.

Lastly, and perhaps most importantly, *accept yourself*. Whatever has happened in the past cannot be changed; we can only change ourselves and our relationship to the past, right?

Never forget that every daily decision counts towards your resilience and growth. Through setbacks and other obstacles, one learns new things about life and a new way to live life—a more positive way forward.

Embedding the Pygmalion effect in your daily life can help you navigate the intricacies of past traumatic experiences, thus making you more resilient and equipping you with all the necessary skills to confront future challenges. Believe in yourself, set meaningful goals, explore different pathways for success, and follow through on the goals you set.

Though it is only a step, resilience begins there. You can overcome anything that stands in your way through endurance and persistence. All efforts compound with time, just like compounding interest in a bank account. This is what it means to H.O.P.E. for a better tomorrow.

***

*"Darkness comes. In the middle of it, the future looks blank. The temptation to quit is huge. Don't. You are in good company... You will argue with yourself that there is no way forward. But with God, nothing is impossible. He has more ropes and ladders and tunnels out of pits than you can conceive. Wait. Pray without ceasing. Hope."*

~John Piper

## Hope Rising: The Bridge to Resilience

As we recalibrate restorative justice toward community resilience, it is appropriate to point out early on the initial gulf between traumatic experience and resilience. It is not as far as the East is from the West, but the divide can create challenges. It's why we are in our current criminal justice dilemma.

There is, however, a bridge to resilience, often overlooked but currently getting widespread attention in the scientific community. The bridge?

Hope. Yes, HOPE.

I made a set of acronyms that align with my ideas about the phases of hope. I imagine someone else has thought of at least one of them already. I'm happy to be in the company of whoever this might be.

## Three Phases of HOPE

Per Charles Richard "Rick" Snyder's "Hope Theory," hopeful thinkers achieve more, and are physically and psychologically healthier than less hopeful people. Snyder's theory probes the intricate interplay between thought, emotion, and gumption. Essentially, our abilities to overcome life's adversities with resilience, determination, and hope as a beacon illuminate how hope drives us toward achieving our goals.

There are three phases to HOPE, as both a concept and an acronym.

The first phase is

>**H**aving **O**nly **P**ositive **E**xpectations

If we can keep our mindset in a "having only positive expectations" mode, we significantly increase the likelihood of our success. Sometimes, it's easier said than done.

> *"Ski the gaps, not the trees. Focus on what you want, not on what might stop you."* ~Cathy O'Dowd

The second phase of HOPE is:

>**H**elping **O**pportunities **P**rogress **E**ffectively

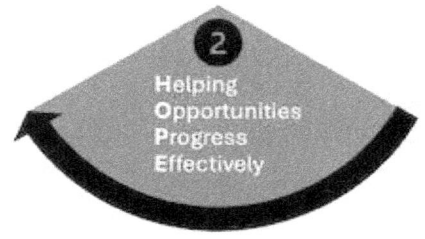

This aligns with Snyder's Pathways (way power: having a carefully considered plan.) However, only when we move beyond his seminal works can we fully appreciate the true meaning of hope and its transformative potential in life.

> *"Simply put, hope reflects a mental state in which we have the perceived willpower and the waypower to get to our destination."*
> *~C.R. Snyder*

Chan Hellman's work on the relationship between ACEs (Adverse Childhood Experiences) and hope adds another valuable piece to the puzzle, becoming a true and clear picture of what Snyder and others like him have been creating.

In my own experience, I am witnessing amazing things in Oklahoma concerning ACEs and Hope where I live (in an Oklahoma Department of Corrections prison facility). Oklahoma's First Lady Sarah Stitt, who had her own experiences with adverse childhood experiences, has partnered with Hellman to bring Hope to Oklahomans in a brand-new way.

It isn't a coincidence that when I was learning about ACEs on my own, the "Oklahoma Hope Rising Movement" (https://hoperisingoklahoma.org/) also just began outside the confined spaces of my correctional facility. Inside the Resilience Prison Project (RPP), we have certified hundreds of men in custody as trauma-informed agents of change. Thousands more await our training.

In the book *Hope Rising: How the Science of Hope Can Change Your Life*, co-authored by Chan Hellman and Casey Gwinn, it is said:

> *"We know we can lose our ability to hope well. But we also know rising hope can change everything."* ~Hope Rising

The book demonstrates these words within its pages, story after story.

When I first read them, I felt such gratitude come up inside. It wasn't so much what was written but the overall context that connected my life and story to a world where I again belonged.

So much from the *Science of Hope* is relevant that I have recognized many parallels between what is being expressed and what we have been doing inside RPP.

> *"Hope is the belief that your future can be brighter and better than your past and that you actually have a role to play in making it better."*
>
> *~Chan Hellman*

We have also incorporated key material from Hope Rising into our program. I'm truly grateful to see this happening outside of our work.

This leads to the third phase of HOPE:

**H**abitually **O**ffering **P**ersistent **E**ffort

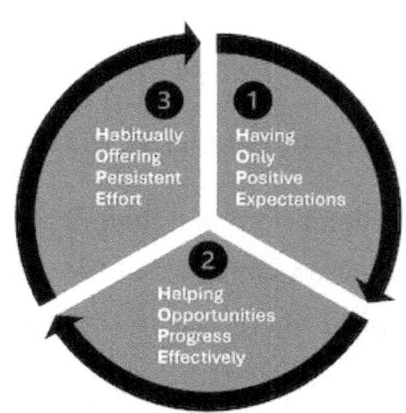

The heart of Snyder's Hope Theory lies in his belief in people's inherent ability to create a better tomorrow, which include:

✔ **Goals**: thoughts focused upon a particular goal,

✔ **Pathways**: plans formed after careful consideration of steps needed to achieve success

✔ **Agency**: a courageous drive or urge to accomplish the set objectives (Synder 2000). This is the agency (willpower to see our goals achieved).

The power derived from thoughts focused upon a specific goal helps us devise various strategies for achieving goals through cognitive pathways. When linked with agency thinking—an unwavering belief in one's capability to navigate such pathways—hope stands as a guide in dark times.

Hope shows where possibility can exist even in seemingly insurmountable obstacles. In Snyder's view, positive emotions fuel individual progressions, making them strong enough to be resilient against challenges.

Hellman points out that all three aspects of hope must be present and involved for success. He points out that all the motivation in the world isn't enough to make up for lack of planning, and no amount of planning can overcome a motivation deficit.

For our hopes to become our reality, we must keep all three components balanced and actively engaged in the process.

## Bridging Hope and Resilience

Hellman's research on hope becomes extremely important when considered against this backdrop because it explains how hope can help overcome ACEs-based trauma. Adverse Childhood Experiences (ACEs) are a range of traumatic events such as neglect or abuse that hover over people's lives and may kill their hope even before it starts to flicker. However, Hellman's study shows an incredible thing—hope is a powerful force that can find its way through the darkest pasts and lead one to a promising future.

Hope is huge for those who have undergone much more adversity than others. By exploring this area, Hellman puts forward that hope acts as a protective factor that works against ACEs by building resilience and empowering those harmed to move on with their lives. Developing hope is also one of the Community Resilience Initiative's *42 Resilience Building Blocks* found at the end of the book. We will be delving into ACEs and protective factors in future chapters.

In my opinion, integrating Snyder's Hope Theory and Hellman's pioneering research is necessary for us to properly understand beyond traditional approaches. These perspectives support the struggle we experience during incarceration while maintaining focus on the end goal.

In light of post-ACEs, hope shows us where we need to be moving forward in life instead of allowing ourselves to be defined by what has been inflicted upon us or what, in turn, we have inflicted upon others. Through adopting pathways thinking and agency thinking, we have taken back powers over our lives, leading us away from ill health, stagnation or stunted growth.

Cognitive flexibility is all about the importance of pathways and the initial reflection on these different paths, which implies that one person may have to consider multiple routes to achieve their goal instead of just single-mindedly focusing on one path. It's the "if at first you don't succeed, try, try again" motto.

The power of intention as captured in Wayne Dyer's philosophy is reflected in agency thinking which embodies purpose, conviction, and willpower to follow through with a number of these differing pathways. This belief underscores the point that transformation can come from aligning one's thoughts and beliefs with desired outcomes in life thereby indicating how clarity, purpose, and positive energy contribute towards manifesting intentions.

## Cultivating Hope in Practice

Ever since we started thinking about the future, full of promise and resilience, it was necessary to find ways of translating theory into practice, which entails creating settings that nurture optimism among individuals. This is because therapeutic interventions and strength-based approaches are promising ways through which individual people can regain agency over their lives as well as develop resilience against adversities.

Similarly, encouraging supportive communities where everyone feels part and parcel of the organization creates a perfect environment needed for hope to grow, thus transforming people's lives and reconstructing society into generations.

This is precisely what happens inside *transformative learning communities* formed by the Resilience Prison Project within correctional environments. We carefully plant hope inside our HEART framework and cultivate community resilience through our training, activities, and individual and collective efforts to restore justice.

We anticipate with sincere hope, the day when these valuable insights will be applied where they matter most - prisons. When *transformative learning communities* become the norm inside correctional environments, hope is crucial to act as a bridge between ACEs and resilience.

Without hope, adverse childhood experiences result in criminal and addictive behaviors as well as physical and mental health problems. Much like a garden tilled and fertilized, the environment must be adequately prepared for the seeds of hope to germinate, sprout, grow towards the light, and bring forth a rich harvest of fruit. This is my hope rising toward the stars.

~~~

When we look at human life in general terms, hope emerges as one thread that holds us together, making a tapestry of resilience, bravery, and unwavering fortitude. Faith, hope, and love are like three powerful threads that, when woven together, create a strong and sturdy rope capable of pulling us out of the worst situations imaginable and lifting us to heights presently unimaginable.

Bruce Lipton's *Biology of Belief* has challenged traditional scientific theories and paved the way toward a clearer understanding of how our "faith" can "make" us "whole," so to speak. Hope Rising and its research also challenge traditional science and show us how hope is fundamental to realizing our goals.

From a Christian context, one I will refer to briefly, the following applies:

> *"I pray that the eyes of your heart may be enlightened in order that you may know the hope to which he has called you."* ~Ephesians 1:18

Love, as we will understand later as the core of our individual experience (along with trust and safety), is where hope leads. Love is how human beings have defined God. Love is considered the highest quality in relationships between human beings. It is the height of self-actualization.

David Hawkins refers to it as the highest emotional vibration in his map of consciousness (compassion - the way of the heart). Thus, Love never fails. So, if what you are calling hope seems to be leading you anywhere other than love, trust, and safety, it is leading you to threat and, therefore, away from your authentic self.

> *"Your task is not to seek for love, but merely to seek and find all the barriers within yourself that you have built against it."* ~Rumi

When Restorative Justice is recalibrated to help seek and find all the barriers that are built against love, it is free to be directed toward creating a more trauma-informed and trauma-supportive worldview. Hope acts as the buoyancy lifting us above the weight of our past setbacks.

As we witness Hope Rising, let us envision it leading us toward the end, described throughout this book as the true path toward wholeness and healing. Hope is too big to be applied to small, trivial successes alone. We must help restore justice so that it becomes politically correct to do the right thing for all members of our society, even when they have created real harm. Only when those most deprived of hope receive it again are they lifted up in the wings of love and aspiration toward who they were brought into existence to be.

Through this visionary work on the science of Hope, we get a glimpse into what hope can do; it's a force that rises above setbacks while leading us into an auspicious future. This is true for those who have created harm, those who have been harmed, and those community stakeholders through whom justice is truly restored.

It's not wishful thinking. It combines "the substance of things hoped for" with a well-crafted plan. We see only the attainable and work at it until our goal is achieved. When faced with growth opportunities, let us use this insight as our compass, ever-guiding us to take bold steps towards uncertain tomorrows with the power of faith, hope, and love, bringing it to fruition.

> *"When infants aren't held, they can become sick, even die. It's universally accepted that children need love, but at what age are people supposed to stop needing it? We never do. We need love in order to live happily, as much as we need oxygen in order to live at all."*
> *~Marianne Williamson*

\*\*\*

*"Resilience is not the absence of adversity but the triumph over it, shaping a narrative of strength and triumph."*

~Angela Duckworth

# Building Community Resilience

A man was traveling on foot in Idaho when he happened to cross a vast landscape of potato farms. As he walked, one such farmer pulled up alongside him and asked if he needed a lift.

He immediately noticed the farmer's truck bed was full of huge potatoes. "Quite a harvest you got there. Look at the size of those things!" he exclaimed.

"Well, thank you," the man grinned as he reached across the cab and opened the truck door from the inside. "But there's more to the story if you'd like to hear it."

Intrigued, the man entered the truck, and away they went.

"I fill this ol' truck up with taters of all sizes," he began. "Once I get the bed full of 'em, I drive about eight miles or so. As you might imagine, it's pretty bumpy drivin'. Along the way, the little taters sink to the bottom, the medium-sized ones shuffle around so that most wind up in the middle, and the big ones, well," he paused briefly for emphasis… "They rise to the top."

He paused again, thoughtfully weighing his words and pondering the subject as a scientist might do with a mathematical theorem. Then he went on, "It happens every time, you see. It's all the bumps on the journey they make. Yep, those bumps put things in their place all right - and make it seem like there's nothing but big taters back there. Brings the best ones to the surface and hides what didn't work out so well. Kinda how life works if ya think about it."

The traveler was amazed. He turned to peer back at that truck bed full of potatoes. Sure enough, it looked like only big potatoes. This was resilience, he thought. Using the bumps in the road to not only grow our best qualities but to bring them to the surface where they can be utilized and valued is how Hope cultivates Resilience. Our strengths are maximized, and our weaknesses are minimized. Wow! He would never forget this man or this lesson." This is me up here, Mister. Thanks for the lift."

And what a lift it was!

The traveler was having a hard time with work. He had just lost his vehicle, and without funds to fix it, he still had hundreds of miles before reaching his destination. Maintaining an optimistic attitude and laboring to realize his goal despite obstacles was a well-timed metaphor for his journey. He needed to hear that. Of all that was inside him to identify with, he had not chosen the failures, the setbacks, or the opposition. Rather, he had chosen Hope based on the possibilities he could realize for himself.

The men shook hands, and each was on their way…onward and upward.

Using this story as a metaphor for our own experiences, even those inside prison - whether we rise or fall is left to our own choices and how we use the opportunities that present themselves daily. We will explore how understanding Adverse Childhood Experiences (ACEs) can set you on course for healing, i.e., being made whole again and building resilience.

In restorative justice recalibrated, which focuses on resilience building, we would like to introduce the "Resilience Trumps ACEs," concept coined by the Community Resilience Initiative (CRI). They have partnered with us in support of our efforts to help mitigate the impacts of ACEs and promote resilience among the incarcerated.

The reason why this has become such an essential part of this work for me is because of my own ACEs. Understanding how certain events and experiences shaped my brain, the concepts that guide my choices, and the predictions that guide my behavior at critical points in my life has helped transform my life and make sense of what used to be so confusing before.

I have applied what I have learned to my parents, their parents, and others who have helped shape my life. Having scored an 8 out of 10 on the ACEs Quiz, I've learned to channel my energies through positive mitigating factors and resilience building.

Much of this occurred long before I learned about ACEs, as perhaps it has been similar for you. In recent years, I have been grateful to learn of First Lady Sarah Stitt's campaign for a more trauma-informed Oklahoma. She has taken much-needed steps to draw from her own ACEs and use them to create awareness and change.

Having someone in her position acknowledge the seriousness of childhood trauma and take preventative steps to help ensure that fewer and fewer suffer inspires hope in me. I also sincerely hope to help this effort and have already taken significant steps in doing so. May you benefit as I have from what follows and experience more love and compassion for yourself and others as a result.

## Adverse Childhood Experiences in Context of Restorative Justice

Adverse Childhood Experiences (often referred to as "ACEs" throughout this book) are an array of traumatic or stressful events that have occurred before your eighteenth birthday and, if left unattended, bear significant impacts on your mental, emotional, and physical well-being throughout life.

Today, one might first learn about ACEs through the "The ACEs Quiz," which has ten questions that help determine whether one's childhood before 18 years old had traumatic or highly stressful events. These experiences can majorly impact an individual's overall health and well-being for the rest of their life.

Participants complete an ACEs Quiz anonymously in a program setting to obtain an ACEs score ranging from 1 to 10. The higher this score is, the more an individual's earlier life has been affected by adverse childhood experiences. (See *The ACEs Quiz Form* at the end of this book.)

The ten questions that comprise the ACEs Quiz follow.

> **#1.** *Did a parent or other adult in your household often or very often swear at you, insult you, or put you down?*
>
> **#2.** *Did a parent or other adult in your household often or very often push, grab, slap, or throw something at you?*

**#3.** *Did an adult or person at least five years older than you ever touch or fondle you or have you sexually touch their body?*

**#4.** *Did you often or very often feel that no one in your family loved you or thought you were important or special?*

**#5.** *Did you often or very often feel that you didn't have enough to eat, had to wear dirty clothes, and had no one to protect you?*

**#6.** *Was a biological parent ever lost to you through divorce, abandonment, or other reasons?*

**#7.** *Was your mother or stepmother often or very often pushed, grabbed, slapped, or had something thrown at her?*

**#8.** *Did you live with anyone who was a problem drinker or alcoholic, or who used street drugs?*

**#9.** *Was a household member depressed or mentally ill, or did a household member attempt suicide?*

**#10.** *Did a household member go to prison?*

Knowing your ACE score (i.e., number of questions that you answer "Yes" to) tells you much about yourself, just like knowing your personal history does. Furthermore, within restorative justice, it is essential to recognize ACEs as a way of understanding how early-life trauma deeply affects individuals responsible for harm, those harmed, and anyone else involved in criminal justice whose roles may be influenced indirectly by their trauma.

With restorative justice recalibrated, trauma-informed approaches are core to restorative community well-being, i.e., practices that foster healing, empathy, and understanding. What your own ACEs mean relative to your own life, and how they may relate to your current incarceration brings immense insight. In other words, through understanding the endured trauma behind your behaviors, you may say to yourself, "Maybe my childhood trauma had a lot to do with shaping my life journey." Ironically, the same could be said of the people harmed (by what you did).

Of course, there are also the people who arrest, prosecute, sentence and monitor you once you are incarcerated. Most of them, too, have their own ACEs to consider. As such, this opens up a whole new dimension of how our criminal justice system has reached its current status in the world (especially if you are from a state with higher levels of ACEs-affected people).

For these reasons, at a minimum, it becomes clear why we must recalibrate restorative justice to accommodate a trauma-impacted society. Acknowledging ACEs can lead you towards self-awareness and compassion for others and yourself. The recognition is not a justification for your behavior but rather a way to untangle complex experiences that might have contributed to your eventual involvement in the criminal justice system.

*Restorative justice recalibrated* calls for empathy and understanding. It offers a platform to understand how ACEs impact your life in a deeper context so you can also learn how to evolve the required resilience that may forever improve your life.

Trauma can be a catalyst for choosing a lifestyle that lulls the authentic self into a kind of slumber. Our goal, therefore, is to find both the courage and the resolve to start waking up to who and what we really are by removing all of the barriers our trauma has set in the way of love and compassion.

As you go through the restorative justice process, exploring your ACEs becomes essential to developing empathy for harm done (and understanding what initially led to criminal behavior). It further sets the stage for a transformative journey that urges you to deal with underlying wounds from ACEs, which contributes to your healing. It enables you to connect and reconnect with community members. Understanding the impact of ACEs' also helps you understand why people treated you as they did during your formative years.

For restorative justice to be effective, it must recognize people who have had ACEs as traumatized individuals who might exhibit harmful behaviors. Rather than seeing your actions in isolation, this approach looks at them as possible manifestations of unresolved trauma.

In restorative justice recalibrated, there is a clear understanding that you are not separate from your past. Yes, our "bad deeds" are symptoms of unresolved traumas, this perspective provides an opportunity for genuine accountability and comprehensive healing. This developmental link might make it much easier for you to accept yourself, which is essential if you want real change.

Carl Rogers, one of the most influential psychologists of the 20th century and founder of humanistic psychology, states, *"The curious paradox is that when I accept myself just as I am, then I can change."* By being honest and vulnerable with ourselves, we awaken an acceptance that quickens the reconnection to our authentic selves. Love never fails.

Over the years, I have grown to appreciate how the most important things I have come to learn seemed to fall from the sky at just the right time. Becoming trauma-informed was just such an instance.

~~~

I have a friend, Tim, who teaches Nonviolent Communication (NVC) in Oregon. Several years ago, he asked me if I knew anything about ACEs. I had no idea what he was referring to. By that time, I had been working on my self-studies, explorations, and teachings in NVC for years. He then pointed me to Fritzi

Horstman, who had been working in California through an organization she founded called Compassion Prison Project.

Fortunately, my job at the time allowed me to view the Internet under the supervision of my boss at Correctional Industries. I watched a brief video Fritzi had made and became intrigued. For weeks, I researched ACEs, trauma-informed care, and anything I could get my hands on that I might incorporate into what was then called the Pathways for LIFE program.

It was then I discovered that I had 8 of 10 ACEs and began understanding more clearly what had shaped my life in the direction it had gone before my incarceration. It was such a revelation! It didn't necessarily make excuses for some of my choices, but it did help make it clear why so many things happened the way they did. I needed to know "the whys" to improve those areas of my life.

I soon found the Community Resilience Initiative, and together, my staff sponsor and I called them. I was put in touch with Rick Griffin, among the most supportive people I had connected with, regarding my goal of incorporating this trauma-informed training. He eagerly asked questions about what I was doing and how the program worked. He then surprised me by volunteering to offer the training to me so that I could teach CRIs courses and train other trainers to teach them.

I was elated and quickly worked to get permission to undergo the training directly from Rick. We spent hours working together, and he was very patient with me, ensuring that I understood the concepts, could reflect on them, and answer questions about the subject matter. He told me how impressed he was with my understanding of subjects that worked alongside his courses and gladly welcomed me to CRI as a certified trainer. I have since accumulated a small library of books on neuroscience, epigenetics, ACEs, and Resilience to improve my own understanding and support others who wish to do the same.

What follows in this next section draws primarily from the training he underwent with me and the material I use to certify others in the CRI Trauma-Informed certification course. Although I have added much to my overall understanding through other sources, much of the following framework originates with CRI.

More recently, I have reached out to Fritzi, who has spent a great deal of time communicating with me. After getting to know each other and discovering a shared vision for the future, we have agreed to work together to change the world in the direction of our goals.

I received her *Trauma Talks,* completed the courses, and facilitated them to the 80 men on the Resilience Prison Project Pod at Great Plains Correctional Center, the first adults-in-custody in Oklahoma to take them. This is preparation for Fritzi's arrival in mid-summer for a two-day *Step Inside the Circle* event for close to 200 residents. We aim to bring thousands through the course as soon as possible.

I am ever grateful to my dear friends Rick Griffin and Fritzi Horstman for their commitment to helping the world reframe its approach to trauma-impacted individuals and helping transform the systems that currently perpetuate and/or retraumatize individuals with trauma.

## KISS Framework for Community Resilience

I'm going to offer you a KISS. Are you willing to receive it?

What comes up for you as you read this? What emotions arise? What judgments?

Well, I don't mean KISS in the way you might initially guess. No, the KISS I offer requires you to reframe your concept of this word, which will, in turn, open you up to understanding the word KISS in a new way.

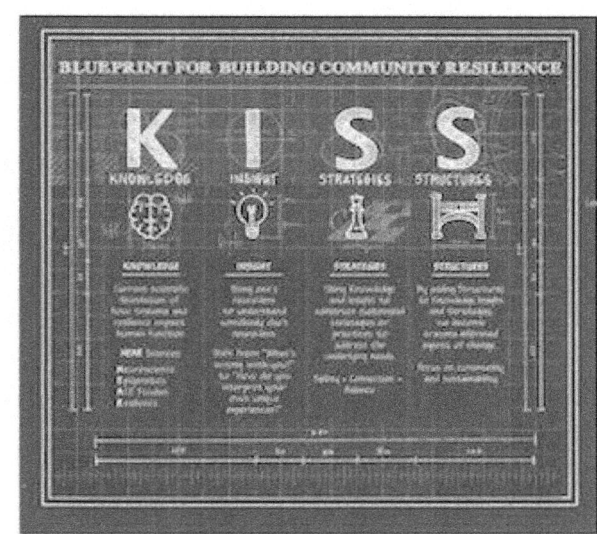

The key to moving through trauma lies in this example. It begins by learning what is happening inside ourselves due to what's going on externally.

We figure out how to reframe and reconceptualize something we think we know so that it can be seen differently. Then, we shift from threat to safety.

KISS is an acronym that stands for:

✔ **K**nowledge
✔ **I**nsight
✔ **S**trategies
✔ **S**tructures

These comprise a blueprint for building community resilience. We will use this framework as a means of becoming trauma-informed. Let's approach each part one by one.

✔ **Knowledge**: This refers to trauma and resilience sciences and how they impact our lives. The relevant sciences that will help us on our way are called the **NEAR** Sciences (i.e., **N**euroscience, **E**pigenetics, **AC**Es Study, **R**esilience).

✔ **Insight**: This is the inner light of your true self, illuminating your experiences with wisdom. We shift from a point of view of "What's wrong with you?" to "How do you interpret your own unique experiences?" Or as Gabor Maté puts it "What is going on inside you because of something that happened to you?"

We take the knowledge we gain from the NEAR Sciences and use our neuro-lens to understand somebody else's neuro-lens. What we know and see in the world truly depends on the concepts guiding our perception. When our thoughts and ideas can connect with what we know about someone so that our predictions about them prove accurate and our strategies are effective, we use insight.

✔ **Strategies**: To adequately address our and others' underlying needs, we must use our knowledge and insight to build customized strategies considering individual experience. As Neuroscientist Lisa Feldman Barrett states, "Variation is the norm." There is no cookie-cutter approach to our own or others' trauma. One thing we can say that maintains its value in each situation is that

$$safety + connection = balance$$

To be balanced is to have the capacity to self-regulate or bring oneself back into a space free from threat. This is the goal.

How people meet their individual needs for safety and connection is based on unique experiences. Much like an interior decorator or a clothing tailor, we must learn to cater our support to each person.

✔ **Structures**: When we apply our knowledge, insight, and strategies to structures (or systems), we become trauma-informed agents of change. Here, we are focused on community and sustainability.

We transform our educational, health care, political, and criminal justice structures, to name a few. By changing policy and procedure so that they are trauma-informed, we began making large-scale changes in our societies.

## NEAR Sciences

*Restorative justice recalibrated* aims to utilize this framework to support safety + connection = balance in our society along lines long overdue for healing. By taking this step and applying this framework to your own life and circumstances, you are pioneering true and lasting change with us.

"Community resilience" means that we are a family of individuals aspiring toward the same goals for the sake of each other, not just ourselves. If we truly want the world to be a better place, we will manifest that dream and vision through our relationships. We can begin right where we are with the people in the communities we find ourselves in.

Ok. So, I hope you feel better about me giving you a KISS…..(framework) because it is the foundation upon which we will reframe our worldview and become trauma-informed agents of change.

~~~

Let's examine each part of this framework piece by piece to gain a clear understanding of the NEAR Sciences. By keeping them near, we have nothing to fear.

The following exploration of the NEAR Sciences is brief but illuminating. You may make whatever efforts you can to increase your knowledge of them, for they will refine your neuro-lens.

## Neuroscience

Neuroscience is the study of the structure and function of the brain and nervous system. What we are now discovering about being human is truly fascinating.

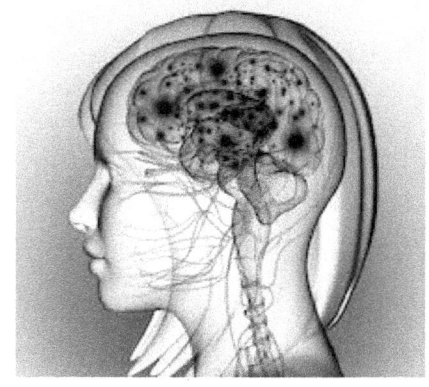

Our brain and nervous system enable us to be internally and externally connected. All of the impacts upon our bodies are experienced by these instruments and translated into what makes up our conscious reality.

> "We don't just passively perceive the world. We actively generate it. The world we experience comes as much, if not more, from the inside out as from the outside in."   ~Anil Seth

Our interpretations of our experiences is the brain's best guess at what's happening out there. So if what's happening appears to be dangerous and unsafe, that will have a significant impact upon how the brain continues to guess. We may start "to generate" a simulation of the world increasingly distorted by unresolved trauma.

Our experiences shape us. Considering this in terms of ACEs helps us understand that what has happened to us is built into our bodies, particularly our brains. These critical developmental years of our lives set the stage for whether we enter a dangerous world we must protect ourselves against, or a safe and nurturing world we can feel safe and happy about. It is in the developmental period of our lives when our brain becomes wired to certain behavior patterns and creates response strategies to deal with what happens to us.

Even as early as two years old, the impacts on the brain from extreme neglect versus typical development is astonishing to compare. Brain scans reveal

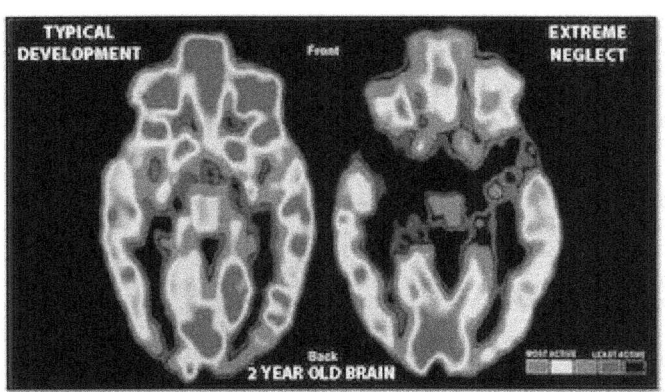

significant diminishment of brain architecture of the neglected and/or abused child. As you can see in the image, the neglected brain is significantly different from the normal brain. Now imagine what this child's behavior might be like.

If the parts of the brain lack the development to function in a certain way, the child can't behave according to what might be considered normal. Do we blame this child for this lack? What about any potential handicaps in his or her social reality that follow? The darkened areas are the result of these networks abeing "offline."

Thankfully, at this stage, the opportunities for change remain optimal. In fact, the brain's ability to change in response to experiences is extraordinary at such an early stage. Over time, however, it takes more and more effort to make the same kinds of changes.

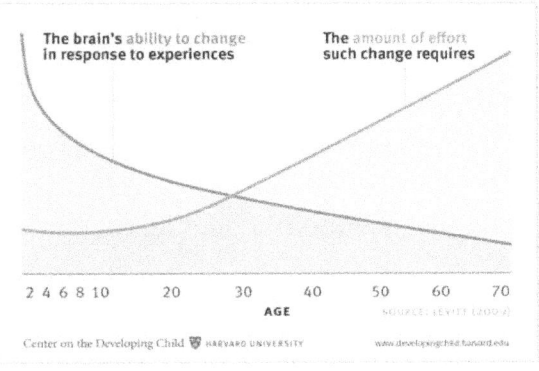

By the time we reach 70, for example, it takes extreme efforts to make even seemingly small changes by comparison. Change can still happen, but the effort is exponentially higher than when we are young and the brain is very pliable. In neuroscience, this ability to rewire the brain is called neuroplasticity.

As it turns out, the brain is not the reactive instrument we used to believe it was. Paul D. Maclean's triune model of the brain is also an inaccurate depiction of its functionality.

The brain is actually predictive and functions much more like the world's global airports with local, national, and international relay stations than hard coded sections.

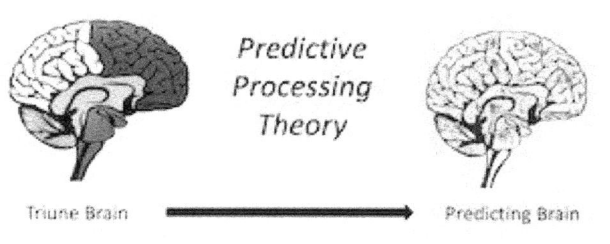

There are flights between local hubs but also a majority of long-distance travels that comprise this network of relationships. Incidentally, how flights are patterned in the brain during adolescence determines mental health in adulthood. Less long-distance flights imply a less developed global airport network so to speak. This has major implications for how the brain will operate.

The brain anticipates. We have proven this along so many lines. Pavlov's dog is the classic example but even the timing of the swing of a baseball bat relative to the pitch demonstrates this anticipatory nature. If the batter had to wait until she could react to the ball's position it would be too late to hit the ball when swinging!

The reason we can anticipate is because we access everything we have learned from our past and use it to make statistical predictions about what is most likely going to happen in the world of our perceptions now.

Much like a gambling bookie, the brain creates real time statistics so that it can make a bet based upon the most accurate information available. With trauma our predictions become skewed. We begin to make high risk predictions because of a distorted connection to the parts of the brain where we access the most accurate data. Here's how it works.

We open our senses to the outer world. All that can be seen, heard, felt, smelled, and tasted is recorded and interpreted by the brain. It takes these perceptions and faster than the millennium falcon in Star Wars (very quickly) cross-references these perceptions with its best guess about what this pattern of experience means. From this activity a prediction arises.

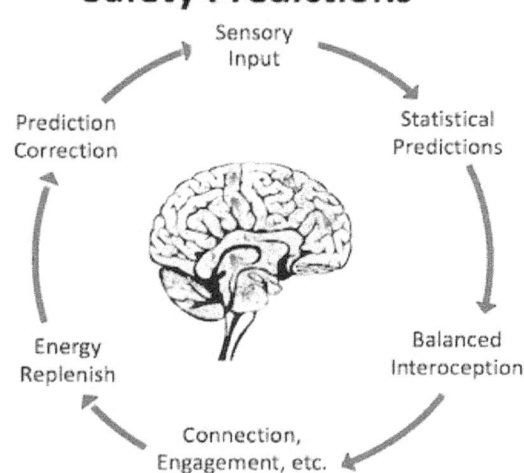

This prediction leads us to engage our inward senses. We call this interoception, i.e. our awareness or perception of what's happening inside rather than outside the body. It is the inward responsiveness to the question, "How does this prediction impact me?"

Normally, or when safe, this leads to connection and engagement. The brain then ensures that our expended energy is replenished, and we continually adjust our statistical predictions much like we maneuver our cars when driving on a busy highway with other vehicles. Gasoline, battery, oil, radiator fluid all continue to take care of the engine in the most efficient manner. This is how it works when we are functioning from a position of safety. An entirely different process unfolds when we are in threat responses mode.

In this case our statistical predictions lead to unbalanced interception. Our body adjusts to the threat by an explosion of stress hormones being released as we choose to fight, flight, or freeze. Our brain reconfigures our body's budget of resources and spends way more than normal attempting to keep us safe. Our heart rate changes as does our breathing and other biological processes. Our blood flees from the surface and goes to the core in case of potential injury. Our reasoning faculties become lethargic if not altogether paralyzed and our energy is quickly zapped.

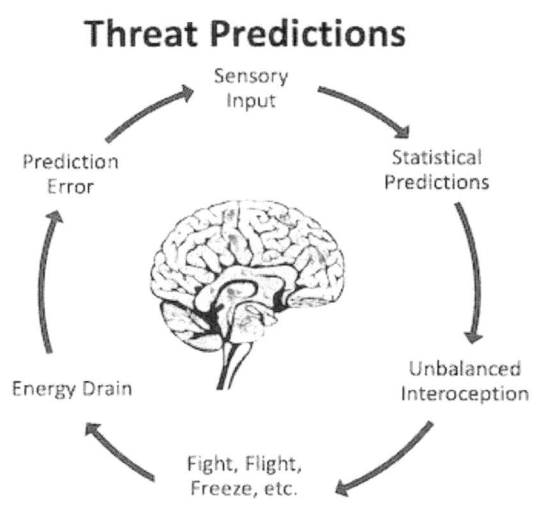

Now as we continue to take in information from the world we begin to make predictions errors because our higher cognitive capacities have literally gone offline. By the way, it's said that when we get angry or scared our IQ can drop up to 20 points! So these prediction errors cause our driving to become more reckless.

We begin to inaccurately anticipate other drivers making moves on the road that doesn't make sense. Our driving becomes erratic, lethargic, or our engine simply shuts down (sometimes right in the middle of rush hour traffic). Thus, we become increasingly susceptible to a crash.

We know all of this because of the discoveries in neuroscience. So, we hopefully begin to understand its value as it helps us to recognize important aspects of our daily lives and what actually underlies our behavior.

## Epigenetics

So, we have genes, which are small sections of DNA that form the blueprint or instructions for building the body. Imagine a computer program composed of code. The code is like instructions for running a program, but someone has to actually run the program. Epigenetics means "above" genetics. The DNA or gene is not set in stone. They can be turned on or turned off and the environment is a major contributor to how these genes get expressed.

The food you eat, which contains particular nutrients, temperature, sleep, exercise, mood, and a host of other environmental factors, play a significant role in the patterns playing out in our bodies. Thus, epigenetics runs the program and adjusts the code according to HOW we live through WHAT our life is from moment to moment. WHY is the core, which will be addressed in a later part of this work and will determine much about the HOW.

According to Dr. Bruce Lipton in *The Wisdom of Your Cells* (which I rediscovered thanks to Fritzi's *Trauma Talks*), we are not victims of heredity but masters of our destiny. Dr. Lipton outlines this with an understanding of how much our environment plays a role in our lives. Since we can change our environment, we can change our destiny.

He proved this scientifically. About 40 years ago he was cloning stem cells. Stem cells are an embryonic cell that divides about every ten hours or so. After a week, according to Dr. Lipton, there are about 50,000 identical stem cells in a petri dish all originating from a single parent cell.

He takes these and divides them into three groups providing a different environment to each group. Inside each environment he provides everything they need to survive much like an aquarium for fish. Each environment is composed with slight differences. The outcome is in one group he gets muscle cells, in another group bone cells, and the other fat cells.

The whole point is that the environment determines what the stem cells become. Now, we can apply this to our own lives. We see ourselves as (enter name here) a single organism, but in reality, we are a community of cells. There are 50 trillion cells that are the living entity, and we are actually the community, a "skin-covered petri dish" with 50 trillion cells inside.

We have an environment, a culture medium called blood. The chemical composition of the blood determines the fate of the cells and therefore the genetics. The cell reads the environment the same regardless of whether it's in the skin or the petri dish. So what determines the chemical composition of the blood?

According to Dr. Lipton, the "brain is the chemist." How does the brain determine which chemicals to send? The answer is the human mind which interprets our experiences. What do we see? What do we interpret? What are we looking for in the world?

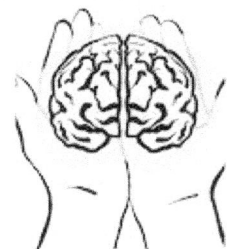

**We can change our patterns!**

*"The beauty of epigenetics is that it's reversible, and the beauty of the brain is that it's plastic."*

-Dr. Margaret McCarthy

Our interpretation of what is happening within and around us causes our brain to release certain chemicals into the blood. When I see someone I love, this is translated by the brain into chemical responses (dopamine, oxytocin, growth hormones, etc.). Now imagine seeing someone you fear. Stress hormones are instead released. This sets us up for fight, flight, and freeze responses and have an entirely different effect on ourselves and our environment.

From these questions, Dr. Lipton took these love chemicals and put them inside the petri dish with stem cells and they grew beautifully. Then he took the fear chemicals and placed them inside another petri dish with stem cells and the cells stopped growing. They went into protection mode and closed themselves off. They died.

The mind interprets and the brain translates these interpretations into electrical and chemical impulses which are released into the blood and therefore the body. This controls our genes. Thus, our cells respond to our interpretation, not what's being interpreted. This says a lot about how we actually control our destiny by HOW we experience what happens to us.

Positive and negative thinking have equally powerful impacts on our destiny because they can override our genes. Wow!

This is terrific news! It means we can change our patterns by our choices and are not bound to heredity or other factors that might otherwise keep us bound to a given destiny. Cases of twins separated at birth help further demonstrate what I'm talking about.

At the same age, they experience significantly different health. One might have heart disease by their mid-forties while the other remains in perfect health. Although they contain the same DNA and the same genes, epigenetics used these in very different ways.

As you think about your own history, including what you might otherwise believe is your destiny because of your genes, keep in mind this epigenetic factor. Depending on our choices today, we can make what we were born with better or worse. Our perceptions and interpretations of our experiences have everything to do with how our genes act.

## Adverse Childhood Experiences Study

This study was released by Dr. Vincent Felitti of Kaiser Permanente and Dr. Rob Alda at the Center for Disease Control in 1995. It demonstrates that there was a crisis in our hands which required our immediate attention surrounding maltreatment/neglect and family dysfunction.

The ACEs Quiz arose to determine which ACEs, if any, an individual has experienced. Since the original study, the term ACEs has expanded to include four more categories of trauma experience.

✔ **Adverse Circuitry Expression**: For example, autism, fetal alcohol syndrome, cerebral palsy, Fragile X syndrome, Asperger's, epilepsy (seizure disorder),

ADD/ADHD, etc.

✔ **Adverse Community Environments**: For example, high unemployment, low access to social services, limited economic mobility, poor housing conditions, food deserts, unsafe neighborhoods and parks, systemic racism

✔ **Adverse Cultural Exposures**: For example, racism, homophobia, ageism, sexism, classism, ableism, etc.

✔ **Adverse Catastrophic Events**: For example, Covid-19, pandemics, extreme weather patterns, war, rising sea levels/flooding, earthquakes, tsunamis, wildfires

As you may already note, these categories relate to events that can potentially change the way we experience reality for the worse and leave us with a chronic threat response.

Consider how much the world has changed since Covid-19. Once we learned how easily we could catch the virus and how devastating its impacts could be, other people became increasingly threatened. Many lost loved ones along the way. Our whole way of life has changed, and we remain affected by it in many ways.

When my mother was already dying of four different cancers, she caught Covid. For her, it was nothing in comparison to what was eating away at her body and ultimately causing her death. A year and a half later, I was among two dozen men in a pod of about 60 who caught it.

I couldn't eat. For days, I experienced a fever and an excruciating headache. Nausea consumed every move I made that required me to get vertical, and after I lost my sense of taste and smell, I wondered if I might die.

At the worst, most dangerous facilities in the state and only six months after arriving there, losing 24 years' worth of accumulated property, and standing within 10 yards of the most gruesome murder of one of my neighbors by members of his own gang, I lay there wondering if I would ever make it out of the cell I had undergone months of time locked inside because of ongoing violence.

The pandemic affected me in ways directly tied to the most adverse experiences I have ever faced as an adult. In the end, I was forced to grow i.e., to increase my capacity to bounce back. I can thank how I worked through those events for the man I am today. The struggle to shift from survival to thriving was not an easy one. It left scars, but the wounds have healed.

> "ACEs are the main determinant of the health and social well-being of the nation."   ~Vincent Felitti

ACEs have several risk factors, including poor mental health, disease, risk behavior, and challenges to one's life potential. Thankfully, as Rob Anda points out, "What is predictable is preventable." We can modify how we respond to events in our lives and, in doing so, recreate our world.

## Resilience

What matters more than our ACE score? Our Resilience score!

Resilience is our capacity to adapt to adversity through the skills and capabilities we develop. It begins with "monkey see, monkey do" and flourishes in proportion to how it's promoted in your environment. So we find examples of it that we can see, learn from them, and build communities where they can become protective factors.

Resilience building is the rewiring of your threat predictions into safety predictions. Protective factors are systems and strategies we put in place to help rewire a threat to safety. They help mitigate the effects of trauma. A high ACEs score with positive childhood experiences makes the impacts of trauma far less than a low ACEs score with little to no positive childhood experience.

- Protective Factors help buffer the effects of trauma.
- Positive Childhood Experiences (PCEs) are among the protective factors that can help to mitigate trauma.

Resilience Building Blocks are Protective Factors in action!

Consider an example from basketball. A rebound is a statistic awarded to a player who retrieves the ball after a missed shot or free throw.

The word resilience literally means to rebound, i.e., to bounce back. So, when a shot is made, and you miss, our resilience is demonstrated by our capacity to reset, take another shot and score. The average offensive rebounding percentage in the NBA is 27%, and defensive rebounding is almost 80%. Consider the points scored in a game and how much that would be reduced if not for rebounds being a part of the game.

Similarly, in life, resilience is about how we deal with missing a shot and our ability to rebound, i.e., to score points despite the initial setback and/or adversity. Our opponent is not another person or people who stand in our way, as with basketball. No, for us, the adversity we face is the interpretations of our experiences that cause us to miss a shot and limit our capacity to rebound when we do.

Because we act on our own statistical predictions, the only opponent we face is the previous version of ourselves. The voice in our heads that speaks all the negative beliefs and interpretations based on our past is what we must transform to find the courage, resolve, and, yes, resilience to give it (life) another shot despite our earlier mistakes.

It is never too late to begin implementing positive lifetime experiences to help buffer the effects of trauma. The *42 Resilience Building Blocks* found at the end of this book are protective factors in action! The more positive relationships we form based on qualities of acceptance, belonging, trust, honesty, integrity, love, and security are the best ways to begin overcoming the impacts of our own trauma.

Again, it is about awakening to the true, authentic self buried under perhaps years of prediction errors and the resulting negative self-image. Community Resilience happens when protective factors are applied to our societies, influencing law enforcement, mental health, social services, businesses, neighborhoods, media, early childhood learning, etc. Is this not the way we "restore" justice? Lacking this kind of knowledge and insight, can we truly say that our methods, i.e., our strategies, can be effectively restorative?

# Brain Networks and Their Needs

We briefly considered how the brain operates in terms of its networks. I described this using the global airport network analogy. Relative to a more trauma-informed world we will now consider these networks as they relate to consciousness. I will categorize these networks and explore them according to their needs. This is crucial to our understanding of trauma.

There are a few reasons we may point out as to why these brain networks are important to behavior.

✔ It helps us to clearly understand each brain network, identify its needs, and recognize the resulting behaviors stemming from such needs.

✔ We must increase our capacity to evaluate and identify our own needs and then shift to and address the needs of others.

✔ Select effective strategies and skills to address needs from a place of connection instead of correction (i.e., empathy vs. judgment).

~~~

For gold panners, panning is a science. There are a few basic principles. Among them, the main one is that whatever precious metal has been deposited in any given location is an effect of what began somewhere upstream from where they were.

The same may be said for our behaviors. They are an effect of what is happening upstream. In this case, the stream flows from the needs the brain networks communicate. Try to keep this image in mind as we explore these networks in greater detail.

## Safety Networks

Like all others, these brain networks seek to predict whether or not their needs are being met and whether what is coming will keep them being met. When triggered, the need to be safe results in various strategies. This network is our body's alarm and arousal system. When activated, our body's instinct is to "Fight," "Flee," or "Freeze."

Fighting instinct may involve hitting, pushing, screaming, biting, kicking, lying, etc. It is a resistance to what is occurring in the present moment. Fighting also represents resistance but manifests as Fleeing in some ways, too. It is a withdrawal, running away, or hiding from what is occurring. This can be literal or figurative, as with the use of drugs and/or alcohol.

On the other hand, Freezing is the opposite of the other two. It accepts what is happening and surrenders to it by complying or giving in.

All of these are attempts to meet the core safety and security needs. They manifest in a range of styles and strategies, but behind what we may judge as ugly or beautiful, there is a life-serving source.

So many people inside prison have brains accentuated to the safety networks. Some fear being assaulted because of their crimes, outstanding debts arising from drug abuse, gang politics, etc. Others bring it with them from the life lived before incarceration, and others have maladapted their response to the world because of adverse childhood experiences.

By arming ourselves with knowledge and insight, we may help them reframe how they see and experience the world. In doing so, we not only increase their safety but the safety of everyone in such proximity that they could be the ones paying the price for such people's trauma.

Among the resilience-building alternatives, we can learn to ask for help, learn to self-advocate, develop communication skills, sense triggers that lead to negative behavior, connect with others' feelings, etc. These are among the *42 Resilience Building Blocks* found at the end of this book.

## Connection Networks

Acceptance and belonging are needs at the heart of our Connection Networks. Behind what we are aware of from moment to moment our body's experience and interpretation system wants to be certain that we are connected to ourselves and others.

When disconnected, we might find that among the strategies employed are attention-seeking, gossiping, bragging, etc. These represent attempts to fill the void perceived to separate someone from being connected. The method will be based on past experiences linking to present predictions. We ask, "What can I do to meet this need for connection?"

We will only attempt to connect in ways we believe meet that need. Our strategies will be limited to what we know. When we don't know what to do, we do all kinds of things that turn out to do the opposite of connecting. Looking to those much wiser than us, asking them for help, and implementing their methods can be a healthy first step in improving our relationships and supporting our brains' safety networks.

As we learn to build resilience, we may find improved success by telling someone we love them, developing self-esteem, forming positive relationships, learning to show appreciation, etc.

## Learning Networks

Almost like a ladder, our needs have levels. Our brains are constantly testing the waters behind the scenes. The first test is the safety test. If our perceptions do not indicate a threat, we move to connection. We look for ways to enrich our relationship with self and others. Once this is satisfied, the doors of learning open. We are now capable of growth and learning. But even in a learning environment, if we do not feel safe or that we belong, our chances of correctly accessing the needed networks to engage decrease.

When our learning needs are met, we are able to initiate things, reason, focus, plan, organize, remember, and self-monitor. These networks have been called our executive networks because they are the integration and management system when everything is in working order. When things are not in working order, it's like the kids running the house while the parents are away.

To improve our resilience so as to increase accessibility to these networks, we can model problem-solving skills, develop hope, develop a growth perspective, share something important, feel empowered to express ideas and ask questions, set clear expectations and boundaries, etc.

## Prediction Drives Behavior

These systems, as described in relation to the networks I have been describing, each activate a prediction pattern. The threat arousal alarm system activates alarm, resistance, and exhaustion as a pattern. When we understand the energy cycle, we can better explain how all behavior is communication of some kind rather than seeing it as mal-intent. Again, behavior is merely an effect of what arose upstream.

We often say, "That's just the tip of the iceberg," when we express only a little of a story to get a floodgate of feedback. Well, as seen above, much like what is truly going on with someone, we see only a fraction. It's 90% behavior and 10% issue. On the surface, we have been taught to ask, "What's wrong with you?"

Below the surface is what this person has been through, neural patterns of behaviors, core beliefs, needs, values, etc. Thus, what we find in someone depends on what we are looking for, i.e., the questions we ask. The remaining 90% of the real issues are root issues like ACEs.

> *"Words seed concepts; concepts drive your predictions; predictions regulate your body budget; your body budget determines how you feel."*
> ~Dr. Lisa Feldman Barrett

I would add, "How you feel motivates action, and action becomes behavior."

## Windows of "Stress Tolerance"

In her book *Help for Billy*, trauma expert Heather Forbes discusses the differences between healthy children and trauma-impacted children relative to their ability to tolerate stress. Like a fully opened window, healthy children have a safe distance between their normal state and breaking point.

Unfortunately, a trauma-impacted child has a window barely opened. The space between stimulus and response is significantly reduced, thereby increasing the use of the threat arousal system.

Baseline levels of stress...

Healthy child's baseline of stress

Trauma impacted child's baseline of stress

Heather Forbes, Help for Billy

So, we learn that there is an entire unseen world behind our own and others' behaviors. This world is created in large part by what has happened to the individual and what has changed inside because of what happened. As we move from trauma to triumph, our threat moves to safety. Fear shifts to love.

# The Individual Experience

Each of us is born into the world with our incomplete brains keyed to love, trust, and safety. This is a natural default we are each created with regardless of our race, religion, or any other distinction that otherwise distinguishes us from one another.

But at birth, our environment becomes a secondary womb for the brain as it quickly seeks to adapt for survival. Along the way, less-than-nourishing experiences occur. That's when this sense of love, trust, and safety begins to compete for supremacy against what arises from such experiences.

When my son was a toddler, he loved it when I would pick him up as high as possible and let him sway back and forth. It was a fun experience, and he allowed me complete control. Not a fear in the world kept him from placing his complete love, trust, and safety in my hands.

But one day, absent-minded of where I was standing, I raised him right up into the dining room ceiling fan. It did not result in injury, but it scared him. From that moment on, something had changed. He never wanted to do this inside the house again. You see, the event was less than nurturing and created fear inside him. This fear modified his concepts of that experience and anything like it. The brain does this to ensure safety and keep such events' negative outcomes from recurring.

At the heart of every fear, i.e., at fear's core, is a primordial fear of losing control. This fear ultimately links to past events when less-than-nourishing experiences arise. This is the spring behind a threat response.

It set into motion defensive behaviors to help meet safety needs. When I would try to pick him up, even without intending to play that game, he would tense up and need reassurance. Sometimes, he would say, "Ehhhh!!" or "Nooo, daddy!!" imagining himself going through the experience all over again. So, these less-than-nourishing experiences generate fears of losing control, which leads to defensive behaviors designed to maintain safety.

Now, let's imagine that despite his attempts to get me to stop, I continued anyway and that in these future instances, he would continue to get hurt. What might he do if his defensive behaviors continue to fail? His defensive strategies would likely change until he eventually became aggressive and offensive.

The brain does whatever it takes to stop the threat. Once the learning networks have gone offline, things like laws being broken and consequences accruing have no place in our awareness.

How do you imagine someone harmed by crime might shift their attention from retribution to restoration, knowing what has been shared about the individual experience? How do you shift your focus toward those who have harmed you after learning this?

This is the individual experience we have each come to know for ourselves. There's no cookie-cutter approach to the process. Although the strategies employed at each phase are similar, they are uniquely crafted to meet the needs of the person under consideration.

We haven't even addressed the fact that there's no guarantee how effective such strategies would be—that would be determined by one's concept of safety and how to meet safety needs. Every child learns their way based on how they are taught by their environment.

Now, replace the above example with abuse. The threat predictions are no longer acute. The more often they are repeated, the more hyper-vigilant the threat responses become. Imagine a system designed to come online only during a crisis, staying online for longer and longer periods of time. The safety networks start to pattern the body's use of resources in the same way during those crises when threats overwhelm.

Under such conditions, connection and learning become increasingly challenging to achieve. The preoccupation with safety needs begins co-opting energy supplies in exaggerated attempts to stay safe. To conserve those resources to not waste them, one may begin to take shortcuts to meet other needs. When the brain repeatedly wires for threat, the condition can become chronic as life unfolds.

Let's return to ACEs. Consider the ten questions in light of the individual experience described above. Without the right intervention, any one of these experiences sets life on a trajectory of obstacles and challenges unknown to those lacking such adversity.

In Bruce Perry and Oprah Winfrey's book *What Happened to You*, I learned about a young boy, Sam, who suddenly and unexpectedly became disruptive in class after a new teacher arrived. It took some time, but with help, it was discovered that Sam's threat arousal system would go on high alert after his brain would register the same cologne his abusive parent wore.

He would smell it as he was getting beaten. Sam wasn't even conscious of why his behavior would suddenly change. He used every resource when triggered to try and maintain safety when his statistical predictions produced a threat response.

When such dysregulation occurs, the goal is to bring a triggered individual back to love, trust, and safety. Once the discovery was made, the teacher gladly changed the cologne, and Sam's behavior completely changed.

Thankfully, a trauma-informed response resulted in strategies that could successfully address the true cause behind the behavior, i.e., the unmet needs. Had it not been for this, Sam might be sitting in a prison cell for committing a crime.

This kind of intervention is consistent with restorative justice recalibrated. It is tailored to Sam rather than seeking to have Sam conform to a generalized corrective measure. The latter lacks the knowledge and insight as defined in this trauma-informed paradigm.

## Know Your ROLES with Trauma

How we respond to triggered individuals matters. We become a part of the equation that contributes to threat or safety.

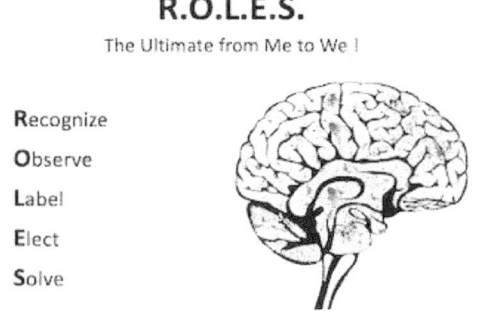

Becoming trauma-informed is about shifting from me to us. Thus, the more effective we become in knowing our R.O.L.E.S., the better the interventions result. It is living with Ubuntu consciousness, i.e., I am because we are. Making this transition begins with our own predictions.

Again, what we see in the world depends upon the concepts guiding our predictions. New concepts seed new predictions opening our world to new behaviors and therefore new outcomes.

Let's look at each of these components individually.

### Recognize

Recognizing what R.O.L.E.S. we play is the first step in practicing a trauma-informed approach to everyday life. If we lack understanding of our own emotional constructions and predictions, we will lack the knowledge and insight to use effective intervention strategies.

Our caregivers shape our mirror neurons, which are responsible for giving us the capacity to understand what it might be like to walk a mile in someone else's shoes, so to speak. This relationship between the caregiver and child is also called "serve and return." This shapes our capacity for empathy. Similarly, our behavior shapes the mirror neurons of others, which helps them empathize with us.

Like the still face experiment, which demonstrates how much an infant's well-being depends on the positive visible indicators of connection with the mother, so do we require support in self-regulation. Thus, our calm sets the stage for calmness in others. Our chaos also sets the stage for the chaos in others.

In the former, the true and authentic awareness of selfhood extends into another human life. We bring our calm to their chaos. In the latter, the false self, in an illusionary space of isolation, extricates itself from connection with another human life.

Some examples often used to demonstrate the impact of mirror neurons are witnessing other people yawn and suddenly getting the urge to yawn. Thus, anything observable has the potential to impact our inner life. If we have negative thoughts and feelings toward someone, their mirror neurons pick up on this at some level.

This is why self-awareness of our own trauma, predictions, and judgments is a necessary first step in knowing our R.O.L.E.S. in practicing trauma-informed care. By knowing what triggers us, we can become more resilient. We can ask for support from others who can help us when we are approaching a situation that, without support, might lead us to dysregulation.

Our family origins shape our triggers, and nature and nurture both influence what we bring to relationships. When we recognize the emotional predictions of threats, we can begin reducing the stressors and restore the energy balance. Being forewarned is being forearmed. Learning basic regulation skills that work for you can become the basis of developing an action plan for threat prediction.

We can also develop an action plan for prevention. It only makes sense to prepare for what's coming, and there is no doubt that someone will trigger us at some point.

Once we become aware of our state of mind, we may help ourselves shift from threat to safety. Deep breathing is considered the best way to self-regulate. It is the number one neurological response to threat.

The ability to calm oneself down is one of the *42 Resilience Building Blocks*. (See full list at back of the book.) Over time we become increasingly able to manage our brain networks.

We become at one with the air traffic control and pilots from our previous global airport analogy. Above all, we must recognize that taking care of ourselves (meeting our own safety needs) must come first.

As a personal anecdote, my friend and mentor Rick Griffin, Executive Director of the Community Resilience Initiative, says that if you genuinely want to be a H.E.R.O. you will:

- ✔ **H**old your tongue
- ✔ **E**xamine your predictions
- ✔ **R**id yourself of threat predictions
- ✔ **O**ffer yourself an affirmation

Another fun way to "recognize" is to make whatever is happening for another person about them (instead of about you!). When you can stay regulated and maintain a balanced energy state, you are more likely to help someone shift their response to you. It's often not about you!

In other words, consider the QTIP acronym (**Q**uit **T**aking **I**t **P**ersonally).

> *"Nothing others do is because of you. What others say and do is a projection of their own reality, their own dream. When you are immune to the opinions and actions of others, you won't be the victim of needless suffering."* ~Miguel Ruiz

Before proceeding to the next component, consider which threat predictions are the most challenging for you to recognize.

## Observe

We can build resilience by learning to sense triggers that create negative behavior. To help us sense these triggers, we must learn how to observe external behaviors accurately, reflecting our internal predictions. Remember, behaviors are downstream from the predictions arising from our met and unmet needs.

Many of these behaviors are observable. A threat response is like a chain reaction. There are usually visible indicators that let us know what is happening with an individual, but first we must have a relationship with someone before we will know what their visible indicators are.

There are three steps to consider:

- ✔ Rage
- ✔ React
- ✔ Regret

We want to help someone regulate before they get to the rage stage. Behavior is communication. It offers insight all the time. There is verbal communication (words), nonverbal communication (body language, posture, facial expressions, breathing mannerisms, etc.), and paraverbal communication (volume, cadence, tone, pitch, etc.). According to Stuart Shanker, author of *Self Reg*, there are five identifiable indicators of threat responses.

- ✔ Biological
- ✔ Emotional
- ✔ Cognitive
- ✔ Social
- ✔ Prosocial

These five categories may help you gain insight as you utilize observation to help yourself and others stay regulated. Shanker says that we need to learn how to become stress detectives so that we can truly understand what is causing people's threat predictions.

The following pages illustrate the five domains.

a trauma-informed approach to rebuilding the web of relationships harmed by crime

**Biological.** These affect our physiological system and take our bodies out of optimal function (These can include noises, smells, visual stimulation, not enough exercise, lack of sleep, etc.).

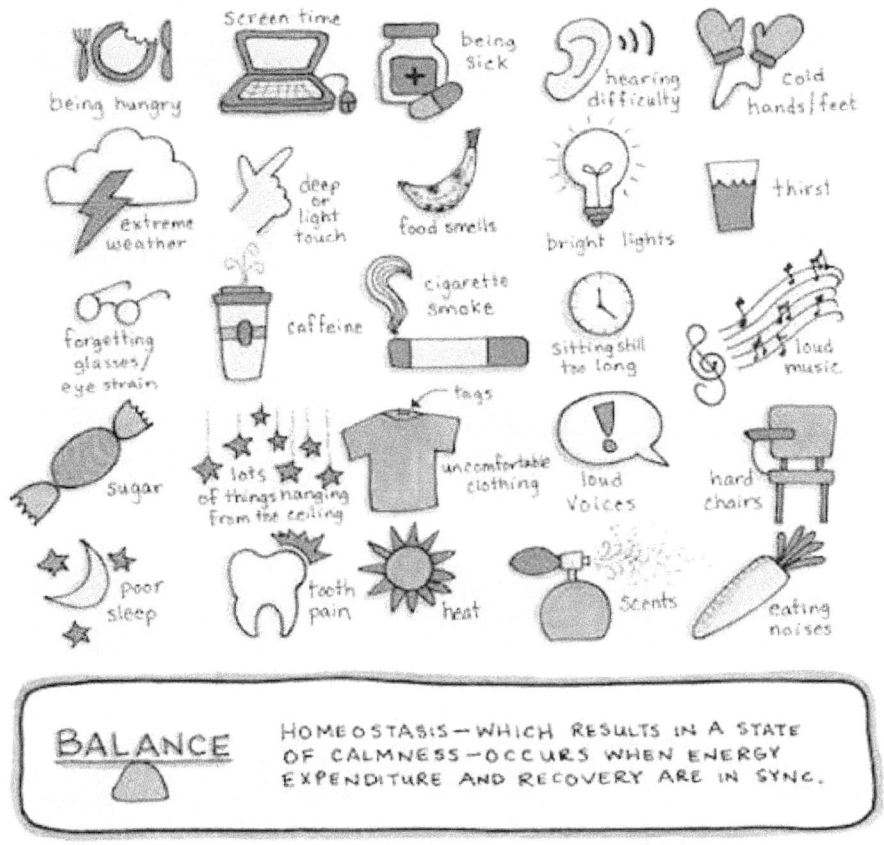

a trauma-informed approach to rebuilding the web of relationships harmed by crime

**Emotional.** Inability to experience and understand emotions. These include grief, loss, disappointment, change of routine, etc.

a trauma-informed approach to rebuilding the web of relationships harmed by crime

**Cognitive**. Usually caused by difficulty processing information. These include organizing thoughts, learning something new, making decisions, and being bored.

**Social.** Caused by difficulties picking up on social cues and understanding the effects of one's actions on others (peer pressure, bullying, exclusion, meeting new people, etc.)

**Prosocial.** This can be tied to the inability to cope with other people's stress (sharing, telling the truth, understanding right and wrong, etc.).

## Label

As a disclaimer, the use of the word label is analogous to what you would put on a file to help organize it inside a filing cabinet with other files. We are labeling the tip of the iceberg elements, not the "below the iceberg" things. It requires us to become like a video camera and take in all of the observable actions. So, this requires us to remove any quality that does not exist for the camera, i.e., only what you see. All judgment is suspended.

This method reduces the risk of being misunderstood because we only express what we see. We can inquire about the part of the iceberg underneath what's visible. Once we have established a connection and permission, we can begin making empathic guesses about what's happening inside them.

Making proper labels of observable details can help us connect the predictions to the behavior and the behavior to the need. We elevate our questions to the true, authentic part of ourselves, free of egotistical judgments, biases, and stereotypes that might further disconnect someone from themselves or us. Like with the Babemba tribe, we are seeking to reestablish love, trust, and safety to restore this person to their true authentic self. By learning to label what we see properly, we lay the groundwork for the next component: electing positive intent.

## Elect

Electing positive intent means that you are choosing to believe that maybe they don't know how to express themselves in any other way than the way they are now. Perhaps this is all they have as a way of dealing with stress.

In a situation where someone has called us names as a way of being defensive about a perceived threat they feel toward us, we want to "elect" (choose) to give them the benefit of the doubt. We want to have a growth mindset vs. a fixed mindset.

A fixed mindset cannot adapt or learn. It remains rigid, refusing to change. A growth mindset sees challenges as opportunities to develop or strengthen abilities. Individuals with a growth mindset believe that their talents aren't fixed and can improve if they put in the effort. This is a resilience mindset!

Meanwhile, those who think abilities are set in stone—and won't change—have a fixed mindset. They're under the impression their skills will never get better no matter how hard they try.

Mindsets are not permanent. People may adopt a growth mindset during some periods of their life and have a fixed one at other times. Your behavior can be entirely different when it comes to separate challenges, and even flip-flop between mindsets over time.

**What Kind of Mindset Do You Have?**

Growth Mindset
- I can learn anything I want to.
- When I'm frustrated, I persevere.
- I want to challenge myself.
- When I fail, I learn.
- Tell me I try hard.
- If you succeed, I'm inspired.
- My effort and attitude determine everything.

Fixed Mindset
- I'm either good at it, or I'm not.
- When I'm frustrated, I give up.
- I don't like to be challenged.
- When I fail, I'm no good.
- Tell me I'm smart.
- If you succeed, I feel threatened.
- My abilities determine everything.

Carol Dweck: Mindset: The New Psychology of Success

A growth mindset is genuinely advantageous for individuals to have. It allows you to reframe your approach to problems and stay motivated to improve your skill set. Instead of thinking, "I can't do this," you'll think, "I can't do it yet."

Carol Deck describes all of this more thoroughly in her book Mindset: The New Psychology of Success. Electing positive intent starts a change from fixed to growth.

The shift from the former to the latter may begin by recognizing that your internal judgment shapes your response. When you are able to see through the drama into the trauma, i.e., through the ego into the true self of the other person, you will demonstrate that you truly understand the language of behavior. The neuro lens will prove effective for having applied the knowledge, insight, and strategies to the unique needs of someone experiencing a threat.

Electing positive intent creates a kind of fork in the road because it is where we are required to choose between drama or trauma. What we decide starts to dictate the intervention we use.

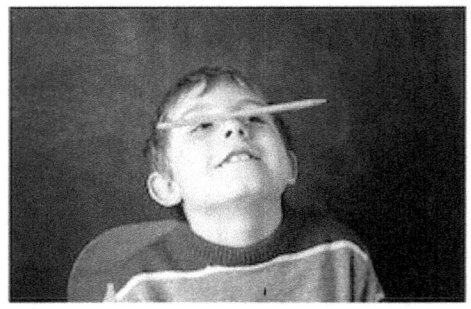

✔ Drama brings out judgment and enlivens our threat response. We are more likely to offer our chaos.

✔ Trauma brings out our natural compassion. We are offering our calm.

When we choose the positive, we reduce our lens of judgment and bias. Use your neuro-lens. What do you see?

Trauma or Drama?

In Star Wars, a pivotal scene is where Luke Skywalker, during his training under Yoda, must undergo a test. He must face himself. As he prepares, he straps on his prized lightsaber, but Yoda makes clear that he will not need the weapon.

"What's in there?" Luke inquires.

"Only what you take with you," Yoda responded as he watched Luke disappear into the cave.

We face in the world only what we take with us. If we see drama it is because we carry within us concepts of drama which seek a perceptual counterpart. If we see trauma it is equally true that we must have concepts of trauma seeking a perceptual counterpart. Thus, we find what we are looking for.

Knowing our R.O.L.E.S. is about awakening the part of ourselves that does not seek to strap on weapons of warfare to face life's challenges. Rather, we bring the C.U.R.E. for judgment and blame:

- ✔ **C**larity
- ✔ **U**nderstanding
- ✔ **R**espect
- ✔ **E**mpathy

As an exercise, the next time you are in a place where many people may be viewed, make some observations of individuals and ask yourself if it's drama or trauma. See if this exercise teaches you about your ability to elect positive intent. Remember that as you evolve the capacity to recognize trauma rather than drama, you are rewiring the brain and creating a new life.

## Solve

The meaning of Solve is to address the needs of the trauma-impacted individuals by reversing the prediction. If someone starts predicting a threat, our R.O.L.E.S. is about moving someone from threat to love, trust, and safety. We can be accountable only when we feel safe and connected. Therefore, as far as restorative justice is concerned, it only makes sense to recalibrate toward a trauma-informed worldview because there cannot be proper accountability without aiming to help someone who has created harm experience what's necessary for this to occur.

No matter what we try, only win/win outcomes that address the brain networks will actually secure safety for someone who is triggered, provide a sense of connection, and ensure that they are ready and able to learn.

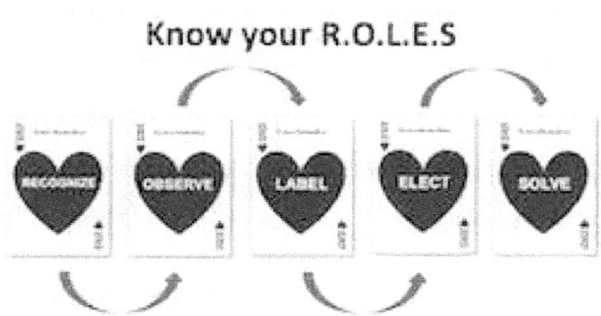

As we aim to solve this problem, we must first recognize that stress behavior is the physiological response to threat. Remember to reframe the behavior, identify what is driving the stressors, reduce the stress, and respond with calm.

Throughout *Restorative Justice Recalibrated* (RJR) we aim to demonstrate how past traumas link up with present behavior. The method employed offers an integrated resilience-building framework seeking to contribute to the restoration of justice as opposed to discussing it or seeing it as some distant goal or lofty ideal better suited for people in other places.

RJR seeks to untangle the webs of influence from childhood trauma. When it is recognized that being abused and/or neglected has led to harmful actions, punishment turns into a compassionate narrative that instead seeks to restore life.

Instead of focusing on punishment alone, RJR embraces the idea of creating a supportive environment for healing. This includes recognizing your trauma history, acknowledging how it has impacted your behavior, as well as providing opportunities for therapeutic intervention and personal growth. It understands that people do not develop criminal tendencies alone; therefore, they will not evolve resilience and prosocial strategies alone.

At the end of the day, the only force in the universe powerful enough to break the bonds of trauma, of criminal thinking, of addictive behavior, and anything else keeping human beings isolated and alienated enough to act contrary to how we were created to be is LOVE.

## Supportive Environments for Healing

RJR goes beyond retributive measures to embrace healing's transformative power.

Imagine an environment that recognizes your history of trauma not as a justification for harmful actions but as a call for you to admit it and grow personally. When we create a supportive space rather than a punitive one, we foster an atmosphere conducive to reformation and well-being. As indicated previously, accountability will not happen outside of safety and connection.

Restorative justice practice transforms rather than punishes as it understands that healing creates an environment where change can occur easily and quickly. Compare this to compelled obedience under duress when one does not intend to change or improve themselves. Such a place is more likely to exacerbate pre-existing trauma than rehabilitate.

This method proves much less effective than a rehabilitative plan designed specifically for the causes behind one's specific unskilled acts. The latter entails actively looking at how trauma impacts behavior and providing pathways for rehabilitation that direct individuals towards recovery rather than shame and alienation from the communities they must re-enter upon release.

Restorative justice, in theory, and by definition, commits itself to a trauma-informed approach. It takes a distinctive stance on addressing harm. Instead of resorting to punitive measures that often perpetuate a cycle of trauma, it envisions a system that explores alternative methods grounded in understanding and compassion.

## Healing Networks Beyond Punishment

A trauma-informed approach in restorative justice incorporates a healing process that involves empathy and community engagement. Restorative justice sees an entire community working together towards understanding, nurturing empathy, and creating an extended support network beyond punishment. Yes, it helps one build resilience, whereas before, there was only succumbing to trauma's unmitigated influence.

"Resilience Trump ACEs" means that developing resilience can minimize the effects of ACEs. Restorative justice enhances resilience against past traumas by focusing on strengths instead of weaknesses. It provides support and offers opportunities for healing.

Imagine a person who has consistently engaged in misconduct stemming from their ACEs but who has been supported by her society to incorporate resilience-building strategies into her life. In restorative justice workshops, members take part in empathy-building exercises where they gain deep insights into enduring impacts caused by trauma. This shared perception becomes a bond between them, opening the door to efforts toward resilience.

Sarah's recovery relies heavily on community involvement, thus acting as a safety net compared with conventional punitive measures that leave one alienated from one's community. Such collective endeavors enhance Sarah's ability to withstand future adversities while addressing wider systemic problems within their society. Such not only helps Sarah but also prevents future adverse childhood experiences from occurring. She has learned to ask for help, developed communication skills, formed healthy friendships, and developed other interpersonal skills. These are but a few of what the Community Resilience Initiative calls *Resilience Building Blocks*. (See the full list at the end of this book.)

## Resilience Inside Corrections

The need to develop resilience becomes even more significant within the harsh correctional setting. Within this framework, "Resilience Trumps ACEs" implies that fostering resilience becomes a transformative way of dealing with ACEs effects. Below are some ways prison programs can promote resiliency.

Instead of merely concentrating on your past traumas or involvement with the criminal justice system, it is vital to adopt resilience-building strategies. Identifying and utilizing your strengths form the foundations upon which resilience is built. It involves recognizing talents, skills, and attributes contributing towards personal growth versus rehabilitation efforts respectively.

A correctional environment requires comprehensive support to build resilience. These may include mental health services, counseling, educational programs, vocational training, and sometimes most importantly, a positive social network.

By meeting the diverse needs of individuals, a prison program can foster a conducive setting for resilience. But as you and I know, there are many reasons why you may find yourself without this support.

It becomes increasingly crucial for you to do everything you can to build resilience even when unsupported by the system. As the individuals who created the harm, the urge to make things right can be enough of a motivating factor to become a different person while incarcerated—and it is within our grasp to do so.

See the *42 Resilience Building Blocks* created by Teresa Basila at Community Resilience Initiative (CRI) at the end of the book. By cultivating resilience through these practices, you build conscience and character, increase your chances of succeeding in life, and make up for lost time in maturing as a human being.

Nevertheless, correctional systems, at some point, must implement trauma-informed programming, which includes accepting and understanding the impact of ACEs on your life. Trauma-informed approaches prioritize creating safe spaces, fostering trust, and providing rehabilitative interventions accentuated to your unique needs.

Educational initiatives are also essential in developing resilience. Educational programs within a correctional setting provide opportunities for you to learn new skills, broaden your horizons, and create an image of a future with hope. Education acts as a catalyst for personal growth beyond prison walls and forms a basis for resilience. It significantly lessens your chances of returning to prison because it grows and accentuates the learning networks of the brain.

Restorative circles incorporated into a correctional environment also promote community spirit and connectedness. These circles help solve collective problems by opening dialogue channels, thereby building connection and empathy. Through these healthy practices, you can develop a support network and strengthen your resilience by forging meaningful relationships.

I recommend Howard Zehr's *Big Book of Restorative Justice* for a detailed look at this. Building resilience goes beyond incarceration. A comprehensive prison program involves careful transition planning and reentry support, which assists in preparing you for what lies ahead upon release and gives you the necessary tools to navigate the complexities associated with reintegration into society.

When restorative justice adopts strength-based, trauma-informed holistic perspectives within correctional environments, it becomes a dynamic force toward building resilience. The focus moves from seeing just through the lens of past traumas to recognizing inherent strengths that contribute towards the rehabilitative journey.

RJR programs prioritize creating safe and supportive spaces for participants by understanding potential triggers and implementing practices that promote emotional safety. As empathic capacities increase, one's natural state of compassion also returns, making creating harm more difficult to follow through with.

Within the restorative process, trauma-informed practices empower you to recognize the impact of your past lack of control by offering choices. This empowerment contributes to a sense of agency and self-determination.

Restorative justice embraces a resilience-building approach focusing on your capabilities rather than solely on deficits. This approach acknowledges that everyone has unique strengths that can contribute to the restoration process.

This approach becomes a conduit for healing trauma through connection, emphasizing dialogue and understanding. Meaningful restorative interactions contribute to a sense of belonging and support.

Trauma-informed restorative justice actively works to prevent re-traumatization. This involves careful consideration of the restorative process's language, approach, and overall structure to ensure it promotes healing rather than further harm.

Addressing ACEs within a trauma-informed restorative justice framework could potentially break the cycle of trauma and damage. In addition to you being directly involved in this transformational impact, there are also families and communities. *Resilience Trumps ACEs (RTA)* is an idea that suggests collective resilience can go beyond individual healing. Communities practicing RJR become more resilient because it fosters an environment that supports the well-being of all.

Much like the principles behind the *Babemba Forgiveness Ceremony* discussed in the earlier historical section of this book, working toward community resilience stems from the idea that we are each other's keepers. We belong to each other, are responsible for each other, and in truth, "Ubuntu," i.e., I am because we are.

This exploration into the intersection between trauma-informed practices, resilience, and restorative justice reveals a deep potential for your healing and transformation. RTA ceases to be just another guiding principle but instead becomes an invitation to restore strength and collective well-being within our communities. By recognizing ACEs, developing your neuro lens, and forming trauma-informed strategies, you can rewrite your story. You can rewire the brain to build resilience and overwrite old, outdated programming behind previous setbacks. Restorative justice as a transformative approach has the potential to heal personal wounds and promote community resilience and well-being, starting right where you are.

***

*"Of all the virtues we can learn, no trait is more useful, more essential for survival, and more likely to improve the quality of life than the ability to transform adversity into an enjoyable challenge."*

~Mihaly Csikszentmihalyi

# Flow: Finding Balance and Resilience

In the pursuit of recalibrating restorative justice and fostering resilience, I want to present a concept that has been meaningful for my journey of self-discovery—it's the state called Flow. Coined by psychologist Mihaly Csikszentmihalyi, Flow describes those moments when we are fully immersed in an activity, feeling energized, focused, and deeply involved. "Being in the Zone" is another way people often describe this state of awareness.

In this chapter, we explore how understanding and harnessing the power of Flow can contribute to building resilience and restoring lives within the context of trauma-informed approaches to restorative justice. Among the most important aspects of addressing trauma is reframing the world from threat to safety and that means changing our concepts.

The concept of Flow as described in the following sections has been an effective way for me to better gauge my own and others well being and form strategies to effectively shift from fear of loss of control to love, trust, and safety.

## Flow in Context of Trauma and Resilience

Imagine a river flowing steadily, navigating obstacles with grace and determination.

Similarly, in adversity, individuals can tap into their innate capacity for Flow, navigating challenges with resilience and determination. I believe understanding flow becomes essential with adverse childhood experiences (ACEs).

Flow provides a lens through which we can reframe our perspective on adversity, recognizing that our responses often reflect an imbalance between our skills and challenges. With trauma, adversity is experienced as a "threat,"

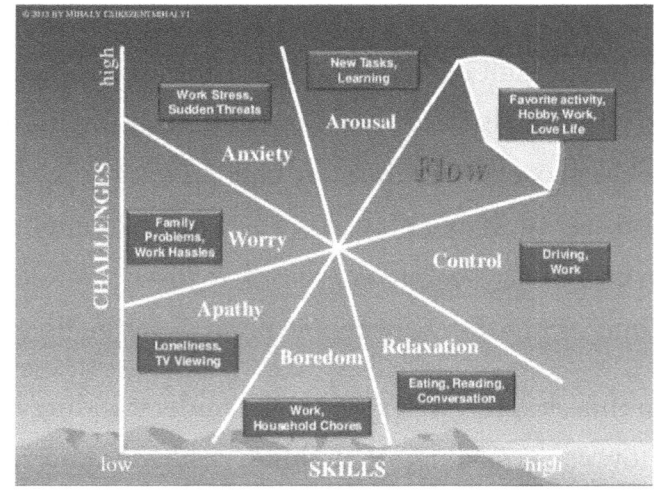

which triggers a plethora of emotions, leading to a negative cycle of experience and making it increasingly difficult to meet needs without creating harm for ourselves and/or others.

As you continue to familiarize yourself with your R.O.L.E.S, what follows will help you recognize your own internal states, make clear observations, accurately label what you are seeing, elect positive intent by realizing what is going on, and solving the problem by efficiently navigating toward skill development.

*a trauma-informed approach to rebuilding the web of relationships harmed by crime*

## Flow Map: Optimizing Skill and Challenge

At the heart of Flow Map lies a delicate balance between skill and challenge. When our skills match the challenges we encounter, we enter a state of Flow, experiencing heightened focus, creativity, and fulfillment. However, we may feel overwhelmed or anxious when the challenge exceeds our skill level.

Conversely, we risk boredom and disengagement if the challenge is too low. As discussed in the previous chapter, whether we are feeling safe or threatened determines our relationship to the world including traumatic experiences. The Flow diagram above can also be used to differentiate between a sense of threat and safety.

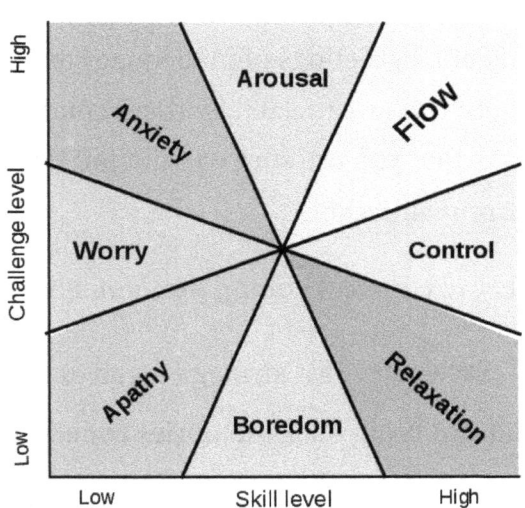

The Flow Map shows how skill and challenge levels are interrelated in their most basic form. We will explain each quadrant, discuss its related emotions, and explore its possible relationship to ACEs:

### Low Skills, Low Challenge (Apathy Zone)

**Emotion Keywords**: *boredom, apathy, disengagement, indifference*

In this area, you may feel blah or uninspired. The tasks at hand do not require much effort or interest from you; as such, you might become bored and disconnected from what you are doing. Consider this in light of ACEs. Traumatic experiences can lead to diminished self-worth and lack of motivation. It can seem increasingly difficult to exit this sense of being "stuck" as we increasingly identify with these feelings.

Alcohol and/or substance abuse is a strategy some use to mitigate this condition despite its ineffectiveness for the long term. The growing problem with K2 inside correctional environments demonstrates an apathetic motivation to doing time. It is an immobilizing escape but temporary avoidance from the responsibility for the unskilled acts that brought someone to prison.

If you have had adverse childhood experiences (ACEs) you might find relief in achieving flow states of low skill and low challenge as a way to cope with stress, triggers, or feelings of inadequacy arising from past trauma. In such instances where you are affected by these conditions, you only take up undemanding tasks that you are sure will not fail because it acts as an escape route from your current situation.

*Here are typical coping mechanisms that lead to the Apathy Zone state:*

✔ **Avoidance**: This strategy involves staying away from situations or activities that can bring back memories concerning your ACEs; you choose to remain within what feels comfortable to avoid being distressed more than necessary.

✔ **Diversion**: Sometimes, you may use mindless activities or substances such as excessive television or other forms of escapism so that, for a moment, emotional pain is taken away.

✔ **Self-imposed isolation**: You may withdraw socially and emotionally, avoiding interaction with others while missing out on personal growth opportunities through social connections.

✔ **Negative self-talk**: You might settle with less challenging activities due to low-effort beliefs about self-worth based on negative past experiences, making you think you don't deserve better.

*For healthier experiences filled with growth and fulfillment, the following measures could help to pull out of the Apathy Zone state:*

✔ **Therapeutic assistance**: You can seek professional help like therapy sessions or counseling aimed towards tackling the root causes of traumatic events in their lives and acquiring skills necessary for managing emotions when triggered. Even self help books or resources on the facility issued tablet can offer helpful insights.

✔ **Identification and questioning of negative beliefs**: You may be encouraged going through this phase by realizing that what you think negatively about yourself might not always be true; reframing these beliefs using transformative learning (discussed at length in a future chapter) can also foster positive self-image development.

✔ **Step-by-step exposure**: You can start by being open-minded about trying new things, which can be achieved by setting small, achievable goals, thereby building confidence over time.

✔ **Skill acquisition**: Seek out opportunities for learning different skills in areas you are interested in or curious about; this could be done through vocational training programs, educational pursuits, hobbies, etc., as these activities provide satisfaction when mastered.

✔ **Social support systems**: Create an environment where those around you act as a backbone when you need encouragement the most. Having a healthy support system makes it easier to step outside your comfort zone.

✔ **Showing self-compassion**: Embrace self-love by understanding that personal growth takes effort and time; any progress made along this path should be acknowledged. Minor setbacks ought not to demoralize but rather serve as lessons for success in future endeavors.

Implementing these strategies and accessing appropriate support services can gradually move anyone with ACEs from low-challenge, low-skill states into more fulfilling, resilient, and healthier lifestyles.

## Low Skills, High Challenge (Anxiety Zone)

**Emotion Keywords**: *anxiety, stress, overwhelm, frustration*

In this part of the flowchart, individuals come up against tasks or situations beyond their current abilities. Such tough challenges can bring up feelings of anxiety about achieving success since you still lack the necessary skills needed to succeed. Increased stress may arise while dealing with such pressures. Again, when threat responses shift from a state to a trait one will be more inclined to self-medicate or act in a manner that will create even more problems for oneself.

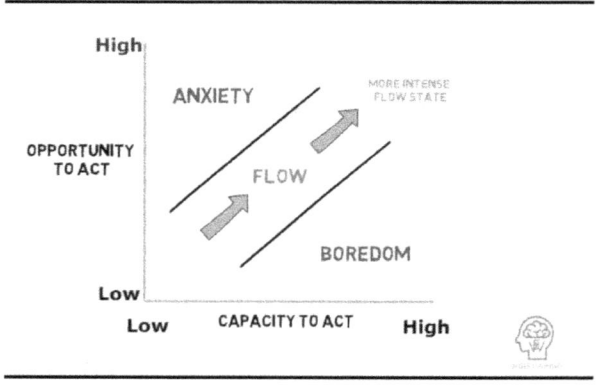

ACEs shape how we face challenges. Crime is essentially "unskilled actions" carried out by challenged individuals. If there had been more skills to meet the needs underlying the behavior, another altogether different strategy would have been employed instead. The nature of the skills we develop often depends on the kinds of challenges we face. During childhood, those with ACEs must develop survival skills different from those whose caregivers demonstrate the love, trust, and safety that often help shape altogether different skills.

If you have an unfavorable social background, getting into a flow state can be tricky as you have to deal with things that are way below your skill level and way above your challenge level. In this state, you may feel inadequate and ill-prepared for the tasks before you, leading to frustration, worry, or lack of confidence.

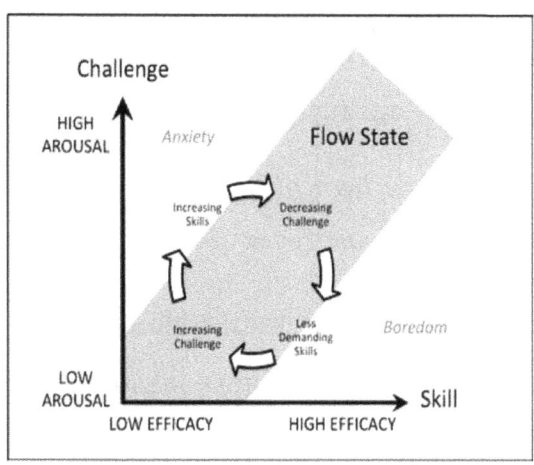

*Here are typical coping mechanisms that lead to the Anxiety Zone state:*

✔ **Evading and procrastinating**: You might avoid taking up difficult tasks completely or postpone working on them, fearing that you will fail or look stupid.

✔ **Self-depreciation and perfectionism**: You may also put yourself down a lot or expect too much from yourself because you feel like nothing you do is ever good enough, making it hard for you to attempt things that seem out of your league.

✔ **Overwhelm and shutdown**: Sometimes, when you face something very challenging, you can become overwhelmed, thus feeling mentally or emotionally shut down. This makes it hard to concentrate well or come up with good solutions. We spoke of this previously as the cortex going offline due to cortisol and adrenaline coursing through the bloodstream and bathing these neurons in response to overwhelming threats (fight, flight, freeze) thereby paralyzing them in the process.

✔ **Imposter syndrome**: Individuals having ACEs frequently suffer from imposter syndrome, i.e., feeling like frauds who don't deserve anything good happening to them; you tend not to recognize or ask for help in areas where you lack skills, especially during times when there is too much at stake.

*To shift into healthier states and better manage high-challenge situations, the following measures could help to pull out of the Anxiety Zone state:*

✔ **Break tasks into manageable steps**: You can learn to divide complex duties into simple stages, which appear more straightforward to accomplish and reduce fear.

✔ **Seek support and guidance**: When faced with demanding circumstances that require more effort than usual, you can obtain assistance and even motivation from peers, teachers, and experts. Ask for help.

✔ **Develop coping skills**: Learn ways of coping, e.g., mindfulness meditation (a relaxation technique), deep breathing exercises, etc.; this equips you with the necessary tools when dealing with stressful events like tasks beyond your abilities.

✔ **Embrace a growth mindset**: Self-motivate by saying things to yourself like, "Abilities can be developed through hard work and perseverance." Let yourself understand that failures or setbacks should not be taken personally since they only serve as learning opportunities for self-improvement.

✔ **Celebrate progress**: Even the slightest achievements must be acknowledged because they boost confidence levels and increase the desire to succeed. This emphasizes effort towards reaching a goal rather than focusing solely on the outcome itself.

✔ **Practice self-compassion**: Encourage yourself to forgive yourself when things don't go well, especially during difficult times. Tell yourself it's alright to ask others for assistance because nobody expects anyone to face challenges alone. Don't beat yourself up when you don't perform as well as you would have liked.

By following these steps and getting the help required, you, as someone impacted by ACEs, can slowly move away from low-skill, high-challenge situations, thus enabling you to become more resilient in facing complex aspects of life effectively.

## High Skills, Low Challenge (Comfort Zone)

**Emotion Keywords**: *comfort, relaxation, ease, contentment*

If you find yourself here, you have all it takes to perform any given task without difficulty due to possessing the required competence levels. Unfortunately, not enough difficulty is involved, which could lead to complacency, where you remain satisfied with mere achievement within known limits without striving for further improvements since everything already seems too easy.

With adverse childhood experiences (ACEs), staying in a state of low challenge and high skill could be a way to cope with or avoid potential triggers or stressors related to previous trauma. This might indicate returning to familiar activities that feel safe and where you have control. But it may also mean not wanting to try new things or face different obstacles due to an underlying lack of confidence or fear rooted in your ACEs. Therefore, it is essential for you in this position to seek support and find healthy ways to gradually increase challenges and engagement while addressing the deeper issues underlying these defensive behaviors.

*Here are methods that can be used to reframe your position and step outside of your Comfort Zone:*

✔ **Therapeutic support**: Consider going into therapy or counseling to work on the underlying trauma and develop coping mechanisms. Therapists can assist you in seeing how previous events can affect present behavior patterns while helping you find healthier ways of dealing with such situations. Again, you may find many self help books along these lines as well.

✔ **Gradual exposure**: Introduce new challenges slowly until you get used to higher levels of complexity over time, starting off with easy tasks that are manageable and then adding more difficult ones as you become comfortable enough.

✔ **Positive reinforcement**: Praise yourself when you take even small steps beyond what feels safe for you; celebrate achievements but also acknowledge how scary it is to try something new.

✔ **Setting realistic goals**: Set reasonable targets that are aligned with your interests and values. Break down larger goals into smaller, achievable ones so that they don't seem too overwhelming at first.

✔ **Mindfulness + relaxation techniques**: Learning mindfulness along with other relaxation skills can help you deal with anxiety brought about by moving out of your comfort zone; deep breathing exercises and meditation, among other things, could help you remain calm during challenging moments.

✔ **Building self-confidence**: Learn to recognize strengths and past accomplishments, thereby reinforcing belief in your ability to overcome any difficulty; this can eventually give you enough courage to take risks or try new things.

✔ **Seeking support networks**: Learn to seek advice from close friends and relatives or even by joining support groups, where you can get encouragement from others who have experienced similar challenges while venturing beyond their comfort zones. (Remember Ubuntu: "I am because we are!")

Through these and other approaches that offer continuous assistance, you can change your mindset over time, thus becoming more willing to move out of your comfort zone, eventually leading to personal development and resilience.

## High Skills, High Challenge (Flow Zone)

**Emotion Keywords**: *flow state, focus, immersion, fulfillment, joy, creativity*

At the topmost part of our flowchart, we see that when both ability and difficulty are high, people get absorbed into what they do best, hence experiencing moments of perfect concentration called "flow."

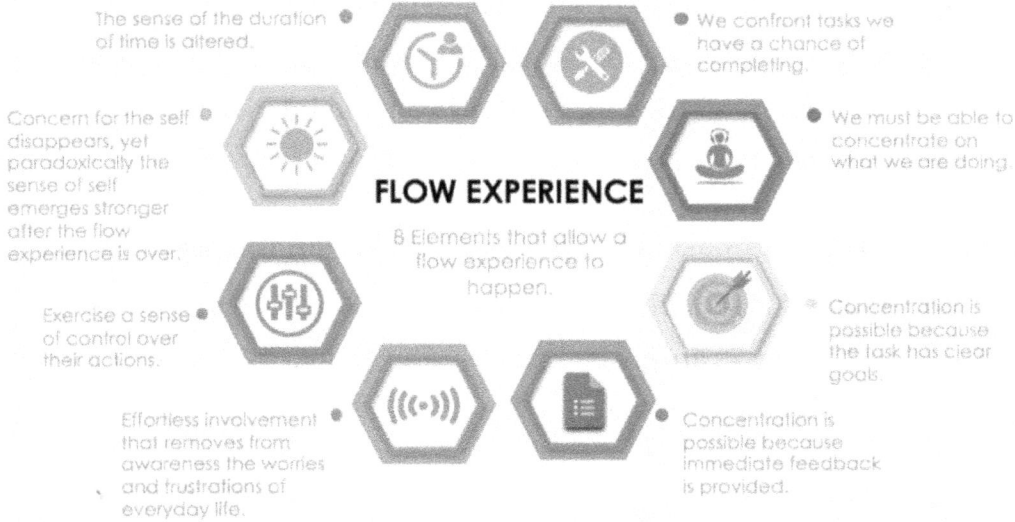

This flow is characterized by a deep sense of enjoyment and intense positive emotions, such as relief after accomplishing something difficult, which leads to higher levels of personal growth and self-actualization.

For a person with ACEs in prison, striving for flow with high skill and high challenge can be life-changing. I have personally enjoyed the experience of Flow through several pursuits, many of which I have learned in prison. Some examples include teaching, writing, public speaking, meditation, yoga, and athletic activities such as handball, volleyball, pickleball, and ping pong.

Here are some ways to find your Flow Zone:

✔ **Naming talents**: Begin by identifying skills and strengths already possessed—abilities that may have been overlooked or not used. Vocational assessments, educational programs, or self-reflection activities might be employed to uncover talents.

✔ **Setting goals**: Start setting ambitious but achievable goals that stretch you beyond your comfort zone and give your life meaning; these could be educational, personal growth or vocational targets based on what you are interested in doing once you are released. They can also be hobbies like art, writing, exercise, yoga, meditation or anything you find interesting but never made the time to do.

✔ **Learning opportunities**: Make sure you access various forms of learning while you're incarcerated; this should match current knowledge levels so that neither too easy nor too hard tasks are given. Even learning to juggle helps to rewire the brain and leads to flow experiences.

✔ **Building resilience**: Learn how to bounce back from failure stronger than before by seeing setbacks as chances for improvement while believing capabilities can grow through dedication rather than maintaining a fixed mindset. Experiment with the *42 Resilience Building Blocks* (found at the end of this book).

✔ **Flow fostering**: Seek an environment where you can immerse yourself fully in activities aligned with your strengths, such as academic engagements or creative works; this could mean having clear objectives coupled with immediate feedback and allowing yourself to choose what you want to do best without being told all the time.

✔ **Making connections**: Encourage connections between yourself and those with similar interests or mentors who have walked the same path successfully; motivation tends to increase when you feel supported throughout the journey, even if only a few steps away from reaching the destination. This makes it much more likely to achieve the desired outcome.

✔ **Reflecting, often**: Foster regular reflection sessions either through writing journals or talking with those you trust as part of sharing experiences while looking back at the progress made so far toward realizing your goals.

Knowing how the flow diagram works can help us understand where we are and what changes must be made for optimal experiences. When we recognize this relationship between skills and challenges, we will look for things that stretch but aren't out of reach, which in turn makes us grow better while performing such tasks or activities. Further, when we realize that we have become bored, anxious, or comfortable, then we should take action immediately so as not only restore balance but also foster our well-being through striving towards maximum productivity at all times.

## Reframing Threat Responses and Applying Flow

In the context of trauma and justice, understanding the Flow diagram offers a powerful tool for reframing our threat responses. Rather than viewing our or others' reactions as signs of weakness or dysfunction, we can recognize them as indicators of an imbalance between skills and the challenges at hand. By identifying areas where our skills can be developed, and challenges can be navigated more effectively, we empower ourselves to respond to adversity with hope and resilience.

Recent studies have shown that when in the Flow state, the brain, because of the developed skill and therefore repeated experiences in a given area, is able to enter a state similar to that of daydreaming when the functions appear to go on autopilot.

We are not overthinking, worrying, or second-guessing, but instead allowing our best selves, our true authentic selves to keep our attention free from the troubled part, the broken or fragmented part we call the ego. In this state, we realize how life can be enjoyed without anything artificial being added to help us escape.

Energy follows thought. Flow helps us to effectively return to love, trust, and safety by centering our awareness hopefully and resiliently toward predictions of happiness and fulfillment.

In practice, you will learn effective strategies for harnessing the power of Flow within the context of trauma-informed approaches to restorative justice. From reframing perspectives on adversity to cultivating environments that support resilience, we are delving into the transformative potential of Flow in support of our own rehabilitation. In our exploration of harnessing the power of Flow within trauma-informed approaches to restorative justice, we delve into practical strategies that bridge theory with tangible action.

Here are some ways we can enrich our lives in the direction of Flow:

✔ **Reframing perspectives on adversity**: We can spend our time constructively by reframing perspectives on adversity through the lens of Flow. Rather than viewing trauma as insurmountable obstacles, feel encouraged to see them as opportunities for growth and development. By reframing adversity as a challenge to be met with resilience and determination, you can shift your mindset from victimhood to empowerment. Every skill you cultivate while incarcerated will also go with you when you re enter society.

✔ **Cultivating environments that support resilience**: Consider the role of environments in shaping individuals' capacity for resilience. This is the epigenetic factor I described in the last chapter. From correctional facilities to community settings, examine how the design of physical and social spaces can either hinder or facilitate the experience of Flow. By doing what we can to help create environments centered on safety, connection, and autonomy, we empower ourselves to tap into our innate resilience and thrive in adversity.

✔ **Restoring relationships**: Flow extends beyond individual experiences to encompass interpersonal dynamics and relationships. In this book, we want to consider how the principles of Flow can be applied to restore and strengthen relationships within trauma-informed restorative justice.

From nonviolent communication strategies to conflict resolution techniques, we provide practical tools for navigating relational challenges and fostering connection, understanding, and empathy. As you increase your skills in these areas, you may approach increasingly challenging relationship dynamics using these approaches and find yourself in Flow states where there was perhaps anxiety or boredom before.

✔ **Fostering growth**: Finally, we highlight the transformative potential of Flow in fostering personal and collective growth. Through engaging activities, reflective exercises, and transformative learning opportunities, you are invited to step outside your comfort zone, embrace challenges, and cultivate your skills and strengths. By harnessing the power of Flow, you can embark on a journey of self-discovery and empowerment, ultimately leading to greater resilience and well-being.

In essence, Flow is a roadmap for integrating the principles of Flow into the recalibration of restorative justice. It offers practical strategies for restoring relationships, fostering growth, and empowering you to navigate adversity with hope and resilience.

Flow emerges as a guiding principle in the journey toward *restorative justice recalibrated*. I personally hope you will take advantage of the opportunities that are yours while incarcerated to develop skills that will enable you to better face the challenges that have continued to threaten your well-being. Learning new ways to heal old wounds is a service you do for yourself and those who have been harmed by your "unskilled acts".

A worthy step of voluntary restitution is to do the work on yourself that may keep you from the happiness that is your birthright. By understanding and embracing the dynamics of Flow, you can navigate the turbulent waters of trauma with hope and resilience, ultimately forging pathways toward healing and transformation.

\*\*\*

*"When you want only love, you will see nothing else."*

~A Course in Miracles

# ACEs, Crime, and Empathy Deficits

Understanding how trauma and Adverse Childhood Experiences (ACEs) affect your life helps us to see why many needs remain unmet and ultimately lead to criminality. A trauma-informed approach means recognizing that sometimes crimes are the result of poor strategies for dealing with unresolved childhood traumas or other unaddressed issues arising out of it.

Crime is a learned behavior. As such, it can be unlearned, too. Deciphering the complexities that drive individuals toward unlawful acts require one to understand the profound connection between trauma and criminal behavior. Traumatic experiences impact how one's capacity for empathy develops. Studies have shown that weak empathy translates into weakness, guilt, and shame, which is another way of saying there is a lack of conscience. As empathy can be improved, so can the criminal tendency be reduced.

Consistently, numerous studies highlight the correlation between trauma and criminal tendencies, usually measured through Adverse Childhood Experiences.

Destructive coping mechanisms can find fertile ground on the scars left by unaddressed trauma, leading individuals down a path marked by criminality. What we must understand is that beyond emotional pain, trauma can shape one's choices to navigate through it.

They say that neurons that wire together fire together. In other words, in the developing brain, neural pathways are formed by repeated impacts of a significant kind. Adverse childhood experiences can heighten threat responses, which keeps us in a panicked state of stress, fear, or anger for extended periods. This depletes reserves and accentuates the brain's growth of safety networks (fight, flight, freeze) while diminishing or paralyzing networks associated with connection and learning.

Imagine a person who, as a child, had parents who taught him that law enforcement was terrible and could not be trusted. The parents told the developing child stories about abusive practices employed by police officers. These stories stimulated fear in the child; the concept of "bad police officers" was shaped by his upbringing.

When a parent was pulled over for a traffic stop, the child was triggered and overwhelmed by the belief that at any moment, he or his parent would be pulled out of the car and beaten without cause by the "bad police officer." What matters in this illustration is not whether or not what he was taught as a child is 100% accurate; what matters is the effect on how the brain is wired to produce threat responses from associations with law enforcement.

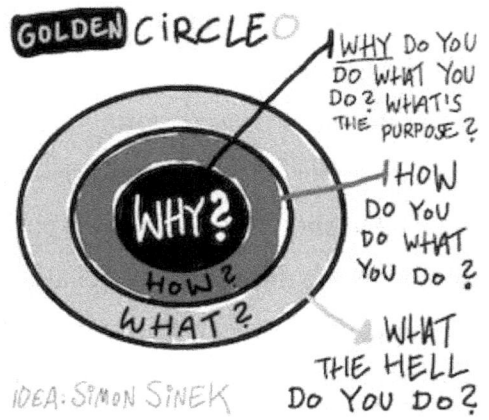

Several years later, the child, now a young adult, finds himself in a challenging situation that has brought conflict into his life. Again, his parents emphasize the danger of trusting law enforcement. He listens to them and, in doing so, finds himself in a much worse situation.

Simon Sinek wisely points out, "Our "why" is our purpose, cause, or belief—the driving force behind everything we do. Our "hows" are our actions when we are at our natural best to bring our "whys" to life. Our "whats" are the tangible manifestation of our "whys"—the work we do daily."

The criminal justice system spends more time on the "what" than the "why." We receive judgments and sentences that some of us may never complete for our 'whats", i.e., our behaviors, while rarely addressing the underlying needs (whys) that caused them.

In this example, because of ACEs and significant developmental trauma associated with law enforcement, bad decisions were made, and the entire context changed for the worse.

Prisons are places where adults in custody are continually re-traumatized because of the ignorance of those whose care they are under. Is re-traumatization an effective deterrent to criminal behavior?

Justice needs to be approached holistically and with compassion because of its complicated relationship with trauma and criminal behavior. Trauma can remain invisible until it propels someone into doing something illegal when it remains unacknowledged and untreated.

These are not simply acts of deviance but rather desperate attempts at finding solace within themselves due to previous traumatic experiences. This connection implies that punishment alone cannot break this chain within our justice system. Instead, it requires a paradigm shift toward acknowledging the underlying source of trauma, treating it, and providing ways for healing/rehabilitation. Bottom line, it is imperative that even if we are part of the criminal justice system, we are not "seen" only for our offenses but more generally understood as people with an entire life history.

If we recognize the trauma behind strategies we have employed that have caused harm, we can introduce approaches that target causes, not symptoms. Shifting towards empathy and rehabilitation will lead to low reoffending rates and restore lives instead of causing more pain. Therefore, we must go beyond punishment to appreciate humans comprehensively and create an environment where compassion forms the basis for true justice.

The criminal justice system's "symptom vs. cause cycle" must be broken. The system must shift its focus towards addressing the unmet needs behind criminal acts from a trauma-informed perspective. There's a recent study released by the *Compassion Prison Project* that shows that 98% of incarcerated individuals have at least one ACEs (as scored on the ACEs Quiz).

In contrast, 34% fewer civilians had ACEs in their background. Trauma is much more pervasive in prison culture than we—or politicians and correctional workers or administrators—wish to acknowledge. ACEs manifest in a myriad of ways while ironically addressed also with violence (i.e., pepper spray, isolation, use of force, etc.).

The penal system is currently ill-equipped to deal with trauma as a a causal factor for criminal behavior. One thing is sure: punitive measures alone do not work. Therefore, if you are a prisoner reading this, it could benefit you to inquire about why you engaged in such behavior patterns first and foremost.

Admitting that there are a host of unmet needs and traumatic experiences in your past are at least a sound basis for which rehabilitation can take place. Breaking out of the belief, you are thrust into means understanding and working to fulfill the unmet needs that led you to engage in criminal acts. It means peeling back layers of experience and understanding how such unmet needs have shaped your life.

Consider trauma as a possible driving force behind behavior rather than just something isolated from reality. Instead of labeling yourself as a criminal forever, the emphasis lies on providing necessary support for healing purposes. By looking at root causes, there can be a complete transformation. Much like the Babemba tribal members, we must be brought back to our authentic selves when we err, not banished or isolated.

This process requires active participation, where your journey towards healing is valued. Therefore, Trauma-informed care creates an atmosphere where your needs are recognized while interventions are designed to promote real change in resilience and prosocial need-meeting strategies. By adopting such an approach, society witnesses meaningful and sustainable reintegration. This breaks the chains involved in recidivism and builds a future based on understanding, support, and personal growth.

However, this does not negate the fact that those who have created harm must be held accountable for their actions. This can be achieved by recognizing the impact of trauma and ACEs as well as creating an environment where acceptance and belonging prevail; this factor plays a crucial role in inspiring authentic accountability as well as evolving empathy toward those harmed.

## The Resilience Prescription

Dr. Dennis S. Charney, co-author of *Resilience: The Science of Mastering Life's Greatest Challenges*, has what he calls: "The Resilience Prescription." The following page describes the 10 "prescription" components. Consider how they can be implemented and applied into your daily life.

## ✔ Positive Attitude

+ Optimism is strongly related to resilience.
+ Optimism is, in part, genetic but can be learned.
+ Cognitive flexibility through cognitive reappraisal.

## ✔ Traumatic Experiences Should Be Re-Evaluated

+ Alter the perceived value and meaningfulness of the event.
+ Stress and trauma can benefit one: one can reframe, assimilate, accept, and recover. These skills can be learned.
+ Failure is an essential ingredient for growth.

## ✔ Embrace a Personal Moral Compass

+ Develop a set of core beliefs that very few things can shatter.
+ For many, faith in conjunction with strong religious and/or spiritual beliefs is associated with resilience.
+ Altruism has been strongly related to resilience. Survivor mission.

## ✔ Find a Resilient Role Model

+ Role models can be found in one's own life.
+ Imitation is a very powerful mode of learning.

## ✔ Face Your Fears

+ Fear is normal and can be used as a guide.
+ Facing your fears can increase your self-esteem.
+ Learn and practice the skills necessary to move through the fear.

## ✔ Develop Active Coping Skills

+ Resilient individuals use active rather than passive coping skills.
+ Minimize appraisal of threat, create positive statements about oneself, seek support of others, and ACT.

✔ **Establish and Nurture a Supportive Social Network**

+ Very few can "go it alone."

+ Considerable emotional strength accrues from close relationships with people and organizations.

+ A safety net during times of stress.

✔ **Attend to Physical Well-Being**

+ PE (physical education) has positive effects on physical hardiness and mood and improves self-esteem.

✔ **Train Regularly and Rigorously in Multiple Areas**

+ Change requires systematic and disciplined activity.

+ Concentrate on training in multiple areas: emotional intelligence, moral integrity, physical endurance.

✔ **Recognize, Utilize and Foster Signature Strengths**

+ Learn to recognize your character strengths and engage them to deal with difficult & stressful situations.

This prescription, when utilized as recommended, can increase your resilience and improve your quality of life. Many of the above components are considered the 42 *Resilience Building Blocks* listed at the end of this book. I believe they are essential for transforming trauma into triumph.

# Rat Park Experiment

Bruce Alexander's Rat Park experiment offers one of the most important lessons for those who want to make real changes in our criminal justice system. I learned about this experiment from Johann Hari in his book *Chasing the Scream*.

Just like rats put into an environment where they cannot meet basic needs, individuals in society who have unmet needs might use harmful coping mechanisms (like the rats preferring "drug water"). However, when these same rats were put in a place called Rat Park, where all their needs could be met, drug usage also decreased by a large margin. This infers that if people can easily meet their basic needs, there will be very little chance of them engaging in harmful behavior, including criminal activities.

This observation corresponds with the urgent transformation we advocate for in our justice system—a move from a retributive model to a restorative justice model centered on meeting individuals' needs. However, this transformation does not mean that one is not responsible for their actions. Instead, the transformation acknowledges that underlying causes need to be addressed. We must move away from the "Marvel Universe," where justice is served when the hero uses retribution to give the villain what he has coming, and everyone cheers the more the villain is abused for what he has done.

By integrating insights about empathy and trauma-informed care with ACEs' understanding into our justice system, we lay down a basis for going beyond mere recidivism reduction. Yes, we move towards creating resilient communities characterized by breaking the cycle of crime through fulfilling basic needs, healing wounds, and embracing each other without condemnation and shaming. Now, let us look at Bruce Alexander's experiment more closely.

The Rat Park experiment was carried out by psychologist Bruce K. Alexander during the late 1970s and intended to study the effects of the environment on drug addiction among laboratory rats.

In traditional addiction studies, rats were placed individually inside isolated cages where both plain water and drug-laced water were available. The rats preferred the drug-laced water over the plain water; there was no surprise in this due to the isolation experienced by the rats. The results show the inherent addictiveness of drug substances when subject to unnatural, isolated conditions.

However, Alexander challenged this interpretation by creating his Rat Park—a large, enriched environment designed to satisfy rats' social interaction, physical exercise, and mental stimulation needs. The cages were equipped with toys and enough space for the rats to run around, so in essence, socialization opportunities existed.

The findings differed dramatically from those of the plain traditional environment experiments. Even when the rats were given access to the same drugs consumed freely by the rats in isolated cages, the Rat Park rats exhibited remarkable resistance against drug-laced water. A very significant implication was that the environment played a decisive role in determining drug-seeking behavior among these rats when able to socialize. In short, when basic needs are met, drugs are less desirable.

This study has illuminated the role of environmental factors and the fulfillment of basic needs in understanding and fighting addiction. Thus, it suggested that drugs alone were not responsible for creating addiction. Still, instead, the context within which people lived had a significant impact on whether they developed an addiction or remained drug-free. The Rat Park experiment challenged prevailing views on addiction. It highlights the importance of supportive enriched environments in mitigating harmful effects due to substance abuse.

Our current criminal justice system often resembles the isolated cages where rats deprived and disconnected turn to unnatural means of coping. When we compare this environment with what Rat Park stands for, we notice a clear difference between it and a restorative justice approach.

I have become aware of entirely different collective behaviors among inmate populations at facilities that can better meet basic needs than those unwilling to do so. Often, less willing administrators ignorantly promote both addictive behaviors and violence among those who did not enter corrections with a penchant for them. Their own threat response inhibits them from supporting true rehabilitation. I have seen it time and time again. Idle time in warehouses

with little to do for meaning and purpose only increases the likelihood of both violence and addictive behaviors.

In other words, those in custody are deprived of basic needs such as socializing, autonomy, and mental stimulation. This makes the whole prison environment seem like a traditional addiction study cage. On the same note, imprisoned individuals might resort to harmful acts just like rats in isolation resorted to drugs as they try desperately to meet their basic needs. In both cases, a longing for stimulation beyond the boredom of being warehoused led to artificial alternative pleasure-seeking strategies.

Conversely, *restorative justice recalibrated* harmonizes with Rat Park's principles. It recognizes how much the environment matters and yearns for a place where people's basic needs can be met. Given chances of rehabilitation, socialization, and personal

advancement, the desire for artificial alternatives naturally disappears.

Incidentally, recidivism rates drastically diminish in countries like New Zealand and others where prisons appear more like resorts than prisons at first glance. It must be easier to obey the laws when the people who hold you accountable show you consideration and respect while instilling values that they expect you to live by.

On the other hand, it would be less astonishing that recidivism rates remain high in conventional prison settings if seen from the viewpoint of the Rat Park experiment. Failure to address these surroundings and deprivation of basic needs keep the criminal wheel turning instead of stopping it.

A new way of thinking is necessary for long-term change and decreased re-offending; this involves shifting away from punitive confinement and isolation towards a restorative model in line with Rat Park's transformative principles. It is that simple.

As we discuss the path toward criminal justice reform, recognize the transformative potential of addressing your unmet needs. This fosters a sense of belonging and ultimately builds a society where you are empowered to contribute positively to the community you call home. When you can uncover the unmet needs behind the actions that brought you to prison, you will only then be able to form more effective strategies to meet those needs without creating harm for yourself or others.

This is within your grasp, with or without assistance or support from the Department of Corrections. Use this time to connect with your feelings and needs (self-empathy). Figure out the needs you aimed to meet by doing what you did to end up in prison. Find a place in your heart where you can sincerely regret the strategies you chose to meet those needs.

Empathize with those you harmed by imagining what it must be like in their shoes. And most importantly, forgive yourself and develop a plan to meet your needs in a way that will not harm anyone else again. This is the best rehabilitation; you don't have to ask permission to provide it yourself. It truly lies within your power to rise above the ashes of yesterday's mistakes toward tomorrow's successes.

Every step forward along these lines peels away a layer currently separating you from the truest, most beautiful, and authentic part of yourself.

## In-grouping, Out-Grouping, and the Retributive Justice Paradox

Continuing our journey forward, let's investigate empathy as a fundamental aspect that shapes our social dynamic. Let's explore concepts of in-grouping and out-grouping. Empathy can be simply termed as the ability to understand the feelings and needs of other people clearly. However, this empathetic response is not uniform; our brains categorize people into ingroups (those we identify with) and outgroups (those we perceive as different).

David Eagleman, in "The Brain," discusses an experiment relevant to our purpose. It demonstrates that when people observe a hand getting stabbed, what's called the pain matrix in the brain lights up. Think of it as an empathic neurological response.

Then, a simple label was added that identified the person's hand getting stabbed with a religious affiliation. These included Christian, Muslim, Buddhist, Atheist, and Hindu. Suddenly, it could be observed that when a hand from an outgroup got stabbed, the brain had little to no response. People we deem as a part of our in-group we easily feel empathy toward. We are more willing to help these people. On the other hand, we feel indifferent toward those who are among the outgroups.

Let's apply this to the criminal justice system. The moment someone is charged with a crime, goes to jail, and takes a mugshot dressed in an orange jumpsuit, they become part of a societal outgroup. Out-grouping is how the brain conserves energy and neutralizes the added expense of caring about another human being.

This energy-saving strategy enables us to continue enforcing the death penalty. Once someone is deemed "out," there is no limit (under these circumstances) to what human beings will allow to happen to one another.

Our language, filled with ready-made "deserve-oriented" and "responsibility-denying" concepts, makes out-grouping all the easier. Being forewarned, we can be forearmed with presence in instances of out-grouping, i.e., when we otherwise feel inclined to shut our hearts to others. RJR is the proper conduit for this presence to re-enter our societies along these lines.

Just think for a few minutes about how your brain responds when it sees "ingroups," or people it identifies with, versus "outgroups," who are perceived differently by the society inside prison. When you are part of the "us," a warmth of shared humanity comes with it. But being marked as "them" by this society puts you outside the circle of empathy, reflecting what many homeless people go through on the outside. Consider the threat prediction cycle. According to Eagleman, similar to the studies mentioned above, another concludes that they belong to the societal outgroup and are perceived more like inanimate objects than humans.

Now consider retributive justice – a system encouraging you to be thrown into an outgroup. Society's narrative justifies this categorization under the belief that you "deserve" punishment for your actions. Prisoners are but one example of marginalized groups or classifications that become a part of the outgroup. It happens in religion, politics, socioeconomic, race, gender, etc.

When individuals are arbitrarily labeled, they become isolated from society, causing increased risk behavior since breaking the law may <u>falsely</u> seem like the only option left due to the lack of basic needs being met. With proper support, such strategies can be employed far less often. When estranged from the in-group, however, it becomes much easier to cause someone else to lose so that we can win.

This fixed mindset stems from a lack of love, trust, and safety among policymakers. They, too, have likely experienced trauma. Therefore, bashing or ridiculing them is not the goal. We must, however, point out how we got here and what needs to occur to get us out of this mess once and for all. Moreover, a fundamental part of this will be how we reframe our interpretation of the teachings of those we identify as embodiments of Divine Love on the one hand while justifying waging war in their names on the other.

Restorative justice challenges the very foundations of this traumatized system. It calls upon society to recognize its flaws for collective unlearning of biases, rewiring empathetic responses, and building a better future based on shared humanity - even amid adversity. It's not just change; it's humanity against all that would hinder its progress toward universal love and friendship.

Early on in my incarceration, I learned from so-called "convicts" the dos and don'ts of prison politics. To keep from being preyed upon, I was taught to outgroup anyone who had certain crimes as well as those who let people pick on them. The thinking was that "birds of a feather flock together", i.e., if we associate too closely with certain people, we must be like them. So, I quickly adopted these generic societal structures at 21 years old to fit in with accepted social norms. It worked well at first, but then something happened that would forever shake the foundation of my developing worldview.

I had agreed to be a caretaker for a man who, after coming out of a heroin overdose-induced coma, had the maturity of a teenager. I would help him with daily tasks, do most of his writing, and help direct his activities, much like a parent. In prison, people like him are vulnerable to being taken advantage of. After some weeks as his roommate, I noticed someone behaving in a way that concerned me. After confirming with him that my suspicions were correct, I asked the man to stay away from my roommate.

The man was a known gang member. He agreed to stay out of my cell, but I returned from recreation early weeks later and found him there again. We had a confrontation that resulted in my being attacked by at least four men wielding "master locks" tied to socks. After a mild concussion, a brief trip to segregation, and my false sense of security quickly becoming a house of cards, I found myself in the very crisis that initiated my transformation.

Everything I thought was true about my life turned upside down. My friends, who said that they'd be there for me if ever in a pinch, stood by watching as I was assaulted. At this inflection point, I was forced to reexamine my beliefs, open myself up to new possibilities, and modify my concepts about reality per this added insight.

When I was exonerated from any wrongdoing and released back into the general population, my in-group, in many ways, was no longer viable for me. I found myself questioning all that had been taught to me by these "convicts".

I began to acquire knowledge on various subjects of interest eagerly using the interlibrary loan system. At the same time, my crisis had opened my heart to people in a new way. Those whom I had previously deemed unworthy or "outed," I tried to be kinder and more considerate toward. It felt wonderful, even liberating.

In one such case, I went out of my way to befriend a man (let's call him Jason here). He came from a background that gave him little experience with physical conflict, and socio-economically, he had lived with very little to be desired. As such, he had been paying a gang to protect him from being robbed or taken advantage of since he had been incarcerated. When I learned of that, I found that repulsive *before my crisis*. I had made it about me, but with a shift in focus post-crisis, I started asking why and trying to imagine myself in his shoes.

As it turned out, hiring protection just as one might employ a dry cleaner made sense for Jason. Why would he want to be subject to combat, which he was no good at when he could pay a few bucks a month to have someone else take care of it? He and I had formed two completely different concepts about acceptance and safety because of how our pre-prison and childhood experiences had shaped our lives.

So, Jason would come by and talk with me every day. He would notice the books I had been reading, and we'd have some interesting discussions that were far more thought-provoking than the ones I had grown accustomed to since incarceration. He would refer to this book he had been reading that he thought I should check out.

Honestly, I ignored him the first couple of times, but then, one time, I inquired more. His description did sound like something I might find appealing, so I expressed interest. To date, the book he brought has been among the most impactful books I have ever read. It changed the course of my life and was a catalyst for the most significant steps toward self-improvement I have ever made.

I am trying to make the point that preconceived ideas and judgments limit life. My preconceived ideas about this man, Jason, were the only things that stood in the way of my progress. My having out-grouped him hurt me more than him in this situation. By segregating him from my social in-group, the wisdom born from his unique experiences remained closed off as an unknown, faraway treasure. Even when experienced naturally, transformative learning challenges us to constantly aspire toward becoming better versions of ourselves. You will never know what is beneath the stone you don't turn over.

Restorative justice does not hide from the fact that it is hard. Imagine what society can welcome back as wisdom inside those who have made mistakes if they could but see the true human being behind each story. What we see in the world depends upon the concepts and labels that guide our predictions. In other words, we see other people according to who we are more than they are.

*Restorative Justice Recalibrated (RJR)* aims to bring people who were once apart closer together. It requires resilience, understanding, and deep commitment. Even when those harmed are unwilling or unable to participate directly, restorative justice may still be applied for the eternal benefit of our species.

We must turn the page on the idea that those harmed must be the ones to initiate restorative approaches to justice. This is the way for specific applications like restorative dialogue, where all parties agree to meet, discuss what happened, and decide how best to move forward. However, our systems need overhauling with the values inherent to a recalibrated restorative justice if our societies are not to become increasingly fractured and segregated into categories of in-groups and outgroups.

By doing the hard work of breaking down walls between us as a society, healing can occur once more within our communities. RJR is the way, but it needs time to expand its reach and enlarge its scope. It needs to incorporate relevant science so that restorative justice continues to be effective amid such added insight. Only because of how far we have immersed ourselves into a kind of justice that creates more harm than helps has it become time to take such a much-needed look into the depths of what truly causes crime and what truly restores all involved.

For the record, I emphasize these points not only as someone who has created harm but as someone who has been repeatedly harmed and traumatized in various ways throughout my life. I have taken this approach toward instances where gang members have tried to take my life while incarcerated, as well as toward those responsible for my high ACEs score. Working through the complex process required by restorative justice recalibrated, all parties reaped a much richer reward and were made better by it.

## Empathy and Social Exclusion

RJR becomes your GPS as you familiarize yourself with the landscape of trauma-impacted behavior, considering transformation through restoring empathy. To better understand this, we will first point to Dr. Fred Sly's doctoral thesis, *Empathy, and Social Exclusion: Re-imagining Belonging as a Mediator of Violence.*

Dr Sly's thesis discusses the profound impact of empathy on shame arising from violent acts. Sly states that when shame for the harm done to others is met with empathy, there is an increased likelihood of the felt sense of social exclusion being replaced by belonging. From that, accountability and prosocial behavior arise. Sly goes on to say:

> *"Empathic failures occurring between individuals, especially failures at a level defined as criminal acts, can be addressed using restorative justice practices that increase the amount of empathy between victims and offenders, with the observed result that prosocial behavior generally increases and community violence decreases."*

Dr. Sly's doctoral thesis drew from those who dedicated their lives to understanding empathy and its relationship to a healthy life. Heinz Kohut's theory about empathic failure during childhood development highlights a fundamental issue – crime may very well originate from empathic failure.

Failing to understand other peoples' needs and feelings creates a disconnection and separation from our shared humanity. Trauma from adverse childhood experiences may diminish one's empathic capacity. This capacity, however, can be restored through empathy-building techniques like those practiced in the *Resilience Prison Project*.

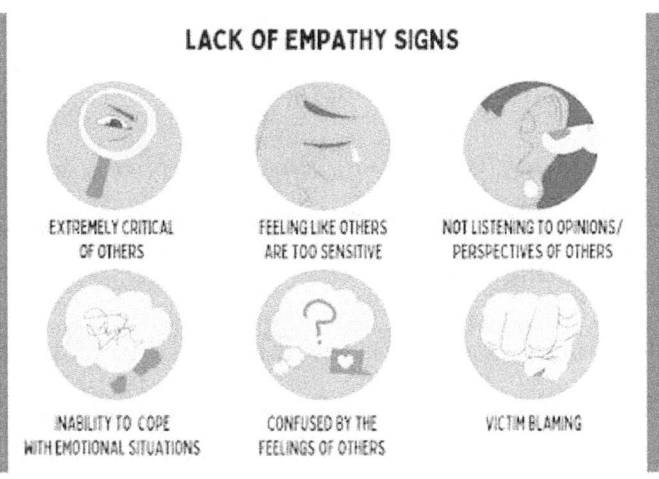

In reframing how we approach the matter, we may learn to perceive crime not just as an act of defiance but as a symptom of deeper empathic issues associated with ACEs. We spoke previously about in-grouping and out-grouping. Now imagine the developing brain minimizing your own in-group as a protective measure stemming from your ACEs. In cases where such adversity has impacted childhood development with minimal positive mitigating factors, it would almost make more sense to consider how we approach child services in our country.

You may ask yourself, "Who supports the idea that empathic failure lies at the root of criminal behavior?"

> *"Empathy is like a universal solvent. Any problem immersed in empathy becomes soluble"*   ~Simon Baron-Cohen

Consider renowned psychologist Simon Baron-Cohen's perspective, where he believes a lack of empathy (what he calls "zero degrees of empathy") is one thing that contributes to various forms of anti-social behaviors.

Rather than seeing people who do "bad" or "cruel" things as evil, Baron-Cohen believes we ought to recognize such behavior as erasing empathy. He argues that effective empathy – the ability to respond emotionally to someone in need – can be drastically impaired by three social factors:

- ✔ obedience to authority
- ✔ ideology
- ✔ in-grouping/out-grouping

Baron-Cohen says, *"Empathy is our most valuable natural resource for conflict resolution."* Baron-Cohen's work underscores how vital empathy can be in preventing crimes.

Kohut emphasizes therapeutic methods to help increase empathic capacity by first modeling what may have been lacking during childhood development. According to him, mirroring and idealizing can be accomplished later in life to compensate for this lack. Thus, having people who exhibit empathy (mirroring) and who we look up to (idealizing) increases our empathic capacity. Are prisons filled with such examples for those who need rehabilitation?

At this point, you might be asking yourself, "Can I change, *really*?"

"Definitely!" says Kohut. He believed in the potential for change within each individual. Crime doesn't define who you are; it simply shows a disconnection from your authentic self, which can be healed with proper support. Recognizing this possibility becomes essential to your transformative journey of healing and rehabilitation.

Empathy has a multifaceted nature. It has been found that empathy can never become a *compelling* catalyst for change. Because empathy arises from within, we are compelled, not compelled, to change. Through the transformative power of empathy, it can affect you and revolutionize the entire justice system. According to this book's vision of restorative justice, we may transition from punishment-oriented strategies to a system genuinely concerned with rehabilitation by deeply understanding others.

Consider the work of Daniel Goleman, a leading psychologist known for coining the term "emotional intelligence." Goleman points out how important empathy is in this framework by arguing that it forms part of social effectiveness (meaning to be emotionally intelligent). Many experts today agree that empathy is vital to healthy relationships and that its development can help prevent criminal behavior.

Consider a paradigm that views crime not just as an act of defiance but rather as a symptom of deeper empathic issues. These perspectives set the stage for your transformative journey that embraces empathy as a catalyst for healing, accountability, and societal reintegration.

## Empathy's Role in Human Connection

At the heart of genuine connection lies empathy as a lifeline to understanding and sharing another person's feelings. It is not just a soft virtue but a link between people who build up their deep sense of shared humanity.

Some argue that empathic failures are not mere missteps; they lie behind many human conflicts, including criminal actions. Now, think about your own life within this framework. Can you recognize a lack of empathy behind the failures in relationships? Restorative justice also sees crime as a violation of relationships. Does this apply to you as well?

Have you ever experienced any moments where a lack of understanding or empathy significantly influenced your actions? There might have been times when people involved in harmful acts could not understand themselves or yearned for their social environment to empathize with them.

Think about how this lack of empathy has affected your journey towards self-perception. Being unable to connect with others empathically becomes burdensome, preventing you from building healthy relationships. This can lead to unskilled and harmful actions. What experiences have you had that make these insights resonate with you?

Let's look at Carl Rogers' insights into this subject to better understand it. Rogers was an influential psychologist who believed in the healing power of empathy. According to Rogers, empathy helps create a safe space for self-exploration and personal growth. This idea correlates well with what we have been exploring. It suggests that fostering empathy can be seen as a practical way of addressing real human dilemmas.

Another person whose views we will consider here is Dr. Lisa Feldman Barrett, a prominent psychologist/neuroscientist investigating the complex landscape of the predictive brain, trauma, and emotions. According to Barrett, feelings are constructs our brains generate based on past experiences rather than natural reactions. Although the departure would be too significant for our purposes, her work offers many insights supporting a criminal justice system accentuating the restorative model. This nuanced understanding delves into the relationship between emotions and empathy within criminal behavior complexities.

In her book *How Emotions Are Made*, Dr. Barrett writes:

> "We're at a turning point where the new science of mind and brain can begin to shape the law. By educating judges, jurors, attorneys, witnesses, police officers, and other participants in the legal process,

*we should be able to produce a legal system that is ultimately fairer."*
*~Dr. Lisa Feldman Barrett*

Until all parties involved with the legal process can get on the right track together, an increasingly traumatized society will fall further into traumatization through our currently failing system.

To reiterate, ACEs, along with other traumatic events, can make our brains predict threats that don't exist. Our body's protective resources are hijacked. When such a "state" over time becomes a "trait," these become unhealthy coping mechanisms. Consequently, potentially addictive behaviors or criminal acts can infiltrate our experiences. While examining crime through these lines, we realize how much our current justice system lacks.

The goal is to help restore these individuals to wholeness and, therefore, back into society. Instead, our so-called "correctional" system has become warehouses where people who are zero threat to society remain.

As a further systemic problem, taxpayers cover this cost of "warehousing" people who are no longer threats. We are currently spending more than a childhood of therapy combined with a college education for traumatized individuals to languish their time away in warehouses filled with all the ingredients for retraumatizing. Please consider this fact alone before moving on.

The human ego says, "That's what they get," without considering the long-term impacts that bring those same people back into our societies with more problems than they left with. It is truly time to recalibrate justice toward restoration.

# Empathic Failure and Crime

By understanding the underlying factors of empathic failure, we will be closer to identifying what triggers the failure and, consequently, a crime.

In terms of fostering or inhibiting empathic connections, it is one's environment that matters most here. In other words, multiple factors in our surroundings often influence empathic failure that can rise to the level of crime.

One factor contributing to crime can be seen from the perspective of an influential criminologist, Robert J. Sampson, who has done extensive research on this issue. According to Sampson, community structures play a significant role in shaping criminal behavior patterns within societies.

The following examines aspects rooted in our upbringing, adverse childhood experiences (ACEs), and the broader social environment.

## Upbringing and Empathic Nurturing

✔ **Parental Modeling**. Kohut emphasizes the significance of early experiences in shaping empathic capacities. A lack of empathic modeling from parents or caregivers can hinder a child's ability to connect with and understand others.

✔ **Emotional Attunement**. The quality of emotional attunement during formative years is pivotal. Children who do not receive consistent emotional support and responsiveness may struggle to navigate their emotions and fail to empathize with others.

## Adverse Childhood Experiences (ACEs)

✔ **Trauma and Disrupted Attachment**. ACEs, encompassing experiences like abuse, neglect, or household dysfunction, can disrupt the formation of secure attachments. Kohut's theory suggests that individuals with a history of ACEs may grapple with empathic deficits rooted in early relational challenges.

✔ **Impact on Self-Image**. ACEs can shape an individual's self-perception and worldview. Kohut posits that a distorted self-image, influenced by traumatic experiences, may contribute to empathic failure as individuals struggle to understand and address their own needs.

## Social Environment and Empathy Formation

✔ **Community and Cultural Influences**. The broader social environment plays a crucial role, including community and cultural influences. Kohut's theory prompts us to consider how societal norms and values impact the development of empathy, particularly when these norms either foster or hinder empathic connections.

✔ **Educational Systems**. The educational system also plays a role in empathy development. Kohut suggests that an educational environment that prioritizes emotional intelligence and social skills can contribute to a more empathic society, potentially reducing the likelihood of criminal behavior.

# PERMA Model and Well Being

Community structures, or lack thereof, expose the origins behind empathic failure and indicate ways out. Through trauma-informed care to address empathic deficits by fostering healthy relationships and creating supportive social environment interventions, the support can help break down cycles leading up to empathetic failures resulting in criminal behaviors.

Regarding post-crime activities, restorative justice similarly acknowledges the need to restore empathy. This view finds resonance with psychologist Martin Seligman's work on positive psychology. According to Seligman, well-being is advanced through strengths and virtues. His PERMA model breaks well-being into five categories.

**P**OSITIVE EMOTIONS
**E**NGAGEMENTS
**R**ELATIONSHIPS
**M**EANINGS
**A**CCOMPLISHMENTS

## P – Positive Emotion

Positive emotions include more than happiness. Optimism, curiosity, and gratitude are examples. According to Fredrickson (2001), cultivating positive emotions is a sign of personal growth that may lead to life fulfillment. This change from negative thoughts can help curtail the effects of negative emotions while promoting resilience.

By purposefully nurturing positive feelings, individuals can develop resources such as social networks, intellectual assets, and psychological strengths that increase resilience, thereby enhancing overall well-being.

**Strategies for Building Positive Emotions:**

✔ Spend quality time with loved ones.
✔ Engage in hobbies or creative pursuits.
✔ Listen to uplifting music.
✔ Reflect on gratitude and areas for personal improvement.

## E – Engagement

According to Seligman, engagement refers to being completely absorbed in an activity, similar to Csikszentmihalyi's concept of "flow". As said before, Flow occurs when there is a perfect balance between challenge level and one's ability level. Studies indicate that using one's character strengths boosts engagement, which leads to increased happiness while reducing depression.

**Ways to Increase Engagement:**

✔ Participate in activities that absorb your attention.

✔ Be mindful of your day-to-day work tasks.

✔ Spend some time outdoors observing the environment around you or find images of nature to use as a focus.

✔ Discover and use various capabilities you have on different occasions.

## R – Positive Relationships

This term refers to community members and friends, colleagues, and others. According to Seligman, these relationships provide support, value, and love that are essential for human well-being. Strong social connections predict cognitive health and physical well-being in older adulthood.

**Strategies for Building Positive Relationships:**

✔ Engage in shared activities or courses of interest.

✔ Enhance understanding by reaching out to mutual friends.

✔ Make friends with those whom you can relate to genuinely.

✔ Get back in touch with old acquaintances or friends.

## M – Meaning

Seeking meaning as well as purpose is a fundamental aspect of human beings. This need for significance can be met through different channels, such as career goals, creativity, social causes, or spirituality. Having a life purpose is related to higher satisfaction with life and overall well-being.

**Ways to Build Meaning:**

- ✔ Align your actions with your values and interests.
- ✔ Dip into new things/experiences to know what resonates with you.
- ✔ Exploring how one's passions can contribute to others' well-being.
- ✔ Spend quality time with loved ones who bring meaning into your life.

## A – Accomplishments/Achievements

Under the PERMA model, accomplishment denotes competence and mastery of skills. It starts with setting goals and persevering through difficulties until personal growth is experienced within each individual.

On the other hand, intrinsic goals (ones you make for yourself), like personal development, lead to higher levels of well-being than extrinsic targets, e.g., money or fame.

**Strategies for Building Accomplishments:**

- ✔ Set SMART goals that are **S**pecific, **M**easurable, **A**ttainable, **R**elevant/**R**ealistic, and **T**imely.
- ✔ Motivation can be strengthened by recalling past successes.
- ✔ Celebrating achievements in creative ways enhances satisfaction and pride.

✔ Consider the triumphs of your past. (Wherever we place our energy and awareness, we get more of)

Using the PERMA model is complex unless one increases one's empathic capacity. Therefore, the reintroduction of empathy among those who've caused harm falls within Seligman's line of thought. It also provides a practical way of addressing the root causes of criminal activities.

The restoration of empathy is not merely sentimental but has several complementary insights by Kohut, Sampson, Seligman, and others. It serves as a transformative step following creating harm for others. The aim is to correct failures in empathic response and foster healing and successful reintegration.

***

*a trauma-informed approach to rebuilding the web of relationships harmed by crime*

*"Dialogue is the bridge between conflict and resolution, where understanding becomes the path to healing."*

~Dominic Barter

# Holistic Transformation in Correctional Education

The transformative power of empathy calls for reimagining correctional facilities as centers where rehabilitation occurs through "Transformative Learning" centered on empathy building rather than punitive measures.

By understanding crime as has been so far discussed here (that is, as arising from unmet needs whose strategies sometimes stem from ACEs and other traumatic experiences), correctional systems may adapt programs to better accommodate proper rehabilitation and restoration.

Correctional facilities can introduce needs-based educational programs that help adults in custody identify their needs and then meet them in positive ways that do not harm others. For example, people incarcerated for property-related offenses due to poverty could learn about finance management or be provided vocational training aimed at equipping them with skills needed for stable employment once released from prison.

Someone incarcerated for assault or violent offenses are prime candidates for conflict resolution, emotional intelligence, and communications training and workshops to allow them to learn how to express emotions or resolve disputes calmly. Chances are these same people have had little to no training to reduce the likelihood of engaging in harmful behaviors in their pre-crime lives.

For those with extensive trauma in their past life (or within prison), resilience-building programs with therapeutic interventions and coping skills development can help break the cycle of trauma-driven criminal behavior. Resilience-building trauma-informed training, mindfulness practice, and empathic development increases self-awareness and self-consciousness for the benefit of both short-term (in prison) and long-term (public) communities and society.

It is a call for empathetic understanding that underscores the significance of emotional intelligence and practical communication skills. This can be done through programs that support individuals in expressing themselves emotionally, resolving conflicts, and connecting with others to reduce interpersonal crime cases.

Going forward, remember that empathy is a moral virtue and a powerful force for change. It opens the human heart to a more compassionate and authentic relationship with us and others.

## Transformative Learning

Programs like the Resilience Prison Project exist for this reason. Transformative Learning Communities inside correctional environments are places where we aim to offer truly effective support for promoting lasting change.

Jack Mezirow developed Transformative Learning, which involves significant changes in understanding ourselves, our belief systems, and our behavior. The process involved begins with a crisis or dilemma that forces one to reevaluate one's worldview and the core beliefs of one's lifestyle.

The process has ten steps or phases, from the initial dilemma through self-discovery and critical reflection to reintegrating the transformed perspective into one's life. Most of us experience this crisis when we enter the criminal justice system. Thus, we are low-hanging fruit regarding its use as a means of rehabilitation.

The framework helps us work critically through crisis points in our lives. When we are subjected to unskilled acts that have created harm and even the trauma that might have led to such behavior, it becomes an essential tool in the tool belt of RJR. These ten phases may also apply to how we approach trauma. The more deliberately you work through these steps, the more effective your transformative journey will be.

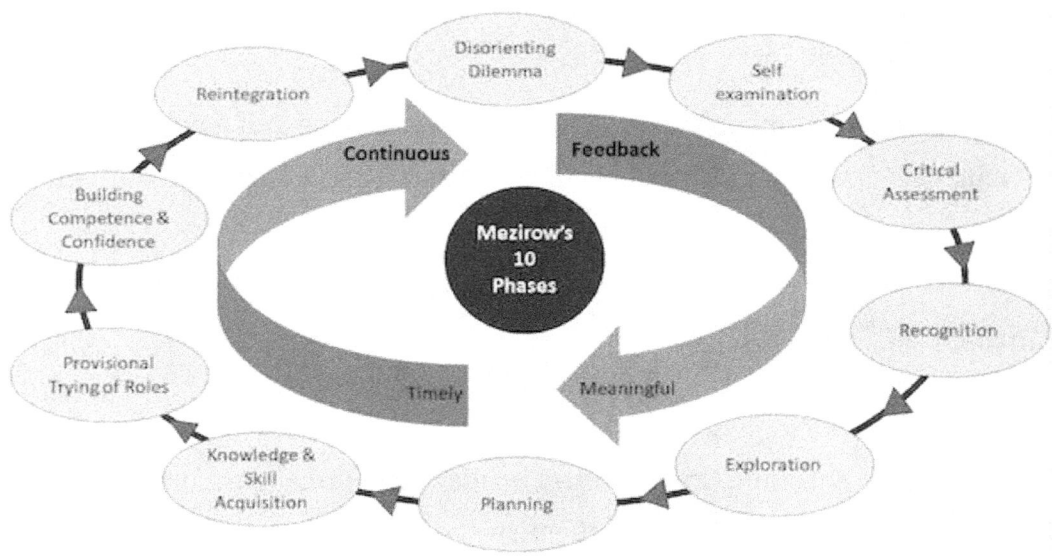

Let's briefly explore these phases in the following sections to better appreciate their relevance. It's like a journey that reshapes your perspective on life.

## Phase 1: A Disorienting Dilemma

Step one of transformative learning involves encountering a disorienting dilemma, i.e., a crisis, which challenges an individual's existing beliefs and perceptions. For many, this dilemma is often the stark reality of incarceration itself or a significant event occurring before or after being sent to prison.

The Resilience Prison Project introduces a fresh perspective at such a pivotal moment, challenging one's values and, ultimately, one's core beliefs, setting the stage for transformative growth. We begin by seeking to help participants shift from threat to safety by providing a wholesome space where connection and learning may thrive.

## Phase 2: Self-examination

Next, incarcerated individuals who have had the scales removed from their eyes, so to speak, engage in an introspective journey. A crisis can encourage you to reflect on past actions. This promotes self-awareness and a recognition of the harm caused to others and oneself. With the proper knowledge and insight, you can begin to reframe your relationship to past events, which may, in turn, set up new experiences.

Within the *Resilience Prison Project*, participants spend 12 weeks undergoing crime sharing and mock parole hearings, following 24 weeks of learning NVC fundamentals, and undergoing trauma-informed, supportive, and practitioner training. This self-reflection is important to transforming lives behind bars and restoring justice.

## Phase 3: Critical Reflection

Making a critical assessment is a core element of transformative learning. As a participant in our program, you can critically examine the strategies you employ relative to the needs you are attempting to meet. Equipped with fresh concepts about needs associated with the brain networks, you may better understand the cause/effect relationship to your choices.

The program helps you understand how specific situations contributed to the unskilled acts that led to incarceration. This phase encourages self-critique. Most importantly, it allows you to recognize the need for change and implement prosocial trauma-informed strategies to live by.

## Phase 4: Recognition of Shared Experiences

The *Resilience Prison Project* helps you identify and address societal expectations and biases. You become aware of how these influences have helped wire the brain. You learn what has shaped who you are. This leads to a deeper understanding of your circumstances and the behavior that led you there.

Moreover, people like you must realize that you are not alone. If others have undergone similar circumstances and overcome undesirable behaviors, you can, too. We can use this time anyway we like. Why not take advantage of the opportunities for self-improvement while we have fewer distractions?

## Phase 5: Exploration of New Perspectives

As an incarcerated person in a transformative learning community, you become open to new perspectives on yourself and your relationships. Plus, you learn win/win strategies to meet your needs.

You begin to understand that safer, more prosocial alternatives exist. This expands your horizons and empowers you to consider new *pathways for life*. This includes forming new relationships and taking on new roles that reflect the new understanding and insight.

## Phase 6: Acquisition of New Knowledge and Skills

Transforming lives behind bars requires acquiring new knowledge and skills. The Resilience Prison Project equips you with essential life skills. It teaches you to express yourself authentically and listen empathetically, among other things.

Learned knowledge and skills through the program are invaluable for self-improvement, healthier personal and interpersonal relationships, and a successful career when released from prison.

## Phase 7: Trial and Experimentation

You can practice your newfound skills in a supportive environment within transformative learning communities. I have witnessed this occur where there are sincere efforts toward self-improvement and a prison administration willing to do what's necessary to help it flourish.

This phase allows you to experiment with the techniques you are offered. You gain practical experience and confidence in your ability to communicate effectively. More significantly, you resolve conflicts peacefully and promote compassionate connections.

## Phase 8: Building Competence and Confidence

As you continue to practice personalizing the concepts and developing skills, you build competence and confidence in navigating your lives effectively.

Relationships no longer represent war—the needs for acceptance and belonging start getting met in ways previously unexplored. Previous threat responses shift to safety. The resulting confidence extends to successful reintegration into society.

## Phase 9: Personal Transformation

Personal transformation is the heart of transformative learning. Through it, you develop a deep sense of empathy, accountability, and a commitment to the evolution of your consciousness.

You undergo a profound shift in self-identity and values, which align more closely with the principles of peaceful living. We, as human beings, create the Babemba circle with humanity as a whole. Ubuntu becomes a part of our neuro-lens as we see each person as an extension of ourselves.

## Phase 10: Integration into New Roles

The final phase involves integrating these changes into daily life. Program graduates are better prepared to reintegrate as responsible, empathetic citizens. Recidivism rates are reduced, contributing to the growth of peaceful, thriving communities. It is also the culmination of the transformative journey.

When analyzed from the perspective of transformative learning, the *Resilience Prison Project* becomes an astonishing chance to experience significant shifts in your life. This will help individuals return to society as responsible, empathetic citizens by encouraging self-critical reflection, skill acquisition, and personal transformation. The positive impacts will then move beyond the confines of prison. Yes, it fosters peaceful, thriving communities and a more restorative criminal justice system.

*a trauma-informed approach to rebuilding the web of relationships harmed by crime*

# Integrated Framework of Resilience Prison Project

Now is the time when we consider this approach as a powerful tool for transformation and redemption for you. Through the insights discussed thus far, we learn how empathy connects to criminal behavior. This lays a foundation for a transformative approach to restoring justice and human connection.

The *Resilience Prison Project (RPP)* is a transformative learning program currently operating in the Oklahoma Department of Corrections (ODOC), directly influenced by most of the teachings (learnings) within this book.

### An Approach from the HEART

HEART is the acronym for the RPP's holistic approach to transforming corrections, which incorporates an all-inclusive and transformative framework. Holistic transformation in corrections is a much-needed addition to a system losing traction on rehabilitation.

HEART stands for a deep dedication to learning communities within a prison.

By applying our HEART framework:

- ✔ **Healing** the root causes of crime
- ✔ **Empowering** individuals,
- ✔ **Accepting** ourselves where we are
- ✔ **Restoring** relationships
- ✔ **Thriving** with resilience

RPP endeavors to break the cycle of incarceration and contribute to the creation of a more just and rehabilitative criminal justice system. We recognize the potential for positive change and growth within individuals who have experienced the criminal justice system.

The first pillar, *Healing*, refers to the fact that most crime comes from individuals who are hurting from past life trauma. Their hurt is not an excuse for the crime but a root cause that most likely led to their crime.

RPP attempts to directly address the hurt that an adult in custody still harbors, with efforts in healing to show that past experiences shape the lives of people who are incarcerated.

RPP addresses the roots of criminal behavior while simultaneously creating a nurturing environment for future stages of the framework. We aim to see the real person behind the criminal act that likely took only moments to carry out.

The second pillar, *Empowering*, signifies RPP's commitment to helping adults in custody learn to take responsibility for their behaviors. By assisting you in gaining knowledge and insight and offering skill-building programs and opportunities for personal development, the project strives to empower you to proactively seek positive change in your lives. Thus, RPP aims to help cultivate a mindset that requires accountability and personal growth for holistic personal transformations.

The third pillar, *Accepting*, provides focused and determined efforts as we help program participants reintegrate into society. Acceptance for the RPP is about breaking down barriers and reducing stigmatization that may impede successful reintegration. RPP does not condone behavior that has led someone to prison.

Still, we can accept the human being whose life can never be diminished to a mere Department of Corrections identification number. Community acceptance and understanding play a critical role at this stage since they ease the transition from isolation and imprisonment to inclusion and societal opportunities.

R for *Restoring* means a decided commitment to restorative justice. Instead of having systemic cycles of punishment, the RPP aims, whenever possible, to repair the harm, rebuild trust, and restore truth to enhance accountability. This orientation towards restoration reflects changing notions of justice as it prioritizes rehabilitation over retribution, two more great R words.

The final pillar—T for *Thriving*—is about creating peaceful, thriving communities. Adults in custody are not meant to "just survive." The RPP program teaches you to thrive in your present conditions. The initiative provides mentorship and personal development opportunities so that you can adequately prepare yourself for re-entry into the community. Thriving does not mean financial sufficiency alone; it means emotional wellness and living meaningfully and purposefully.

The *Resilience Prison Project*'s HEART framework is a comprehensive and compassionate approach to transforming lives inside correctional environments.

## Resilience Prison Project's Integrated Framework

The key course areas of the *Resilience Prison Project* (RPP) are outlined as follows:

- ✔ **Bare Bones Biz Course**: Financial literacy courses and vocational training to address economic struggles, providing individuals with the tools to meet their financial needs through legal means.

- ✔ **Emotional Intelligence/NVC Course**: Conflict resolution and communication workshops focusing on emotional intelligence, providing alternatives to violence to express emotions or resolve disputes.

- ✔ **Resilience Trumps ACEs (RTA) Courses**: Resilience-building programs addressing trauma through therapeutic interventions, support groups, and coping skill development to break the cycle of trauma-driven criminal behavior. This transformative approach addresses Adverse Childhood Experiences (ACEs), whereby 95% of the participants score (2) or more on the ACEs Quiz.

- ✔ **Trauma Talks**: As a logical follow-on from the RTA courses, this program is a part video/workbook series which educates prison residents about their traumas, so they can find resilience, self-regulate to calm their nervous systems, reduce prison aggression and become productive members of society upon their return. Through Trauma Talks, we create conversations to bring awareness about the devastating effects of childhood trauma.

- ✔ **Nonviolent Communication (NVC) Course**: RPP's integrated NVC workshops equip individuals with skills for articulating their emotions and needs, reducing the likelihood of resorting to harmful behaviors.

Participants increase their empathic capacity, improving their connection with themselves and others, expressing their needs and feelings without violence and other skills directly tied to learning and practicing NVC.

✔ **Mindfulness**: Mindfulness training enhances self-awareness and impulse control, providing individuals with alternatives to impulsive actions that may lead to criminal behavior.

Mindfulness practices are required "homework" for all RPP participants, providing tools for self-reflection and emotional regulation. Including mindfulness programs within correctional education helps individuals acquire self-awareness skills and effective coping strategies.

✔ **Restorative Justice Recalibrated**: Recalibrated restorative justice practices with program participants include surrogate-based Restorative Dialogue and "mock" Parole Hearing sessions.

Restorative justice circles to facilitate dialogue between individuals and those affected by their actions, allowing for empathy-building and restitution

~~~

Collectively, these studies move forward transformative change for the participants and the prison environment. While the training courses are helpful universally across a prison population, I have provided categories where particular program agendas are especially poignant for specific crime categories.

The RPP's framework provides individuals with comprehensive tools to increase empathic capacities, meet needs constructively, and cultivate resilience for positive reintegration upon release. The idea is to rekindle the flame of the authentic self and move forward more equipped to succeed both inside and outside of prison.

***

*"If punishment worked, there would be no prisons, because most of the children that have ended up in prison were all punished, were all destroyed. They were physically abused, emotionally abused, sexually abused, neglected, told they were nothing. So, that's punishment. They've already been punished. Violence for a violent act doesn't work. The only thing that works is love. The only thing that changes anything is love."*

~Fritzi Horstman

## Restorative Justice: A Needs Centered Approach

This chapter explores how true reform must focus on meeting the needs of all those affected by crime to reduce recidivism and build stronger communities.

Within the criminal justice framework, we stand at a critical point whereby attending to one's needs (which is often ignored) becomes central.

Retributive systems that are more concerned with punishment fail to address the driving force behind crime. Instead, they merely deter the behavior for a period, hoping that the miserable and, at times, inhumane conditions will act as a deterrent. Something that centuries have proven otherwise.

The shift towards a more effective criminal justice system lies in recognizing and meeting the basic human needs of all parties involved in crime. Importantly, acknowledging the gravity of offenses committed and their effects does not negate the value of tending to the needs of those who have created the harm. We need to realize that needs are at the core of every behavior. Thus, focusing on the behavior alone cannot restore justice. As said before, upstream behaviors are the underlying needs.

Retributive systems inadvertently contribute to a plethora of societal problems by focusing almost exclusively on punishment, especially when it leads to resentment and isolation as experienced by incarcerated people. When punitive measures are taken against individuals with minimal effort towards understanding or addressing their underlying needs, the result is merely deterrence, which often translates to delayed re-offense. It does not facilitate rehabilitation, as its significant impact is perpetuating resentment and retraumatizing trauma.

Therefore, the danger lies in maintaining this vicious cycle. The retaliatory features of retributive justice fail to recognize the intricacies involved in criminal behavior and its causes. Instead of promoting understanding, it deepens the divide between those with unmet needs and those who could help facilitate these needs getting met in a way that creates zero harm for others.

Suppose convicted felons feel estranged from the very communities they are expected to be accountable toward. Imagine their primary relationship to it has been retribution for acts some even feel justified in doing. What result ought we to expect?

We are not discussing how people "should" feel for the harm they've created. Instead, we are talking about how much accountability gets deterred because of the kind of treatment the person who created harm received for their crime. Accountability cannot be compelled and will not happen where there is a lack of safety and a sense of belonging.

With isolation, the appearance of no freedom, limited connection to those you love, inability to support yourself with the few dollars per month you receive from the state for your prison job, and forced to live with people of the state's choosing, what is the intrinsic motivation for true repentance, restitution, and reform?

On the other hand, an enlightened, comprehensive approach requires a finer understanding of each person's basic needs. Behind a criminal act is a real story of a real person with real problems. Somehow, crime is where you end up. A rehabilitative system recognizes and seeks to adequately address the root causes behind criminal acts.

Such a proactive stance aims to prevent re-offending and reintegrating those who've created harm into society as productive members. This method emphasizes empathy, which acknowledges that mere punishments without considering the complexities surrounding someone's circumstances may worsen instead of resolving these issues.

> *"A man convinced against his will is of the same opinion still."*
> ~*Dale Carnegie*

Dale Carnegie knew this one hundred years ago because he had the intuitive insight to see things, i.e., he was awake. We cannot change someone unless they want to change themselves. Any attempt to do so costs us in the long run; we are currently well into the long run.

Behind every action are the concepts that shape and guide behavior. These concepts have been formed over time and influenced by many environmental factors. If we truly seek to change people's behavior, we must win over those whose behavior isn't working for us. There's no winning someone over by hurting them, stripping them from their lives and families, etc., without actually proving to help them.

Moreover, a system that tries to make those harmed by crime feel better because now the person who hurt them will get what they've got coming is equally shallow and offers no depth to the healing process. Our criminal justice system is arming crime victims with violence-perpetuating strategies as a faux method of recovering from the harm they've experienced.

> *"A culture is strong when people work with each other, for each other. A culture is weak when people work against each other, for themselves."*
> ~Simon Sinek

This is true for both crime and punishment.

Restorative justice points out your need for accountability first and foremost but also acknowledges your need for acceptance and belonging. These needs must be met for someone to want (out of their energy) to express accountability for harm done to others. What's being said, it is also not a get-out-of-jail-free card. Harm has consequences, and individuals who act with violence upon others must be detained.

The point is for our deterrents to be effective for those harmed, those creating harm, and members of our communities. So far, restorative justice has emphasized two out of three. Recalibrating means emphasizing help toward those who have created the harm because it's now irrefutable that adverse childhood experiences have contributed to harmful behavior.

*"If you study prison populations as I have, you see a common preponderance of childhood trauma and mental illness. The two go together. So a lot of the people are being punished for being mentally ill and they are mentally ill because they were traumatized as kids. So what we have in [prisons] are the most traumatized people in our society."*

~Dr. Gabor Mate

By incorporating these principles into our justice system while acknowledging the gravity of the crimes committed, an environment is created where those of you in custody feel you can belong and even thrive. This feeling of acceptance is a powerful incentive towards good behavior, reducing chances for further criminal engagement.

In the meantime, finding a connection to your self-worth and value is vital to moving forward with life, even inside a prison cell. You must not wait until the "Powers that Be" transition to more suitable arrangements before you tap into the unlimited resources inside that can both figuratively and literally set you free from all that binds, restricts, limits, and condemns.

## Understanding Your Needs

Restorative justice Recalibrated, at its core, is personalized to individuals. This sets it apart from conventional justice systems by being sincerely focused on understanding and even meeting the needs associated with the harms created by criminal acts.

From this angle, we will break down the concept of restorative justice as a needs-centered approach to addressing harm. I hope this will help you see and understand the intricate process of healing these harms as much as possible.

a trauma-informed approach to rebuilding the web of relationships harmed by crime

Your behavior is driven by universal needs shared by all human beings. Understanding these needs is based on and forms the foundation of your experience.

Needs can range from survival needs such as food or water to complex emotional ones like love and acceptance. Restorative justice recognizes that you have unmet needs as someone who may have caused harm or experienced it. Addressing these constitutes one major aspect in restoring you to wholeness.

Let it be reiterated that focusing on the unmet needs of someone who has harmed others is NOT condoning the unskilled acts that caused the harm. Rather, it's lifting the veil to the actual underlying causes of those acts to support true and lasting change.

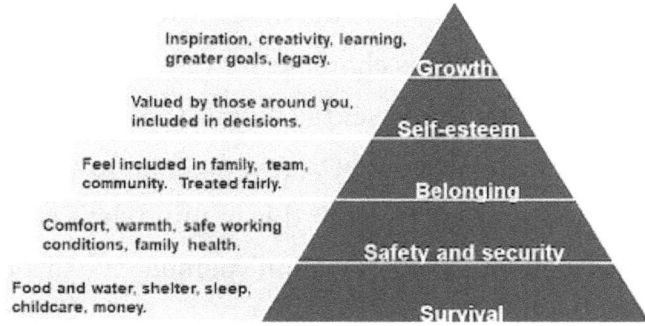

Needs are different for everyone

The very people who claim that an empathic response toward those creating harm is soft on crime have simply not undergone the process involved. Comparatively speaking, a brief look at what's required to approach so-called "offenders" with either empathy or indifference, the latter wins every time.

It could be argued that our current approach to criminal justice requires prosecutors to enter into what Martin Buber calls the "I—It" relationship with the accused. This is the perspective "offenders" (those creating harm) descend to during empathic failure when crime as a strategy is embraced.

This perspective of "I—It" diminishes the person to an object or thing to be used as a means to an end; in this case, "justice" as understood by the prosecutor.

The accused is seen as something used to achieve one's goals and desires, a conviction and a sentence that will teach the accused a lesson.

Buber calls this dehumanizing as it strips the individual of any inherent dignity or value. This is the out-grouping we mentioned previously, considered in a slightly different way. Buber emphasizes how common it is in our modern society to take this perspective. Thus, it seems almost ironic that those involved with criminal justice use it when actively engaged in their roles, i.e., both the crime and the following punishment.

On the other hand, the "I—Thou" relationship is the ideal restorative justice approach as it engages the other with mutual recognition, respect, and value. This relationship is characterized by vulnerability and connection. Buber goes on to say that it is essential to cultivate this "I—Thou" relationship if we are to overcome the disconnection and alienation growing increasingly common in our modern society. With this in mind, let's continue approaching the development of this "I—Thou" perspective through the Resilience Prison Projects integrated framework.

To integrate nonviolent communication (NVC) practices with restorative justice models, foundations must be established about understanding that needs are at the core of all human experience. NVC serves as an introduction to the subsequent exploration of restorative justice within this program. Early on, we look at language use based on universal needs rather than moralistic judgments.

A profound connection between these two approaches exists when considering how essential understanding human needs is to driving behavior.

Restorative justice does tend to focus on the fact that individuals creating harm and those affected by it have unmet needs directly associated with the event that brought them together. NVC provides the tools and vocabulary to articulate, recognize, and empathize with these unmet needs. We believe NVC is a necessary component to improve behavior out of one's own energy to bring lasting change.

By immersing ourselves in the NVC process, we may ensure a heightened consciousness about what is most important. Rather than getting caught up in "right-wrong" judgments that promote disconnection, we learn to uncover what's truly behind our actions.

Engaging in these restorative practices requires a nuanced understanding of the underlying needs that drive behavior. Restorative justice applications inside a correctional environment include but are not limited to crime sharing and mock parole hearings. Our whole way of life may reflect these values.

Moving into restorative justice requires a change in perspective. Blame and shame shift to understanding and acceptance. Traditional justice systems usually involve determining guilt, assigning blame, and executing punishment.

Conversely, RJR invites you and other stakeholders to discover what happened, the harm it created, the unmet needs remaining, and how best to restore relationships with trauma-informed care.

## Meeting Your Needs via Restorative Justice

What distinguishes restorative justice is its unwavering commitment to meeting the needs of everyone affected by a harmful act and restoring relationships as best as possible. That includes yourself, those harmed, and the wider society. This feature underpins a holistic restoration plan.

I hope that even if any party refuses to involve themselves in restorative practices, the remaining parties may still find a way to participate. The same has been confirmed for retributive justice for quite a long time.

It is time for the consciousness of restorative justice to graduate to the next phase in its evolution. With retributive justice, those harmed are not always involved with the outcomes, but the process is executed the same way.

Similarly, we must install restorative justice infrastructures in our communities that make it available to all parties as opportunity permits. Why hasn't this become our standard? We make restorative justice applications depending upon whether they are initiated by those most harmed and possibly traumatized by what happened. Is this the healthiest use of the kind of justice most concerned with healing harms and rebuilding the web of relationships harmed by crime?

By recognizing and addressing your needs, restorative justice acknowledges immediate and long-term factors ranging from a vital sense of safety and security to emotional and psychological well-being. In this process, you are allowed to honestly express what was driving your behaviors and the feelings and unmet needs that arise now about those events.

It also provides opportunities for you to understand the impact of your unskilled acts on others. We must understand the impact our actions have on others. When we connect empathically, feelings of shame and regret may transform into what fertilizes the growth of conscience and character.

Contrary to punitive measures, restorative justice does not limit your role to one category but tries to understand the unmet needs that could have prompted your actions. Many who harm are often those who have been harmed. In other words, hurt people hurt people.

Restorative justice redefines accountability beyond mere punitive measures. Instead, it becomes a dynamic process within this complex setting involving recognizing the harm done, taking responsibility for what was done, and actively working towards addressing any unmet needs that may have led to the harmful behavior or remain because of it. Through this redefinition, you become more personally empowered, making active contributions to the healing process as much as possible.

It does not follow that conflicts and crime arise out of the actual needs we seek to meet. They come about due to the strategies we use to meet them. Even on opposing sides of war or American politics, the values driving each opposing side are similar. They find themselves at odds because of differing views on HOW to meet their needs.

This is the most vital lesson for those who have harmed others, i.e., learning new approaches to meet the needs they share with those they hurt. Restoring empathy paves the way to a successful reintegration because "needs consciousness," which is knowing how to love one's neighbor as oneself, is centered on empathy.

In our continuing search for restoration based on effectively meeting needs, we must grasp that this principle is at the heart of restorative justice. It represents a dynamic framework where an individual like you can end the vicious cycle of harm and rebuild the web of relationships broken through such unskilled acts.

In restorative justice, the central element of the restoration process is the lives of those most affected by the harm created. As one of the crime participants, it includes recognizing and understanding the unmet needs associated with the harm created.

Examining needs in the context of restorative justice reveals their importance to holistic healing and transformation.

*a trauma-informed approach to rebuilding the web of relationships harmed by crime*

# Holistic Spectrum of Needs

Within restorative justice, our needs and others go beyond mere survival; they comprise emotional, psychological, and social dimensions representing the various facets of the human experience. Recognizing the whole spectrum is essential for understanding why harm happens and finding a way back to normalcy.

Restorative justice requires a combination of meeting the diverse needs of those harmed, those who've created harm, and communities to work efficiently. Recognizing and responding to these needs helps shift focus from punishment towards a complete recovery journey that encompasses everyone involved – including you. This is the vision of justice arising from a collective cry for restoration, second chances, and wholeness.

Refer to the following list per your needs and your situation. It is also helpful to look at the needs of the person(s) on the opposite side of the spectrum.

### Needs as Someone Who Has Experienced Harm (Victim)

✔ **Safety and Security.** An intense sense of insecurity may be experienced by someone after being harmed. Building trust cannot begin without attending to this need for security.

✔ **Acknowledgment and Validation.** It is crucial that we have our hurt acknowledged and validated by others to heal appropriately through restorative justice. This pain platform allows for its expression as well as recognition from others involved with it.

✔ **Empathy and Understanding.** To be understood by both the person(s) responsible for the harm and fellow citizens could be something a person harmed longs for deeply when going through such an ordeal. The experience of being able to share the hurt associated with having been harmed makes room for proper recovery on their part. Many have also benefited greatly from receiving verbal or written expressions of regret and remorse for the harm they experienced.

## Needs as Someone Who Created Harm

✔ **Accountability and Responsibility.** You also have needs, one of which is accountability or responsibility for what created harm for others. Restorative justice enables you to commit to your actions, actively participating in healthy processes alongside others involved.

✔ **Understanding Root Causes.** Your harmful behavior might have been due to some underlying factors which, when investigated, revealed to be an attempt to meet another need – knowing the deeper "why" will serve not to repeat these strategies to get the need met in the future.

✔ **Opportunities for Redemption.** This need for redemption, and the opportunity to rebuild one's life is inherent to human beings. Restorative justice provides you with tools through which personal growth can be achieved.

## Community Needs That Impact You

✔ **Safety and Cohesion.** A collective need for safety and cohesion exists among communities affected by crime. This involvement makes everyone here feel responsible for each other's welfare.

✔ **Prevention and Education.** Many communities ask for prevention measures as well as education so that they can avoid future occurrences of similar incidents. This creates a culture that equips its members with better, more prosocial strategies to meet needs. The method creates win/win outcomes for all involved.

✔ **Restoration of Social Fabric.** When harm has been caused, an entire web of relationships gets torn apart. It is up to us to help rebuild this web. Restorative justice attempts to fix these societal threads, thereby making communities more robust due to an increased connectedness of its parts.

***

*"In the end, reconciliation is a spiritual process, which requires more than just a legal framework. It has to happen in the hearts and minds of people."*

~Nelson Mandela

# Unlocking Healing Through Restorative Dialogue

For someone who has created harm, restorative dialogue (RD) goes beyond mere words to a carefully planned conversation to bring about empathy, understanding, and restoration.

We have taken what has been called victim-offender dialogue and recalibrated it so as to reflect an approach which values all parties equally. By restorative dialogues we intend to learn a process which may be applied in any situation where harm has arisen and the relationship needs restoration.

Despite the fact that we can justifiably refuse to condone the behavior of the person who created harm, (and rightfully so) by also refusing to accept them as an equal, a human being with dignity and value, it is unlikely they will genuinely seek accountability. With this approach, we are throwing the baby out with the bath water so to speak. Therefore, starting off by defining the dialogue as "victim-offender" or right wrong, we lack the trauma-informed care necessary for such dialogues to produce the desired result for all parties.

It is important to get this specific because in the "victim-offender" dialogue, the label says to the offender, "You are wrong." By changing our reference to a person who created harm, we are saying, "What you did, i.e., your actions were wrong." This shift helps support change as the static label of the "offender" is removed—the first step in helping someone who has created harm restore their humanity as well as their place in society. As long as accountability is compelled, we risk it being inauthentic.

Much like the advice given to a snow skier when first learning. You must keep your eyes on the slope before you, not the trees you try to avoid. Energy follows thought. If we look at the trees, our body moves toward them. We are more likely to crash.

Similarly, if we focus on the "wrongness" of an individual, our actions follow in many respects - at least in terms of our identity. Thus, like with the Babemba Forgiveness Ceremony, we remind people who have missed the mark of who they *really* are and what they are truly capable of living. This keeps them on the course and not continuing to hit trees, so to speak. It also helps the rest of us see the humanity in someone who has erred.

We will, therefore, not use the terms victim, offender, or victim-offender dialogue in context to anything designed to restore justice. It is time to return to better times when things like the *Babemba Forgiveness Ceremony* helped a community draw out the best in each other.

This unique space enables those harmed and those who've created harm to connect deeper, diverging from past events. For most people in custody, RD is likely going to involve surrogates; nevertheless, our exploration provides insights relating to the process to better equip you for a surrogate-based RD, which may be a beneficial part of the rehabilitation process.

As you embark on this journey, be aware that this style will ensure the dialogue is practical and emotionally safe for everyone involved. Through this infusion of compassion, you will understand how much more transformative restorative dialogues can be.

In going deeper, consider how much the process contributes to personal growth. It resolves conflicts and becomes a means of understanding, empathy, and healing. Therefore, by embracing such conversations, you are involved in restoring justice and embarking on a personal path toward holistic well-being.

## Critical Components of Restorative Dialogue

In the Restorative Dialogue approach, a framework exists meant to ensure your well-being and the effectiveness of restorative dialogue. RD is voluntary; if you participate, you consciously decide. Safety always comes first; measures are implemented to create an environment where open communication can be done honestly and effectively while observing threat predictions and our R.O.L.E.S.

Envision moving through an emotional journey with a neutral guide always present to ensure fairness and balance. The facilitator is a companion who understands the complexities and will support you.

Thorough preparation is made before entering into a restorative dialogue. It goes beyond understanding. Preparations set clear ground rules to create a safe and respectful atmosphere for all parties. This foundation allows for fruitful engagement.

RD provides an avenue within the conversation where you can share how much pain has been caused by what happened. In this case, it becomes an opportunity for self-reflection. This leads to genuine regrets as well as feelings of responsibility. Sometimes, during these meetings, participants end up agreeing on compensation or any other kind of action that can be taken by the concerned person(s). These agreements are reached mutually.

Consider the following guidance as navigational tools that shape an encounter and not only address harm but also foster actual understanding, accountability, and transformative growth for all parties, not just those who have created harm.

## Facilitating Restorative Role Play

Starting on the path of restorative dialogue carries excellent weight. This structured conversation presents a way for those harmed and those who've created harm to heal. For instance, when participants feel safe enough, they can share actively in discussions concerning their experience(s) related to the crime rather than being spoken to about it by a third party, like a prosecutor.

During the preparation session, participants are informed of what to expect from the dialogue and its voluntary nature. Those who have created harm provide support for those harmed and express ownership for the harm that has arisen through unskilled acts.

After each role-play session, have a debrief where feedback is offered about what happened, allowing insight into each party's challenges surrounding the event. The negotiation part emphasizes agreements on restitution or future actions leading to restoration.

Finally, a collective reflection involving all parties involved is conducted so as to wind up with some lessons learned from the whole process. This reinforcing value is attached to restorative dialogue. This step-by-step guide ensures that everyone gets a comprehensive, transformative experience while navigating the complexities of healing and reconciliation.

## The Transformative Potential of Dialogue

This Restorative Dialogue journey can have lasting transformative effects if handled well and according to these principles. It goes beyond what traditional justice systems offer because they enable a person harmed (or surrogate) to talk about their experiences while helping you understand how your actions have affected them; both can actively help to restore justice.

Your involvement is prominent among the many threads making up restorative dialogues. Always remember that it's not a cure-all, but when used appropriately, it becomes a powerful tool for fostering empathy, accountability, and, hopefully, reconciliation.

## Unlocking Your Journey with Nonviolent Communication

Nonviolent Communication (NVC) emerges as a harmonizing force in restorative justice, weaving through the intricate threads of longing for accountability and connection.

Let's look at the seamless integration of NVC principles within the restorative justice framework, exploring how this synergy enhances empathy, fosters understanding, and propels your restoration process.

### Connecting NVC with Your Restorative Journey

Nonviolent Communication (NVC), developed by Marshall Rosenberg, is grounded in the knowledge that all human behavior stems from attempts to meet universal needs. NVC provides a compassionate and practical framework for expressing, receiving, and understanding the needs underlying our actions. It is a matter of where we are focusing our attention. With NVC, the goal is to focus attention where we are most likely to meet our own and other's needs successfully.

Promoting empathic communication aligns seamlessly with your restorative justice journey. It emphasizes the principle of fostering empathy between you and others. This process encourages the expression of your feelings and needs and the reception of the same in others. This lays the foundation for a deeper understanding.

Addressing your unmet needs is a crucial goal of restorative justice, but that does not mean catering to your wants. This very interpretation keeps ambassadors of retributive justice from transitioning toward restorative approaches. Because attempts to meet universal needs were undoubtedly behind the acts that caused harm and brought you to prison, finding more prosocial ways to meet those needs is what true rehabilitation is about. NVC provides a language and methodology tailored for identifying and articulating these needs, creating an essential framework for your comprehensive restoration.

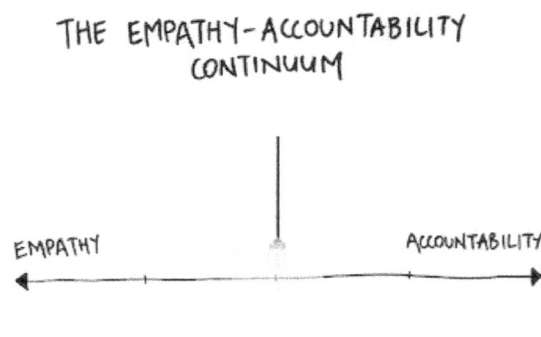

NVC and restorative justice share a central tenet—the significance of dialogue and the centrality of needs. NVC's emphasis on compassionate dialogue aligns perfectly with the structured conversations inherent in restorative justice processes. This intersection provides a shared space for authentic expression, contributing to healing.

Crucial to your restorative justice journey is the balance between empathy and accountability. NVC strongly emphasizes empathic listening and understanding, reinforcing these essential elements. This approach aids you in navigating the delicate balance between holding yourself accountable for your actions and fostering genuine empathy for your experiences.

Mutual clarity, understanding, and respect are three basic needs that result in empathy. Within the *Resilience Prison Project* framework, we use this formula: C+U+R=E. And yes, we see this formula as a CURE for all violence, including that which is involved in crime and the resulting disconnect between creator and receiver of harm.

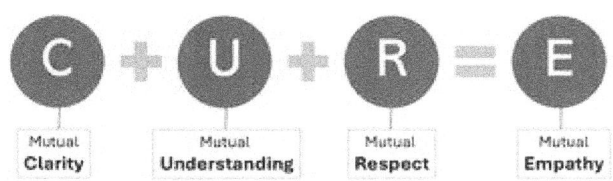

When all parties have mutual clarity as to what happened, mutual understanding of what is alive (feelings/needs) in oneself and each other, and mutual respect for this reality, empathy becomes the natural bi-product.

## NVC in Restorative Dialogues

In restorative dialogues guided by nonviolent communication (NVC), openly expressing your feelings and needs is paramount. Vulnerability is a golden key for connection. It sets the metaphoric lemniscate current of honest expression and empathic reception into motion.

NVC principles play a crucial role in guiding this. This enhances the depth of communication and fosters a profound understanding between parties. Imagine restorative justice as a country and NVC as a kind of "Rosetta Stone" for language barriers between people.

The transformative potential of NVC unfolds in restorative dialogues, where cultivating empathy is a central focus. Infusing NVC principles into these dialogues transforms them into 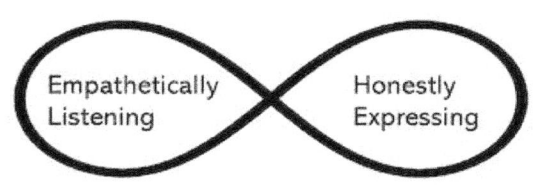 encounters where empathy becomes a powerful catalyst for your healing and restoration.

When we share feelings and needs about painful events that have happened (no matter how hard to hear), what's said becomes more readily received by those listening.

## Exploring Surrogate Practice for Enhanced Empathy

With restorative justice, one engages in a unique exploration that weaves together the principles of nonviolent Communication (NVC) with the intricacies of restorative dialogue. This is where the concept of surrogates comes in—individuals selected to participate in a controlled and supportive environment, serving as stand-ins, skillfully simulating the nuanced dynamics inherent in authentic dialogues. The purpose is clear: to provide a platform for honing NVC skills, deepening empathic understanding, and cultivating the readiness required for genuine, real-world interactions.

When you are engaged in surrogate practice, you enter a sanctuary where you refine NVC skills within yourself. This controlled setting mitigates the immediate emotional intensity often associated with real-life restorative dialogues, creating a secure space for experimentation and growth. As needs are universal, empathy enables us to take on the role of someone harmed by tapping into their unmet needs.

The methodology gradually unfolds, offering an immersion into the complexities of dialogue. Participants navigate through at their own pace based on their comfort level. By incrementally exposing themselves to the multifaceted nature of these interactions, confidence and competence build organically over time.

Surrogate practice is more than just a script; it is a feedback loop. By engaging in reflective discussions and giving constructive feedback later, communication skills continue to improve, creating an environment where they evolve through intentional introspection.

Surrogate practice within restorative justice's bounds is a transformative tool for developing empathy and honing skills. It transcends mere theory by providing practicality and immersion. When we reverse roles and experience what it might have been like on the other side of our unskilled acts, it becomes much easier to understand the harm we have created.

This process helps you comprehend NVC consciousness and prepares you for real-life restorative dialogues, whether formal or informal. Through judicious use of the surrogate process, one embarks on a self-discovery journey that gradually replaces shame with acceptance and confusion with understanding.

As we examine how NVC relates to your restorative justice journey, it becomes clear that these two approaches have something in common, which is their heartbeat-a commitment to developing empathy within oneself, recognizing one's needs, and promoting a justice system that is centered in what NVC calls a partnership paradigm (cooperation vs competition).

***

*"If your relationship to the present moment is not right—nothing can ever be right in the future—because when the future comes—it's the present moment."*

~Eckhart Tolle

# Mindfulness in Restorative Justice

In our approach to restorative justice, you are invited to embrace the transformative experience of mindfulness—a powerful current infusing the restoration process with presence, awareness, healing, and an intimate connection to the present moment.

My initial exploration of mindfulness was independent of restorative justice. It was the result of my curiosity about spirituality and the practice of meditation by people from diverse backgrounds and traditions. Over the years, the process has helped to deepen my self-awareness, improve my focus, and connect compassionately with myself and others when it matters most.

At first, it seemed almost impossible to focus my mind for even moments without soon realizing that my attention was wavering. But my patience and concentration grew over time. What might surprise you is that my abilities developed most from focusing on inanimate objects I had no personal interest in. At one point, I could easily meditate on a pencil for an hour with the slightest loss of focus. As a result of this practice, seemingly insignificant things became all the more interesting to me.

Forming a clear mental image and asking straightforward questions like "What is the object (size, shape, color, material, etc.)? How did it come to be this way? What was the process? Why was it designed as such? What are various types of this object?" We can become so engrossed in contemplating that we become like the director of our own *How It's Made* podcast episode inside ourselves.

We move from forming a clear image to imagining all of the various steps of its coming to be, why it was designed this particular way, the development of the object throughout history, where it originated, etc. We learn to extend our focus to things beyond the ego simply for the sake of acknowledging the totality of a given thing we might normally never consider.

Before we know it, this activity sharpens the mind and opens the heart to ask similar questions about more complex foci for our attention, like people we are challenged to understand. Thus, it prepares us for empathy's invitation to connection when evaluations and moralistic judgments bar us from seeing what's alive in others.

There are numerous approaches to mindfulness practice. In what follows, you will find ways to initiate your practice and apply the principles in the service of restorative justice. Another consideration you might make based on what has come before is this. In the *Community Resilience* section, I mentioned that:

safety + connection = balance

With justice, we find the justice scales to be a symbol because true justice is also about balance. Thus, mindfulness practice is one of the best ways to balance our inner and outer lives. As we move to recalibrate restorative justice, mindfulness plays a significant role in creating a restorative lifestyle.

This chapter takes you on a journey that reveals how mindfulness may work in conjunction with restorative justice while showing how being present contributes to healing.

## Foundations of Mindfulness

Mindfulness means being fully present in the moment without judgment; it invites awareness about thoughts, emotions, and sensations inside us – going beyond mere appearances into the roots that have shaped their significance in our lives. Yes, it sounds like how NVC has been described and practiced. That's because NVC is a mindfulness practice as well.

Mindfulness is rooted in ancient contemplative traditions that span different cultures around the globe. It began with practices still found in Buddhism, Hinduism, Christianity, Islam, etc. Meditation has stood the test of time to bring along with its wisdom from mystics and sages who recognized how being present could transform lives.

One of the primary characteristics of mindfulness is its demand for total presence – fully immersing oneself in the present moment with a compassionate heart and a curious mind. Through this practice, you can gain insight into your mental landscape on a deeper level than ever before. It is simply observing thoughts without judgment or feelings alongside sensations without trying to change them. This practice reveals how intricately linked they are together within you.

The value of mindfulness extends far beyond any one moment of practice. Research from various fields, including psychology, neuroscience, etc., has shown that mindfulness has positive effects on mental well-being. Examples include reduced stress levels, better emotional control, and improved overall cognitive functions.

Luminaries like Jon Kabat-Zinn and Thich Nhat Hanh have played pivotal roles in popularizing and adapting these ancient practices for the modern world, drawing inspiration from contemporary sources in the mindfulness realm. Even within the confines of incarceration, their teachings offer practical insights into integrating mindfulness into our daily lives.

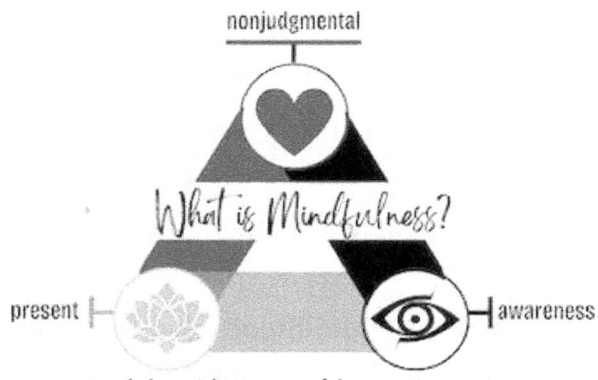

> "When we are mindful, deeply in touch with the present moment, our understanding of what is going on deepens, and we begin to be filled with acceptance, joy, peace, and love."    ~Thich Nhat Hanh

Think of it beyond a technique as you explore the foundations of mindfulness. Across time, it unfolds through this journey, connecting you with ancient wisdom while providing tools for navigating the complexities of our modern world.

Mindfulness is a gift to yourself that can lead to inner peace, resilience, and a profound connection with the universe, your higher power, or whatever you call the spiritual source of your existence. We initially experimented with techniques handed down by others. Eventually, we learn to personalize what we learn to create our inner life rich with insights from our experiences.

> *"Letting go gives us freedom, and freedom is the only condition for happiness. If, in our heart, we still cling to anything—anger, anxiety, or possessions—we cannot be free."*  ~Thich Nhat Hanh

## Recalibrating Toward Mindfulness in Restorative Justice

Within our exploration and practice of restorative justice, mindfulness becomes an invaluable ally since it matters when delving into the unskilled acts that created harm for others and transformative paths towards avoiding future harm. It is so much more than just something you do; mindfulness acts as a window we may use to see past behaviors and honestly engage in restoring what has been broken. Mindfulness helps us minimize recidivism through prosocial behaviors such as trauma-informed care and nonviolent communication (NVC).

> *"Awareness is like the sun. When it shines on things, they are transformed."*
>
> ~Thich Nhat Hanh

Again, mindfulness can mean entering our thoughts, feelings, needs, or body sensations without judgment if one wants to understand the causes behind the behavior better. This reflective process marks a significant turning point for individuals who, like yourself, have engaged in unskilled acts identified as "criminal." This may be your first time exploring the actual needs underlying your behavior. An NVC framework supports a space where you may reach the universal needs upstream from guilt, shame, or even justification of your behaviors.

This increased self-awareness within restorative justice is foundational to meaningful dialogue. It enables you to approach the journey towards restoration genuinely while recognizing how your actions have affected others and accepting responsibility for the harm they caused. Therefore, mindfulness leading towards present-moment awareness aids in building an authentic relationship between those harmed and those who've created harm. It encourages active involvement in restoring what has been lost or damaged.

> *"When another person makes you suffer, it is because he suffers deeply within himself, and his suffering is spilling over. He does not need punishment; he needs help. That's the message he is sending."*
> ~Thich Nhat Hanh

Mindfulness also plays a significant role in addressing harms perpetrated within incarcerated populations by creating an environment where people, including yourself, become more aware of the outcomes of their deeds. This technique fosters empathy among adults in custody, promoting collective responsibility toward positive changes within correctional institutions.

Moreover, mindfulness also helps prevent future offenses. Practicing mindfulness can develop emotional regulation skills, resilience, and heightened awareness of triggers that may lead to harmful actions. Victor Frankl once said,

> *"Between stimulus and response, there is a space. In that space is our power to choose our response. In our response lies our growth and freedom."* ~Victor Frankl

Such words of daily wisdom point out that cultivating these qualities helps us make conscious decisions that reduce the chances of falling back into destructive patterns again.

As I considered mindfulness in relation to restorative justice, it became apparent that this practice is more than just meditation; it can be a way of finding yourself, being responsible for your actions, and making the world a better place.

> "None of us has to be a helpless victim of what was done to us or what was not done for us in the past, nor do we have to be helpless in the face of what we may be suffering now." ~Jon Kabat-Zinn

In what follows, we will discuss ways you can incorporate mindfulness into your everyday life. It provides pragmatic techniques for self-improvement.

# Mindfulness Exercises for Restorative Justice Participants

With these exercises incorporated into your daily life, you can participate genuinely, and the restoration process becomes more observant and compassionate.

## Breath Awareness Exercise

Breath awareness exercises are best implemented daily.

> "Bliss begins with the breath. We breathe in and accept all that is new. We breathe out and release all that has passed." ~Sara Wiseman

✔ **Find a comfortable space.** Go to a quiet and comfortable place where you can sit or stand without interruption. Relax your posture, keeping your back straight to breathe comfortably, freely, and naturally.

✔ **Inhale deeply.** Begin by taking a slow and deliberate breath in. Fill your lungs in this breath. Notice how much broader your chest is getting, as well as the abdomen. This deep inhaling sets up the moment of now.

✔ **Mindful exhalation.** Exhale slowly and deliberately. Release any tension or distractions as you breathe out. Every exhale is like an anchor gently pulling focus away from wandering thoughts towards peaceful rhythmic breathing.

✔ **Repeat the cycle.** Keep going with this breathing pattern consistently. Inhale deeply, feeling the life-giving breath, and exhale mindfully, grounding each breath in the present moment. Let the flow of air act like a constant reminder of your current experience.

✔ **Cultivate awareness.** Feel the different sensations of your breath, such as temperature, the rise and fall of the chest, and the subtle pause between inhales and exhales while practicing this technique. Cultivate an increased sense of presence through your breathing process.

✔ **Gentle redirecting.** If your mind wanders, it's normal. Just softly bring it back to focus on breathing again. Use every inhale/exhale to guide you back into calmness and the present moment.

✔ **Reflect and conclude.** Spend some moments reflecting upon small changes within consciousness. Observe any shifts in your mental state or emotional well-being. When ready, gently end the practice session.

As you commit to this practice, you'll find it becomes a powerful tool for grounding yourself in the present moment. It fosters mindfulness in your restorative justice journey.

## Body Scan Meditation

Take this mindfulness with you as you journey through restorative justice and connect your spirit, soul, and body.

*"Caring for your body, mind, and spirit is your greatest and grandest*

*responsibility. It's about listening to the needs of your soul and then honoring them." - Kristi Ling*

✔ **Set the scene.** Start by finding a quiet space where you can lie down or sit comfortably. Allow yourself to rest and close your eyes once you feel safe.

✔ **Connect with your breath.** Center yourself by taking a few deliberate breaths. Breathe deeply in and breathe fully out. Use breathing as an initial focus point for bringing your attention here now.

✔ **Scan your toes.** Focus on your toes. Can you feel any sensations like tingling, warmth, or coolness? Slowly move awareness from toe to toe, observing each sensation.

✔ **Travel upward.** Gradually shift your attention up to your feet, ankles, and calves. Feel the weight of your legs and how they touch the ground or the seat beneath them.

✔ **Explore each region.** Scan through every part of your body further. Bring awareness into areas such as knees, thighs, hips, abdomen, chest, etc. Observe tension, warmth, or subtle movements within each region.

✔ **Acknowledge sensations.** As you scan, allow yourself to notice whatever is happening without judging it, just accepting their presence and gently seeing what arises about yourself.

✔ **Observe your breath.** Reconnect back to breath at various points during this exercise using it as a guiding force towards staying present. While scanning, observe how different parts feel when affected by your breathing.

✔ **Mindful exploration.** Continue being conscious about what's happening inside while traveling down your arms, neck, and head and ending at your fingertips. Be curious about every single part encountered with full attention to its uniqueness.

✔ **Conclusion.** When you get to either the top of your head or the tips of your fingers, spend some time enjoying the whole self. Gradually return to an outward focus, opening your eyes if closed.

✔ **Reflect and integrate.** Take a moment after finishing today's practice to consider what happened today; did anything change?

## Observation of Surroundings

You develop a greater appreciation for the world around you by participating in the observation of surroundings practice. One wise philosopher has noted that intelligence is heightened by increasing our capacity to make precise observations without judgments.

After some time, practicing this will lead to an even stronger connection with the present moment in your restorative justice journey.

> *"There is a great beauty in observation, in seeing things as they are."*
> *~Jiddu Krishnamurti*

✔ **Find a tranquil setting.** Look for a peaceful place with minimal distractions. This could be inside or outside, where you can relate to your surroundings. It may be that with limited choices, you find a time inside the cell or accessible location when it is most conducive for beginning this practice. Over time, it will become easier to practice anywhere.

✔ **Breathe and center.** Take several deep breaths to help yourself focus. Release all tensions and worries, allowing your mind to be open to the present moment.

✔ **Engage your senses.** Start by opening up your awareness to what is happening around you. Use your five senses to experience the colors, shapes, and sounds surrounding you.

✔ **Release judgment.** Forget about any judgments or assumptions about anything. Approach your observations with a sense of curiosity and openness.

✔ **Notice details.** Explore all the intricate details found in your surroundings. Pay attention to subtle nuances that usually go unnoticed.

✔ **Appreciate the present moment.** Allow yourself to stay with whatever is happening right now. Just appreciate any beauty that becomes present in your awareness before you move on.

✔ **Feel a connection.** Establish a relationship between yourself and everything else around you. Notice how different pieces fit together, including where you belong within this larger context.

✔ **Reflect on your experience.** Spend a mindful period observing, then take some time afterward to reflect on what happened during that moment. Record insights or shifts in perception experienced during meditation practice if any occurred—for example, note changes made from worrying too much about plans versus appreciating the present moment. Contrast moments of openness and peace to feeling anxious over things we cannot control, such as other people's opinions about us.

## Gratitude Journaling

This means that whenever Gratitude Journaling becomes part of your everyday routine, then it keeps you in a positive mood and makes you realize the beauty in ordinary moments, which enhances your restorative justice experience.

> *"The soul that gives thanks can find comfort in everything; the soul that complains can find comfort in nothing."* ~Hannah Whitall Smith

✔ **Choose a journal.** Get a book that will be your gratitude journal or notebook and keep it aside for this purpose only. This way, writing in it becomes sacred and dignified.

✔ **Set a daily time.** Decide on when to do this every day. You could choose the morning hours before going to bed at night as well as some other times during the day that are convenient enough for you. Count times are excellent for this because it provides a consistent window of opportunity. Avoid getting "hung up" if you forget to be consistent at first. It takes time to train the brain. This in itself becomes a part of being aware of such moments without judgment.

✔ **Reflect on three things.** Be deliberate about thinking of three things that make you happy today. They might be simple or deep, referring to personal experiences, relationships, and joyful moments.

✔ **Be specific and detailed.** Whenever expressing gratitude, try being more specific and detailed than generalizing. Instead of talking about big ideas, talk about small ones so that each entry is unique from one another.

✔ **Feel the emotion.** Take a moment once again when writing those entries down just to feel those positive feelings that come with each one. Let gratitude sink into yourself deeper by connecting it with the underlying need being fulfilled.

✔ **Acknowledge the ordinary.** Realize that even ordinary aspects of daily life have their beauty within them. Gratitude journaling helps you find joy in little things.

✔ **Build a positive mindset.** This practice gradually builds up your mind to think positively over time. It enables you to shift attention toward the good, the true, and the beautiful parts of life rather than focusing on the negatives.

✔ **Review and reflect.** At regular intervals, go back through what has been written so far as part of thankful entries. Think about how far you have come since starting this journey and how your perspective has changed because of fostering thankfulness.

## Mindful Listening

It takes time before one becomes skilled at listening mindfully. Every conversation is an opportunity to learn more and strengthen connections between people living within the same environment.

> *"Wisdom is the reward you get for a lifetime of listening when you would have rather talked."* ~Mark Twain

✔ **Prepare the space.** Find a quiet and comfortable space where you can engage in mindful listening without distractions. Remove all your distractions and create an environment conducive to focused attention.

✔ **Set your intention.** Before you enter into a conversation, set your intention. Remind yourself to listen without judgment and open the space for authentic understanding. At first, you might choose the most accessible examples, like someone you care about. Then, increase the challenge so that eventually you find yourself resourced to listen with mindfulness to even the most opposing views from those you are not as close with.

✔ **Focus on the breath.** Take a few deep breaths to center yourself. Allow your breath to become your anchor. It can help you remain present in this moment. At this point, your mind is ready for focused listening.

✔ **Engage with curiosity.** Go into the conversation with curiosity as if it were a gift revealing itself over time. Imagine a brooding hen patiently sitting on a nest of eggs, trusting that a breakthrough will happen adequately. Let the words wash over you rather than immediately framing responses: Notice the subtleties; observe how things are said.

✔ **Avoid interruptions.** Feel compelled to remain silent while someone else is speaking. Give them enough room to express their hearts. Create an atmosphere where their needs to be heard and valued may both be met.

✔ **Observe non-verbal cues.** Mindful listening goes beyond verbal communication. Take note of the speaker's body language or facial expressions. Allow these aspects to speak to you about who this person is. Allow their feelings and needs to communicate themselves as well. Such added awareness brings about another dimension of interpreting someone's speech.

✔ **Refine your focus.** If your mind starts wandering off track, bring it back gently to what was being said by the speaker. This way, there will be no disruption between them and you during deep connection stages.

✔ **Reflect before responding.** A moment of silence after someone has spoken helps one reflect before replying: Think about what they said, get clear on this and then try and guess what feelings and needs might be driving their words;

then think about your response. This particular pause encourages better communication through empathy.

✔ **Express understanding.** Afterward, respond by acknowledging their point of view and guessing their feelings and needs. It shows that you listened while also creating room for mindful exchanges between each other.

✔ **Practice regularly**. Make mindful listening a daily practice: Each time you do this type of intentional hearing, it gets easier and leads to richer connections. This contributes toward stronger relationships and peaceful, thriving communities.

## Walking Meditation

Make walking meditation a part of your daily routine to bring mindfulness into your everyday life. The simple activity of walking can be an occasion for transformation. It grounds one in the present moment and fosters a deeper connection between oneself and the surroundings.

> "We can train ourselves to walk with reverence. Wherever we walk, whether it's the railway station or the supermarket, we are walking on the earth and so we are in a holy sanctuary. If we remember to walk like that, we can be nourished and find solidity with each step." ~Thich Nhat Hanh

✔ **Choose a tranquil path.** Find a quiet place where you can do your walking meditation. It could be inside or outside. If it is peaceful, you can walk mindfully there. Recreation time, a trip to the cafeteria, medical, or even pacing in your cell can all be times for practicing this technique.

✔ **Stand mindfully.** Start by standing still. Acknowledge the distribution of weight in your feet as they touch the ground. Take some deep breaths to center yourself.

✔ **Set your intention.** Before you start walking, decide what you want this meditation to achieve. Make it clear whether it is mindfulness, stress relief, or being in touch with nature around you.

✔ **Start walking slowly.** At first, take slow steps on purpose. Be attentive to every step. Lift your leg by bending your knee joint, and notice how it feels when your foot touches down again. Allow these thoughts to fill your awareness as you begin. It is about being here now.

✔ **Focus on sensations.** Concentrate on what sensations come from your feet and legs as they move about in space and time. Feel the pressure changing, note how feet raise then fall smoothly, finding balance all along this process.

✔ **Mindful breathing.** Synchronize your steps with inhalation and exhalation processes taken during each movement: inhale softly while lifting your foot off the ground; exhale gently whenever putting it back again, thus linking together mental activities with physical activities.

✔ **Maintain present awareness.** Stay focused on the now. If thoughts begin wandering away—just return them gently to sensations within your soles like before. Stay present with what you are doing with each step.

✔ **Expand awareness.** Gradually expand awareness beyond just yourself into the environment surrounding you. Note sounds, colors, plus textures, among other things included in this way. Allow your senses to make walking more meaningful.

✔ **Embrace imperfections.** Walking meditation is not about being perfect but rather about being aware. If you find yourself getting lost or losing focus, just acknowledge it without any judgment and gently bring yourself back into the present moment.

✔ **Conclude mindfully.** When you decide that it's time to stop doing walking meditation, do so consciously. Pause for a while; enjoy what has happened during this exercise; carry such mindfulness with you into the next activity.

## Sensory Awareness Exercise

Doing this exercise will help you connect more deeply with the world around you. If you make it a habit, you will be more present in each moment and more mindful.

> *"Self-awareness is your awareness of the world, which you experience through the five senses (sound, touch, sight, taste, and smell). Pay attention to your sensory impressions and be aware of those five ways that the world comes to you."* ~Deepak Chopra

✔ **Prepare a quiet space.** Find a comfortable and quiet space where no one will bother you. If this is not possible, find the best opportunity available to you. Sit or stand in a relaxed position, ready to explore your senses.

✔ **Begin with sight.** Open your eyes and look around. What colors do you see? Are there any shapes moving? Are there things that no one ever notices but are actually really interesting to look at?

✔ **Explore sound.** Now close your eyes and listen to sounds. Pay attention to all the noises around you – both near ones and those from far away. Can you tell what made each noise? How does it sound altogether?

✔ **Engage with touch.** Next, focus on what your body feels like when you touch different things. What does it feel like when your hand brushes against something rough or smooth? How does temperature affect how we perceive touch?

✔ **Taste mindfully.** If you have something small to eat, take the time to taste it. Do not just chew on food; notice its flavors while chewing slowly before swallowing them. If there is nothing edible nearby, try remembering an unforgettable taste that lingered inside your mouth for a long period.

✔ **Explore smell.** Now bring your attention back toward the sense of smell. Just breathe deeply and find out what kind of scents are coming from everywhere else in here or elsewhere. Nature can have its scent just as food or any other thing. Try to notice this without any personal sentiments. If you notice pleasant or unpleasant feelings, acknowledge them and let them go.

✔ **Rotate through senses.** Take some minutes for each sense one after another by going through them systematically. One sense is unique from others, yet they all work together. Try to relate your sensory experiences to the way the external world speaks to us.

✔ **Integrate multiple senses.** You can use more than one sense at a time. For example, while opening your eyes, listen to sounds and feel what is happening around you so that it creates rich combinations of sensory experiences. How does adding other senses help increase our overall awareness?

✔ **Reflect on the experience.** After you've completed this exercise, take a moment and think about how it has changed the way you see things around yourself. Do you now notice any previously invisible details for some reason or another?

Once these exercises have been practiced independently with some success, they may be combined to create your unique mindfulness experience. Bringing elements of two or three of these activities together may be a natural result of your evolving self.

## Mindful Reflection

Each day, we go through life unaware of the many lessons and insights that are being communicated to us. It's said that of the 11 million things we could pay attention to each moment, we typically pick up on about 40. By spending time at the end of the day moving backward through the day's events, you can gain clarity and understanding about the "missed" happenings and harvest a rich reward.

> *"We pass through the present with our eyes blindfolded. We are permitted merely to sense and guess at what we are actually experiencing. Only later when the cloth is untied can we glance at the past and find out what we have experienced and what meaning it has."*
> ~Milan Kundera

You begin by observing in the mind's eye what you did just before lying down. Starting with the behavior, you recreate a clear image like watching yourself on a movie screen. Once you create such an image, you examine the motives behind your actions. What feelings, emotions, or impulses drove you to do or to say that? What need was behind this motive?

As you approach this activity with mindfulness, you make no moralistic judgments (good/bad) about the behavior under examination. You simply move from effect to cause, i.e., from behavior to met or unmet needs/values.

The exercise is about measuring effectiveness impersonally. You can consider how you might improve your methods to meet your needs in the preceding day. This helps you integrate these gained insights into your life the following day as the opportunity arises.

"Did this meet my need for _____? Is there something else that might have been more effective at meeting this need? What might I do to make life more wonderful in such instances?"

You move through your day in reverse order, seeking clarity and understanding about your own and others' words and actions. You move from consequences to causes, from behaviors to the underlying needs. Perhaps you make guesses about what feelings and needs might have been underlying what you could see with your eyes. You can also imagine ways to improve your own strategies to meet your needs. "What would I be willing to do differently in this situation so that I and/or others are more fulfilled?"

When you find something that you or others have done that is unfulfilling, you might ask what could have been done better to meet needs without there being any expense to others. Such contemplative reflections help you to better create "win/win" outcomes through your actions.

Through repeating this exercise day after day, you may feel a shift inside when you connect with your own or others' needs that may have been previously veiled to you.

You strengthen a relationship to a deeper part of yourself in these precious moments.

Over a longer period of time, hopefully, you might find that you have improved the way you accept and live with yourself, among others. This exercise harvests wisdom from simple events in everyday life. It can help discharge and dissolve negative energy tied to previous events and help you discover what lies at the core of your own and others' actions. More importantly, the exercise can help you appreciate the truth, the goodness, and the beauty within and around you.

Once you have become proficient in reviewing the day's events in this way, you may benefit further by going back to other events in your life where you wish to gain clarity and understanding. Perhaps even those events associated with the unskilled behaviors that brought you to prison may be examined this way.

Over time, you may find yourself reviewing difficult moments from your past and searching for the inner causes of those outer events, ideally with a calm you couldn't find in the past when the actual events occurred. Thus, this is good because you extend a compassionate eye toward what brought you only pain before (and possibly to others around you).

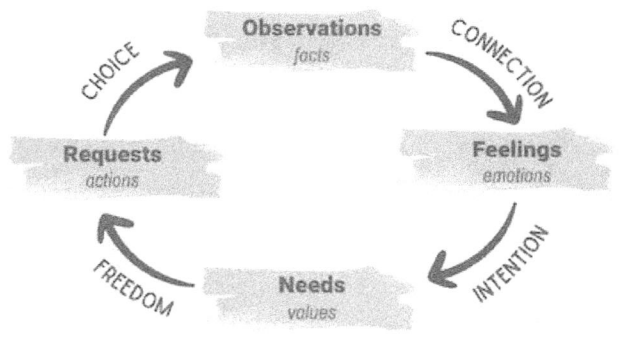

In my own life, this exercise has been among the most beneficial mindfulness practices for personal growth. The insights gained during these quiet pre-bedtime moments become building blocks of conscience and character. If we are attentive, we may find that the gleanings from last night will help us tomorrow and beyond - provided we intend to act upon the insights we gain during this practice.

## Emotional Regulation Strategies and Framework

Mindfulness techniques foster a more constructive and healing dialogue within the restorative justice framework, providing individuals with a foundation to manage their emotions.

Because keeping our emotions under control is such a key factor in maintaining overall well-being and enjoying wholesome relationships, it's vital to have a mental roadmap to guide us through challenging experiences. Using NVC, for example. NVC helps us to direct our mindful awareness toward key aspects of our moment-to-moment experiences.

Another useful framework, OFNR (**O**bservations, **F**eelings, **N**eeds, and **R**equests), as shown in the following table, helps maintain ownership of what comes up for us when triggered by events in the world. Incorporating these strategies beyond the restorative justice context will enhance your ability to navigate intense emotions in various real-world situations.

**Observation leads to...** "I observed that there were elevated voices during group discussions."

**Feeling leads to...** "I feel concerned and uneasy."

**Need leads to...** "I have a need for a supportive and harmonious environment where all parties feel comfortable and their need for respect is met."

**Request:** "Could we take a moment to breathe together and then express our feelings and needs? This way, we can work towards resolving conflicts with understanding and empathy, creating a more positive atmosphere for everyone."

## Emotional Regulation Methods

Let's now nuance our approach using a real-life example of when it may prove most effective. With practice, we learn to observe our inner life with objectivity that frees us from succumbing to the temptation of reacting on impulse. We discover our awareness extending to a place beyond personal reactivity, as Rumi once alluded:

> *"Beyond right and wrong there is a field; I will meet you there."* ~Rumi

By incorporating these strategies, you can develop emotional regulation skills that extend beyond the restorative justice context. This enhances your ability to navigate intense emotions in various real-world situations. This is how we may become restorative justice practitioners from moment to moment in everyday life.

✔ **Mindful Breathing.** Take a moment to focus on your breath. Encourage slow and intentional breathing to create a pause and prevent immediate reactive responses.

✔ **Acknowledge Emotions.** Acknowledge your own emotions without judgment. Recognize any feelings of discomfort or defensiveness. Accept them without immediate reaction.

✔ **Cultivate Empathetic Presence.** Ground yourself in the present moment and cultivate empathy. Listen to the message without internalizing or immediately responding to the emotional intensity.

✔ **Nonviolent Communication (NVC).** Apply NVC principles by focusing on needs rather than reacting to emotional expression. Identify the unmet needs underlying the outburst and consider how these needs can be addressed in the restorative process.

✔ **Take a Brief Pause.** Suggest a short break if necessary. Use this time for further mindfulness practices, such as a brief walk or moments of solitude, to regain composure before continuing the dialogue.

✔ **Reflect Before Responding.** Reflect on the message and your emotional response before formulating a thoughtful and empathetic response. This reflection allows for a more measured and compassionate engagement.

## A Victim's Emotional Outburst Scenario

*Response Scenario with Mindfulness & Restorative Justice Principles*

During a restorative justice circle in a correctional facility, a victim, Sarah, whose personal belongings were taken by another person in custody, Barbara, has an emotional outburst.

Sarah expresses deep frustration, fear, and a sense of discomfort in front of the group. Contrast the more generic example above with the following realistic scenario.

✔ **Observation and Acknowledgement**: *"I observe the intensity of your emotions, Sarah, and I want to acknowledge the pain I think you're feeling right now. We must address this with understanding and compassion."*

✔ **Mindful breathing (Feeling).** *"Can we take a moment together to breathe? Inhale deeply, and as you exhale, release some of the tension. This will help us approach the situation with a clearer mindset."*

✔ **Validation (Need).** *"Your feelings are valid, and everyone here needs to listen and understand. Barbara, I invite you to listen to Sarah's experience without* *judgment mindfully."*

✔ **Empathetic Reflection (Need).** *"Sarah, it sounds like you need a sense of safety and assurance. Is that accurate?"* (Allow a response)

*"How can we, as a community, work together to address your needs and restore a sense of security?"* (Allow a response.)

✔ **Accountability and Amends (Request).** *"Barbara, I'd like to hear from you as well. Mindfully consider Sarah's feelings and needs. How can we move forward in a way that fosters understanding, accountability, and restoration?"* (Allow a response)

In *restorative justice recalibrated*, combining mindfulness with active listening and empathy helps create a space where emotions are acknowledged, and participants can collaboratively work towards resolution. Mindfulness techniques provide a foundation for individuals to manage their emotions. This fosters a more constructive and healing dialogue within the restorative justice framework.

~~~

Practicing mindfulness during your journey behind bars can be a powerful tool for understanding yourself and others. Taking a moment to reflect on your feelings and needs (self-empathy) lays the groundwork for building empathy (connecting to the feelings and needs of others). It's about recognizing what's alive in you and, in turn, finding a deeper understanding of the experiences of those around you. Thus, we connect to our reservoir of empathy and compassion, refueling as needed to be better equipped to connect with others.

Within restorative justice, this self-awareness is even more important because it focuses on healing the wounds caused by the unskilled acts that led you to prison. By embracing mindfulness, you're not just looking inward but also opening the door to empathy, another key principle of restorative justice.

Empathy is necessary in fostering connections within these confined spaces. Communication stemming from understanding and compassion can go a long way toward improving emotional well-being. It isn't just about what's said. Use connection as a stepping stone for personal growth and rehabilitation.

However, when exploring your emotions, you aren't only on a path of self-discovery. You are also laying the foundation for your transformative journey. Understanding how your actions have affected others is essential to rebuilding oneself internally and preparing for reentry into society.

## Mindfulness in Restorative Dialogue

*Centering the Conversation*

Consider incorporating mindfulness techniques into conversations within restorative dialogues' unique setting. Doing so deepens connections between participants. Deep breathing exercises like grounding could be an anchor, allowing one to be emotionally centered during such engagements.

Mindfulness forms restorative dialogues, thereby creating an enabling environment for open communication. Being fully present enables you to navigate the complexities of these dialogues; hence, it is a place where both parties can speak from their hearts.

In these dialogues, mindfulness techniques become particularly important since they often involve discussions about sensitive and emotionally charged topics. You enhance your capacity to listen actively and respond empathically by centering yourself. This promotes a more constructive exchange of perspectives.

Hearing feelings and needs regardless of what is said is an example of NVC as a mindfulness practice. This skill is among the peace offerings we can give to those harmed by our unskilled acts.

Studies have shown that incorporating mindfulness practices into conflict-resolution processes improves outcomes. These techniques help people understand their emotions better and build a bridge between those who caused harm and those who got hurt.

Regarding restorative dialogues, mindfulness acts as a guiding principle for creating authentic connections and facilitating healing paths. Grounding oneself in mindfulness is an empowering step towards building bridges of understanding and empathy in the intricate landscape of restorative justice.

## Active Listening and Nonjudgmental Awareness

As you enter these crucial dialogues, make sure you bring the practice of active listening and nonjudgmental awareness. Both are vital parts of mindful communication. Active listening is more than just hearing words; it means understanding them to create a basis for empathy and connection.

Mindfulness promotes non-judgmental thought, which enables you to put aside your assumptions. This openness allows for a real conversation between those harmed and those who have created harm, where both can express what comes up inside without fear of being condemned. It's about creating a safe space for vulnerability and understanding, acknowledging that everyone brings their perspective to the conversation.

Incorporating active listening and non-judgmental awareness into restorative dialogues aligns with restorative justice principles. It recognizes the humanity in all involved parties and seeks resolution rather than revenge.

I must highlight how powerful active listening and nonjudgmental awareness can be during resolution and reconciliation. These mindfulness principles help us contribute effectively to dialogue, ensuring that such interactions become more empathic and focused on healing.

Mindfulness becomes the guiding rhythm amidst this process of restorative dialogue. Here, active listening intertwines with non-judgmental awareness, resulting in understanding between these two sides. This helps create a connection.

During your time in prison, mindfulness may serve as an agent of change, leading you toward personal growth and strengthening prison communities. By practicing deep breathing or grounding exercises, one can create room for mindful reflection on what led to the crime, thus setting the stage for transformative learning.

Beyond individual change, mindfulness has a communal effect that helps build up collective resilience in communities affected by harm. The shared strength developed through this awareness assists societies in navigating post-harm situations and actively taking part in restoration.

To conclude, mindfulness may be seen as a support but a foundation for your journey toward restoration. This light guides you toward healing, understanding, and a justice system that recognizes the power of authentic connection and reconciliation.

Embrace mindfulness as your companion on this journey, and may it lead you toward a future marked by growth, connection, and positive transformation.

***

*"Human progress is neither automatic nor inevitable… Every step toward the goal of justice requires sacrifice, suffering, and struggle; the tireless exertions and passionate concern of dedicated individuals."*

~Martin Luther King Jr.

# Integrating Restorative Justice into Daily Life

Let's now look at how we can put these ideas into practice within the correctional environment as we continue our exploration of restorative justice. Some people may not be comfortable with direct communication, and they have a right to choose not to. Here are a few points to consider.

✔ **Respect.** Respect is key in this process. It is up to each individual if they want to start talking. If it is not possible for people to talk directly, it is important that other ways are found through which accountability can be shown.

✔ **Restitution.** Restitution comes in different forms, such as repairing what was broken and giving back positively to society. Genuine empathy goes beyond just words. However, where direct dialogue is impossible, thoughtful and creative alternatives may be sought to acknowledge and address the harm caused.

✔ **Commitment.** The commitment towards positive change may remain the same regardless of whether or not those harmed in your case seek reconciliation.

✔ **Communications.** Where there can be no direct communication, efforts may focus on meaningful alternatives. For instance, paying it forward might involve community service within your immediate surroundings.

~~~

You might write or speak with young people who have been in trouble with the juvenile courts. Someone younger with similar charges may be mentored at the prison. There are several ways in which you can make restitution efforts.

We will be considering mock parole hearings. They go beyond role-playing. Even if the injured person isn't present, they provide room for deep reflection and accountability. This symbolizes an intention toward transformative change that surpasses traditional forms of justice.

Throughout our discussions on empathy, understanding, and connection, bringing restorative justice into the correctional setting means embodying these values. Therefore, either through words or actions, it becomes a shared journey towards making things right.

Within prison walls, implementing restorative justice involves more than just talking. It involves taking purposeful actions. There are many ways to restore justice from right where you are. It does not require participation from any other person.

Restorative justice is a way of life, a mindset, a consciousness of connection and healing. Anything you choose to do that helps humanity rebuild the web of relationships harmed through crime, is an act of restorative justice.

Be creative and use this time on the inside to implement some of what's been shared here or perhaps something you have come up with on your own. This kind of freedom does not require you to be on the outside to experience. You can start right here and right now.

***

*"A real friend is one who walks in when the rest of the world walks out."*

~Walter Winchell

# Stories of Transformation

## Jeremy: From Victimhood to Victory

When I first met Jeremy, he was working as a maintenance man at the facility where I was housed. Early on during my incarceration, I became skilled at cutting hair, so at the request of the Warden, I took a part-time job as the Staff Barber. Jeremy would come in from time to time, which is how I got to know him.

One night, he, his wife, and his two sons (one seven years old and the other still an infant) were driving home when a man high on street drugs hit them head-on when suddenly losing control of his car. Jeremy remained trapped in the vehicle as he watched the life leave his wife's body, never to return. His sons, amazingly enough, survived the accident with minor injuries.

Immediately following the tragedy, Jeremy took some time off work, but understandably, he was a wreck himself, so it didn't help much. He began drinking to numb the pain and to help him cope with daily life as a newly widowed father of two boys. Nothing he could do helped to erase the images of watching his wife die. Nothing softened the blows of his 7-year-old son repeatedly asking where his momma was.

One day in the cafeteria, a new DOC cadet was checking IDs and was getting some flack from a man in the line. He started to get a bit aggressive. Jeremy saw the commotion and came over to help. However, the man pushed Jeremy, and "the fight was on". The two men rolled around on the ground until other officers pulled them apart. Ultimately, Jeremy was escorted out of the facility and lost his job. He had been drinking early that morning, which made him a risk despite what had happened.

A few years later, I was at a different facility and established Pathways for LIFE (PFL) as an inmate club. Classes were underway, and we were about to have a guest trainer from out of state come down. At the same time, a Kairos 4-day event was underway, and a surprise volunteer, Jeremy, showed up.

Since I'd last seen him, he had gone through some soul-searching and formed a solid bond with his faith in Jesus. We talked a little between sessions, and I invited him to our PFL classes, explaining that I thought it might be something good for him to be a part of. He agreed and soon joined our weekly meetings.

We were in phase three, which was all about Restorative Justice and crime sharing. There were thirteen of us, and we each shared our story of what led us to prison. We used the structure of nonviolent communication (NVC) to stay connected to feelings and needs throughout the process. It was deep.

I acted both as the facilitator and participant. Tears flowed as men who had become comfortable enough to be open and honest told the raw version of what happened in their crime. It was cathartic and fulfilling, even though painful to revisit.

Jeremy spoke occasionally but, in the end, surprised us all with his own story. He talked about what the experience had meant for him - as someone harmed by crime (his wife's death), and it was truly inspiring.

He talked of what it was like to lose his wife and how, for so long, he had wanted to kill the guy who took her away from him. He spoke of how that had seemed to be killing something inside of him and that, after listening to our testimonies, something had shifted inside him. Even after his conversion experience, he still found it hard to let go of it all but he explained how these moments shared with us changed his heart. He told us that he believed everyone harmed by crime ought to undergo the process we had undergone with him. Now, he was going to try to reach out to the man who killed his wife and work to reconcile as best as they could.

Not long after, Jeremy and another volunteer who had also been coming and experiencing what was happening inside our classes started talking about forming an official non-profit organization with me. In 2019, they became two of three founding members of Pathways for LIFE, 501c3. It was another step in the right direction, led by forces much more significant than me or anyone associated with our program.

Jeremy continues to support this work and speaks about his transformation at Kairos 4-day events across ODOC.

## Louise: How Being Believed In Helps Us Reclaim Our Power

In 2019, I met Louise through a prison pen pal program. After the first introductory letter, we began writing regularly. I quickly learned that she was my age, a single mother of two girls, and had not been in a relationship since 2004.

She admitted having a drinking problem, diabetes, anxiety, depression, and a mild learning disability. Her youngest daughter's agenesis corpus callosum brought its own challenges as well. Louise just needed a real friend.

The timing for me becoming that friend could not have been better. I had been practicing nonviolent communication for over a decade and underwent significant changes in my spiritual life. My understanding of the impacts of ACEs and trauma had grown. I was sincere in my efforts to help others and needed purpose.

The relationship developed slowly but became a space for trust, openness, and vulnerability. I shared everything about why I was in prison and what I've focused my efforts on while incarcerated, and Louise shared many details about her life, including her pains and hopes.

Growing up with a disability made her a black sheep of the family, and her mother and siblings treated her poorly, keeping her at a distance and not allowing her to enjoy family events or holidays.

When we first corresponded, Louise was 293 lbs. She had gotten married at 21 and had two girls by the man who had sexually abused her. They divorced when she walked in on him cheating when both girls were very young. Her weight and inability to relate to others easily caused her to isolate and escape through food and alcohol as she got older.

Less-than-nurturing experiences quickly triggered Louise, and she always felt exhausted from stress and worry. Her drinking and eating were her best efforts to rid herself of the pain that she just didn't know how to do anything about.

I avoided offering her any advice except when asked; even then, I was cautious. This and my openness made her increasingly vulnerable about things she had never shared with anyone else. It was a gift to experience a slow but constant shift in her attention, well-being, and way of life.

About eight months in, and two months after she quit drinking, Louise was told that if she didn't change her lifestyle, her diabetic pill would go away, and she would be required to self-administer an insulin shot. Within a week, a separate doctor visit scared her to the core. She felt panic and did not know what to do.

This time, I empathized while asking if she would be willing to hear my concerns about her general lifestyle. She welcomed it, so I did my best to explain how diet and lack of exercise were contributing to her health issues without insulting or offending her. I told her that if something didn't change, she might have serious concerns, affecting her ability to care for her daughter.

Because of my experience with exercise and diet as a fitness instructor and trainer before being incarcerated, I shared my willingness to assist her improve. My only condition was that she would be required to follow the guidelines to the letter and could not give up.

I wrote that unlike the people she was used to, I would never push her or make her feel bad about her choices. I knew she needed complete autonomy if this was to bring true and lasting change. As a believer herself, I suggested that we both pray about it.

A week later, I got a letter that said she was ready, promised to follow the instructions, and knew she had to change. She said this "was from God " so she had to do it. If she didn't, she would never forgive herself. I wrote a basic dietary and exercise plan. We were both vegetarians, so it was relatively easy to develop some basic dietary guidelines:

- ✔ No bread, pasta, rice, potato, or snacks.
- ✔ Three wholesome meals per day

✔ A fruit/protein powder smoothie between breakfast and lunch

✔ A veggie smoothie with protein powder between lunch and dinner

✔ Five small meals would increase her metabolism, and high protein would eliminate excess calories; our bodies do not store protein.

At first, her exercise plan was rather basic: a brisk walk twice a day for a half hour and another thirty minutes on her old-fashioned Aerofit machine (which had never gotten much use until now). She started a journal documenting everything she ate, her exercise routine, and her weight at the beginning of each month.

On the day she started, she weighed 293 lbs. I suggested she take a photo of herself in the same position every time she weighed to see her progress. I remember how nervous I was for her after those first 30 days. It had been so hard for her to accept herself when she made a mistake or was compelled to feel guilty by her mother.

Her letter came, and I opened it eagerly. I went right to the numbers and couldn't believe what I saw. In month one, she had gone from 293 to 264. YES! I thought. She said she was in tears when she saw the results on that scale. For the first time, she had taken charge of her own life in a way that proved good for her.

Her self-confidence quickly grew, and she seemed much happier. Her dietary changes were going well, but she admittedly battled food temptations. She wrote of how hard it was to even go into the supermarket and see chips and candy bars. In my response, I expressed how important it was to begin reframing her thoughts about those foods. I tried to help her see that the way she felt was not about the foods but about the thoughts she had, the programming she had built into her life.

When the temptation arose, I recommended she think of new thoughts to replace the old, e.g., how much better she feels without them. My real job was to encourage, empower, and enthuse.

In month two, she was at 240 lbs. At this point, it got real. Her doctor's visit came back negative for anything major. She was gaining control over her life and had been sober for several months before any of this dietary/exercise stuff. Now, Louise was buying new clothes because of all the weight she was shedding.

Month three, 220lbs. This month, Louise had to see her parents. She was excited to impress them, but her mother acted like she couldn't tell. She told her she was making it all up and shouldn't lie. It took her a week to recover from that ordeal. I did notice with her past success behind her, though, her mother's abuse had less of an impact. To further ensure no depression, we increased her exercise so that she could add some aerobics from YouTube to do with her youngest daughter.

After almost 20 years of being over 200 lbs. in month four, she was 198 lbs. I noticed from her letters that the rest of her life was also beginning to change. She got a new job and was taking charge at home in new ways. Before, her eldest daughter pretty much ran everything, but with this added confidence, she enjoyed directing her own life's affairs.

Month five: 182 lbs. When Louise started, she wore size 22 pants cut by at least half. Over the next seven months, Louise lost weight and became stronger inside and out. A year after starting the process, she was 151 lbs. She was a size 6 and had lost a total of 142 lbs.

But that wasn't the half of it. She had also returned to her doctor several times along the way. Her doctor hated her vegetarian diet and told her several times that she needed to change it. But as the blood work continued to show progress, it led to her diabetic pills being reduced over and over. Her doctor began to change her tune.

The most amazing part? Well, the diabetes disappeared. She had reversed it and was taken off the medication completely. Her doctor became her biggest cheerleader, even advocating for others to follow the dietary and exercise guidelines I had provided for her. It was a fantastic experience. She saved her own life, given the trajectory she was previously on.

In hindsight reflection, several things became clear.

When we are at a low point in our lives, we need someone to lend us their belief in us and their hope for us, i.e. to see in us what we can't yet see and help us do what we cannot yet do for ourselves. This is the epitome of rehabilitation.

We need someone to accept us just as we are without trying to change, judge, or advise us. Just being there and showing love without expecting a return on their investment. This is the foundation for accountability.

When this occurs, the sense of acceptance, belonging, and love invigorates us, out of our energy and allows us to do what is best for ourselves and others. This is the basis for prosocial living.

At some point, the scaffolding of our support can be safely removed, and the individual may be left to self-governance. This is the beginning of a healthy, happy life.

## Safety + Connection = Balance

Fast-forward three years: Louise has never looked back. She continues to eat healthy and exercise. Other women learn about her journey as she inspires them to consider new possibilities. Her relationship with her parents has changed some. Although her mother continues to behave the way she always has, Louise has found ways to self-regulate her responses to maintain peace and poise. Sobriety has been hers for almost four years now.

Louise profoundly shifted her perspective and, therefore, her life. She moved from faith to firsthand knowledge, from hope to happiness, and from fear to love. It was indeed a miracle.

## Devan: Finding the Faith that Leads to First Hand Knowledge

It was midnight, and when the cell door swung open, a large white man walked in with his mattress and personal belongings. He stood 6 ft 3 in, weighed about 250 lbs., had a cleanly shaved head, and tattoos ran up his arms and disappeared behind his shirt. He had apparently gotten into a fight with his other roommates and had to move.

It didn't take long to see why he had been beaten up and kicked out. Devan was a drug addict and regularly "flopped" on K2. That means he would do the drug and fall to the ground, sometimes shake, and seem out of his mind. This drug was cheap and dirty. It totally changed who a person was. He would do and say whatever he could to get more.

Once in our pod dayroom, he fell to the ground, turned white as a ghost, and lay still for so long that some thought he was dead. Then suddenly, he made a shivering move, opened his eyes, and then slowly came back online, enough for me to help him up and escort him back to our room.

This happened as we were about to be moved to the Resilience Prison Project Pod. All of my roommates wanted him gone. There was something about the guy that made me feel compassion for him. I had an urge to help him. I shot straight with him but showed love when he seemed most alone. That connection led us to communicate about spiritual matters, the moral life, and what addictive behavior really meant. I knew he wanted better for himself, so my role was to be the one person in his life who believed in the version of him already freed from those bonds.

It had some effect because he gradually started coming around. I invited him into our workout group and shared books with him that got him to do some soul-searching. I could see he was feeling good about himself, and people started to enjoy his company.

One day, out of the blue, he said he was done with drugs and began counting each day of sobriety. Our talks became more profound and intimate on spiritual subjects, and I encouraged him to search for these ideas in his heart. On the day he left prison, he had been sober for over 100 days. Our roommates had transformed into friends, and he left with a new lease on life. Just a few days before he left, he wrote one of the most touching letters as he said, "I love ya Oz and I want us to be friends forever." The letter follows in its entirety.

*"My name is Devan Donovan. I'm currently in prison in Hinton, Oklahoma. I'm from a little town next to Portland, Oregon. I have had a very abusive and trauma filled past that has destroyed everything I've ever worked hard to achieve. By my choice to usoed drugs and alcohol to escape feelings of shame from mental and sexual as well as physical abuse from my childhood. I can look back today and see I was a ticking time bomb. Fueled by resentment.*

*I'm 40 years old and I do have some great things I'm proud of. Such as being a hard worker. Being a father and it seems like God has always found me in my mess and sent a person to help me understand I have a purpose and the reason*

*I'm writing this because after a very dark place in my life when I had just about decided drugs were always going to be my way to heal my pain and when self pity had blinded me to my actions, I met Alexis Osborn.*

*There is no reason why this man who has a life sentence for murder should even care about a hopeless drug addict. I moved into D pod after a fight with previous cellies and I had really just given up on trying to even get clean or get close to God and I did not want to think of all my past failures that getting sober always reminded me of.*

*When I first met "Oz" he was very friendly, almost too friendly. But there was nothing I had he could possibly want. So I was curious why he even cared. I would get so high that I made everyone in the cell uncomfortable. We were in 8 man cells so peace was important. But I didn't care about how my actions were affecting anyone else.*

*If you had my past and failures you would do what I do also. Well at least that's what I thought until I would "come to" out of a black out from being so high that I lost control of my mental faculties. And Oz would be either guiding me back to the cell or helping me see how my actions were affecting others.*

*I really don't know why he broke through to me except I would speak to him being sober for a day or two and he would give me challenging thoughts about my behavior and how I was actually creating my own turmoil and he had answers about God that have always been hard for me to understand. But I would always go back to getting high.*

*Finally, I asked Oz if I could use his tablet pin number to call my son. When Oz realized I was calling my son for more money for drugs he let me know how foolish I was being. And for some reason instead of lashing out in anger I could hear what he was saying.*

*Now mind you, I have been praying for years to stop using drugs and I've been diagnosed bipolar, schizophrenic and all sorts of antisocial personalities. But Oz would let me have it.*

*He wasn't scared at all to tell me what I was doing was very selfish and he would share the story of his father and wife and son. And I could hear him because I knew he knew what pain was. But it wasn't affecting him like it was affecting me. Well months went by and I would get clean for a day or two and relapse. But Oz never gave up on me. And I always remember something he said to me one day.*

*He said "for some reason God had told me to help you. But everyone else wants you to leave this cell. You're toxic." That statement hit me hard. I didn't want to move to another cell. I was tired of fighting and things were getting more dangerous each move. Prison is a hard place to learn lessons and there are no warning shots. But Oz had enough influence on the cell that for some reason they let me stay.*

*I remember crying to Jesus that night. Saying, "God, I'm not going to be able to fit in here if I can't get clean. Please help me!" Wouldn't you know the next day and for two weeks we were on lockdown in the cells. Man it was tough! I was so emotional and angry I didn't think I could make it. But Oz would always have just what I needed to hear to keep me in the fight of sobriety.*

*Man, long story short I get out of prison in three days and I have four months clean. I've been a heroin and meth addict for ten years and a divorced father of three sons.*

*I'm going to a program called Adult and Teen Challenge. But I would have never decided to make a plan or stick to it had I not met Alexis Osborn. He has been to me what Jesus must have been to his disciples. A man of boundaries but also patience and love and a whole lot of wisdom.*

*I'm very grateful to have met him. And I'm even more grateful God told him not to give up on me. I could tell you all the darkness I shared with Oz but because of his direction today I choose to look forward in the light. I've spent enough time in the dark. I know it's a choice today and I finally realized that bad things happen. But that's not who I am.*

*Sincerely,*

*Devan Donavan*

<div style="text-align:center">~~~</div>

Your life matters. You can help change the world for the better. Everything you grow to become can positively impact people all over the world. Isolation and exclusion are not mandatory parts of your sentence despite where you may find yourselves at the moment.

Everything that follows is about practicing Restorative Justice. I hope what's been written here has been helpful for you and might encourage you to become increasingly restorative in your approach to life. Each day we spend inside these walls is like a sentence in a paragraph of a chapter of our lives. We write each one through the choices we make. I pray that the chapters you write from this day forward may be fulfilling for you and inspiring for others.

***

*a trauma-informed approach to rebuilding the web of relationships harmed by crime*

*"We see the world not as it is, but as we are."*

~Anaïs Nin

# Facilitation Guidelines for Mock Parole Hearing

Unlike earlier sections of this book, this section is an activity to provide a framework for undergoing a parole hearing using the skills and consciousness evolved through 24 weeks of rigorous nonviolent communications practice. Having familiarized yourself with restorative justice, you may approach the mock parole hearing with new meaning and purpose.

You should review the parole members' questions and hard-to-hear messages. Then, write down your most authentic responses so that you will be prepared. The more you treat this as real, the more you will benefit from the process.

## Overview of Purpose
*Insight, Empathy, and Accountability*

As the facilitator, it is vital to begin by stating what the mock parole hearing intends to achieve: insight into the crime, empathy among participants, and a sense of accountability for their actions.

Let the participants know that it is not punitive but a means towards personal development, understanding, and rehabilitation.

## Introduce the Approaches
*Using Nonviolent Communication (NVC) and "Resilience Trumps ACEs" Trauma-Informed Approach*

Marshall Rosenberg created NVC as a communication model. It consists of four elements: observations, feelings, needs, and requests. NVC encourages individuals to be open with their feelings while listening to create empathy-based connections. During this mock parole hearing, participants will be encouraged to communicate using NVC, thus helping them understand more about their own experiences and those of others.

Introduce the concept of adverse childhood experiences (ACEs), emphasizing that specific life experiences can impact behavior and decision-making. The trauma-informed approach focuses on understanding the effects of trauma and promoting resilience.

Participants will examine their negative experiences and identify strengths and coping mechanisms for overcoming such life challenges. With this approach, we can stop blaming ourselves or others, creating a space for healing and growth. (By this time, participants of the Resilience Prison Project will have completed the following courses: *Trauma-Informed, Trauma-Supportive*, and *Trauma-Practitioner* certifications from the Community Resilience Initiative.)

As the facilitator, ensure that participants understand how these frameworks promote healthy communication, empathy-building activities, and addressing crime-related root causes. Encourage openness among them, assuring that through this process, one can be transformed personally, leading to rehabilitation from criminal activities.

## Set the Stage

*Create a Safe, Confidential Space for Participants*

For this mock parole hearing to succeed, there must be safety and confidentiality agreements agreed upon by participants. The facilitator will establish this.

Choose a neutral, comfortable space where people can freely express themselves without fear. Avoid setting up seats so that others are seen as superior to others.

Make it clear to participants that what is discussed in the session remains confidential. This will encourage openness and honesty. Each individual can speak their mind without feeling judged by others.

### Establish Ground Rules

✔ **Respectful language.** Maintain a constructive atmosphere by using respectful language throughout this activity period.

✔ **Active listening.** No interruptions. Allow each participant to express himself fully through active listening practice.

✔ **Raise hands for speaking.** Participants must agree to raise their hands and be recognized by the facilitator to avoid disrupting others while talking.

✔ **One speaker at a time.** During conversations, ensure that only one person speaks at any given moment for clarity and understanding purposes. You may use a talking stick or the like to designate who is to speak.

✔ **Confidentiality.** Ensure all personal information shared during the hearing is kept confidential, thus building trust among members present.

✔ **Constructive feedback.** Give feedback based on what was said rather than who said it. Focus on content rather than comments that may seem personal towards someone else's character or personality traits alone (use constructive criticism).

✔ **Stay on topic.** Let discussions be related to matters concerning parole hearings. Avoid getting into other things that might not have anything to do with it or those sensitive ones, especially if they are likely going off track (irrelevant/sensitive subjects).

✔ **Empathy and understanding.** Approach the hearing with empathy; understand where others are coming from so that you can also consider their feelings and experiences (empathy and understanding).

✔ **No side conversations.** Do not engage in any other conversation while the hearing is going on since this may distract attention from what is happening in court. We will offer respect towards its proceedings (no side talks).

✔ **Follow time limits.** Finally, stick within the time limits assigned towards making statements and responding, ensuring fairness and effective hearings throughout your session (time boundaries).

✔ **Parole hearing dress code.** We recommend that you be dressed professionally to maintain its seriousness and formality.

✔ **Be clear and simple.** Make sure you speak and use fewer words for communication efficiency.

✔ **Avoid disruptive behavior.** Refrain from disruptive behavior, like gestures or facial expressions, which may disrupt the hearing.

✔ **Recognition of feelings**. Acknowledge the emotions of all participants, stressing the need to stay composed throughout the process.

✔ **Being committed to decision**. Agree to abide by the decision, knowing well that it will be made through a mutually just and thorough procedure.

Recognize that talking about personal experiences, especially those relating to crime, can be an emotional challenge; therefore, encourage participants to be aware of their own feelings/needs and those of others. Understanding each other's perspectives is the main goal here.

## Emphasize Active Listening and Empathy

It would be nice if you define active listening so that participants know how important it is for them not only to understand what someone else is saying but also to feel satisfied that they are being understood; encourage non-verbal cues such as nodding or eye contact showing interest during conversations too.

Tell participants why empathy matters in this case; let them know that they will share their stories with others while listening empathetically at the same time; through connecting emotionally with one another, a sense of humanity is established, thus breaking down barriers between people who have different experiences with life.

Introduce reflective techniques, such as paraphrasing when necessary, to ensure mutual understanding among members; summarization will help avoid misinterpretation of statements made by others, hence promoting trust within groups.

These elements work best when carefully planned to create an environment conducive to constructive dialogue where respect prevails. Authentic participation can only occur when individuals feel safe enough to express themselves honestly. This leads to positive results such as insight, empathy, and accountability.

## Roles, Briefings, Expectations

Each participant who has created harm will take on the role of "the person who has created harm" in the Mock Parole Hearing. They are to share their perspective, feelings, and experiences related to the crime. Let them express themselves genuinely so that they may reflect on themselves and be accountable.

Assign roles to people who will act as parole board members. These members ask difficult questions, deliver hard messages, and respond empathetically through Nonviolent Communication (NVC). Striking a balance between seeking accountability and providing a supportive environment for rehabilitation is crucial.

As a facilitator, you guide the entire flow of this simulated parole hearing. Facilitate communication using the NVC process while ensuring that it stays focused on insight, empathy, and accountability. If necessary, intervene when a conversation goes off-track or emotional tensions arise. This maintains a safe space for constructive discussions.

The facilitator will be briefed about the general structure of mock parole hearings, indicating where intervention may be needed most. Strongly point out key safety aspects and maintain the neuro lens and NVC adherence, among others. This leads to constructive and insightful dialogue between participants.

Conduct a private briefing with the person taking this role. Explain why they are participating, emphasizing that it is about personal growth and understanding rather than judging someone else's actions. Guide the participants on being cognizant of their own predictions using NVC when expressing themselves and promoting self-reflection.

Hold a briefing session with the parole board members either individually or collectively. Clearly outline their R.O.L.E.S. in asking challenging questions and delivering hard truths. It is essential to do so with empathy, considering that it only aids rehabilitation purposes. Show them how NVC applies by giving instances from past interactions between them during such exercises.

By assigning roles and giving detailed briefings, you ensure all participants know what they are being asked to do to contribute effectively towards achieving transformative objectives. Preparation helps create collaboration and purposefulness during the exercise.

Examples of NVC exercises during the mock parole hearing include:

✔ Clarify the NVC Process: Observations, Feelings, Needs, Requests
✔ Provide examples relevant to the specific case
✔ Role-play exercises for participants to practice NVC

## NVC Preparations
*Clarifying Principles, Providing Examples, and Role-Play Exercises*

### Clarify Basic Principles of NVC: Observations, Feelings, Needs, Requests

Make clear, non-judgmental observations about particular events or behaviors. Encourage participants to focus on facts rather than interpretations. This will pave the way for an open conversation.

Feelings and needs play major roles within NVC. Encourage individuals to identify and connect their emotions with a need without blaming others. This creates a shared understanding of what is happening inside.

Behaviors are expressions of universal human needs. Each person may explore their own needs and recognize those of other people. This promotes empathy and understanding, which are vital during the rehabilitation process.

State things that one is requesting of others. Let participants know how powerful it is to make specific positive, doable real-time requests that encourage collaboration and inclusion.

## Provide Examples Relevant to the Specific Case

Tune these examples according to the specific case being discussed now. If crime arose out of relationship conflicts, give similar situations, making it easier for participants to relate their experiences using the principles of nonviolent communication.

Consequently, you can use real-life situations to show how to apply NVC when difficult. These might be conflicts, misunderstandings, or tense moments like those that may occur during the mock parole hearing. Participants' ability to incorporate NVC into their communication is enhanced by its real-world relevance.

## Role-Play Exercises for Participants to Practice NVC

Create scenarios related to the crime so that participants can practice NVC in a controlled setting. Take turns playing different roles so that every perspective is fully understood.

Immediately following each role-play session, hold feedback meetings where learners may think deeply about what happened. Making explicit expressions about what arose by observers during the session about NVC principles will be encouraged.

Allow groups to discuss challenges faced, and achievements reached during role-playing activities. This group reflection leads to a common understanding of the principles behind NVC and motivates individuals to support their fellow participants in practicing it.

By involving participants in preparations for employing NVC, you equip them with the tools for efficient and empathic communication. The theory and knowledge combined with practical examples like the role-plays make it possible to integrate principles of nonviolent communication into the very heart of the mock parole hearing. This makes it more meaningful and transformative.

## ACEs and a Resilience Perspective

Open by introducing adverse childhood experiences and the resilience-focused perspective. A brief overview of the KISS framework and ROLES will help participants stay conscious of their significance. Remind all involved that ACEs are traumatic or stressful events experienced during childhood, such as abuse, neglect, and household dysfunction. Emphasize how ACEs can affect emotional and behavioral outcomes.

Transition to the resilience-focused perspective, noting that resilience means adapting positively despite adversity. While ACEs can be highly influential, people must recognize the role played by resilience in shaping their responses to challenges. This perspective aims at identifying strengths and coping mechanisms that help overcome adversity. (See the *42 Resilience Building Blocks* at the end of this book.)

## Discuss How Trauma Awareness Helps Rehabilitation

Following are key discussion topics for participants to understand how being trauma-informed can help rehabilitation:

✔ Help participants understand how past traumas affect current behaviors.

✔ Recognize that behavior, especially within contexts of criminal activities, might be influenced by unresolved trauma.

✔ This knowledge forms the basis for a trauma-informed approach towards rehabilitation.

✔ Highlight the importance of empathy and compassion when exploring trauma impacts.

✔ Work to acknowledge that some behaviors were adopted for protection, thereby addressing root causes that might facilitate recovery and personal development.

✔ Explain how trauma-informed approaches could help break the cycle of negative consequences.

✔ It provides individuals with an opportunity to develop healthier coping skills through addressing trauma issues. These further foster resilience within them and positively influence their future decision-making process.

## Explore Participants' Own and Others' Resilience

Following are vital topics to guide participants to explore their resilience so far and others' over time, which also helps in rehabilitation:

✔ **Create a guided reflection** where participants explore their strengths in the face of difficulties. Furthermore, encourage participants to find moments when they have shown strength despite adverse circumstances. Reflecting on oneself helps build resiliency from within.

✔ **Allow participants to tell stories** about how they have been resilient. Doing this will give them a sense of belonging and support from other people. Remind them that their past does not define them and can be overcome.

✔ **Use strength-based language** during conversations. For example, during interviews, participants ask questions and give feedback using an appreciative inquiry approach, recognizing the strengths and resilience of parolees. This creates a more favorable climate for everyone involved.

By incorporating the resilience perspective in the simulated parole hearing, participants get to know the whole person, enhancing empathy and supporting rehabilitative goals within the program. Moving away from judgment towards understanding lays the foundation for personal change and better choices.

## Mock Parole Hearing Structure

This section outlines our Mock Parole Hearing Structure, which will be used for a restorative justice approach to a process many will undergo at some point during their incarceration. Among the goals of this section is to provide a space where challenging confrontations relate to the participants' crime.

This structure thoroughly examines critical elements of the rehabilitative process and enables participants to face these confrontations with presence and stability. I believe familiarity and practice of nonviolent communication are essential for those involved in this process. Resilience Prison Project participants undergo 24 weeks of NVC Foundations to acquire knowledge, gain insights, and develop the skills and consciousness to prepare for restorative justice activities such as Mock Parole Hearings.

## Opening Statements
*Introduction of the Crime and Its Impact*

*[The opening sets the tone for the mock parole hearing, emphasizing understanding, empathy, and accountability rather than judgment. It suggests a purpose beyond punishment where participants self-reflect to gain insights about themselves.]*

*Parole Board Member 1*:

> "Good day, ladies and gentlemen. We are here to discuss an incident on [date]. This case involved [brief description], which had a major impact on individuals and the community. Mr. or Ms. _____, before that, let us know what happened."

*Person Who Created the Harm*:

> "I want to acknowledge the pain I have caused. On [date], I did [describe the incident using NVC], and I feel sorry for other people affected."

## Acknowledgment of Purpose
*For insight, empathy, and accountability.*

*Facilitator*:

> "First, it will help if we understand why we are having this mock parole hearing. Here, we aim to explore the circumstances surrounding the

harmful acts committed by [name of parolee], fostering empathy among participants and laying grounds for accountability and rehabilitation."

*Parole Board Member 2*:

"This is a space for us to be honest and understand each other well. We don't come here to judge but to work together for personal growth and positive change."

## Individual Sharing of Feelings and Needs

*Parole Board Member 1*:

"Mr./Ms. _____, What was alive in you when these events occurred? Describe in terms of your feelings and needs surrounding these events."

*Person Who Created the Harm*:

"I felt lost and overwhelmed that day. I made bad decisions because my needs were not met (for security, connection, or understanding). All I can say is how much I regret the pain I caused."

## Board Members' Response

*Using NVC principles, expressing their feelings and needs.*

*[This section of the hearing creates a conversation based on nonviolent communication (NVC) principles whereby the parole candidate expresses their feelings and needs while board members respond by showing empathy through expressing their feelings and needs. Therefore, it helps understand why they did what they did and creates room for constructive communication and rehabilitation.]*

*Parole Board Member 1*:

"Thank you for sharing your perspective. You said you felt _____ because your _____ needs were unmet. I would like to say that in this process, safety is important to me. Therefore, could you please tell us more about what led to your actions so that we can be sure that we can prevent such happenings from occurring again?"

*Parole Board Member 2*:

"I appreciate your honesty. When I think about the impact on the victim, it worries me. My need for justice/fairness is great. On my part, I am willing to understand where you are coming from, but at the same time, let's not forget about others who were affected by your actions. What do you imagine those harmed by what you did felt because of what you did?"

## Resilience Exploration

*Discussing identified ACEs and building resilience.*

*Facilitator*:

"We have already discussed how adverse childhood experiences affect individuals. Now, let's find out how we can build up resilience. Would you mind sharing any known ACEs from your life with us and how you have built resilience despite these challenges?"

*Person Who Created the Harm*:

"Things like [mention specific ACEs] greatly affected me in my early years. I have been working hard towards building resilience through [describe personal strategies, therapy, support networks.]"

## Sharing Examples of Resilience by Overcoming Challenges

*[This part of the mock parole hearing asks participants to think about what they've been through and how they've managed to cope. When talking about ACEs and giving their examples of resilience, it becomes more about strengths and ways they deal with things. This ties into how the program wants people to start seeing things in a trauma-informed way.]*

*Parole Board Member 1*:

"Thank you for sharing. Resilience is a powerful force. Can you provide examples from your life where you've demonstrated resilience in overcoming challenges unrelated to the incident? How have these experiences contributed to your personal growth?"

*Person Who Created the Harm*:

"There were times when I dealt with [mention specific challenges] and through it all [describe coping mechanisms, support systems]. From this, I learned that sometimes you must be resilient."

## Challenge Questions and Hard-to-Hear Messages

*[After each challenging question and hard-to-hear message made by a parole board member, the person who created the harm has an opportunity to answer. The queries/messages that follow are examples that will require modification to match the particulars of each individual undergoing the process.]*

### Contextualization and Accountability

*Parole Board Member 1*:

"Take us through the background facts leading to this incident. We need to understand what happened and what contributed to it."

### Exploring Personal Responsibility

*Parole Board Member 2*:

"How do you accept personal responsibility for how your actions affected those harmed and the community?"

### Addressing the Impact on Others

*Parole Board Member 1*:

"What do you know about this impact on those harmed emotionally or physically? How have you demonstrated a commitment to change, given these realities."

## Examining Risk Factors

*Parole Board Member 2*:

> "What risk factors or triggers were present that led to your involvement in this incident—and what are you doing or going to do about them."

## Understanding Emotional State

*Parole Board Member 1*:

> "What were your feelings during that time, and how did they influence your decision-making? What does it mean about managing such emotions now."

## Exploring Rehabilitation Efforts

*Parole Board Member 2*:

> "Tell us about the rehabilitative steps you have taken. Have you participated in any program that addresses the reasons behind your criminal act?"

> "Please give an account of your misconduct history. (Adapt to the specific misconduct history in question). Does this demonstrate the kind of behavior of someone who should be given a second chance?"

> "What program or programs have been most effective at helping your own personal growth. Tell us a bit about this and how this will impact your life on the outside."

## Community Reintegration

*Parole Board Member 1*:

> "How are you going to reintegrate into society upon your release? What plan has been set in place? How will this affect those around you."

## Impact on Personal Growth

*Parole Board Member 2*:

> "As you reflect on where you have been since that incident, what would you say about personal growth and self-awareness? How has empathy and accountability come out of this process for you."

## Handling Future Challenges

*Parole Board Member 1*:

> "If there is another difficult situation like this, what will you do differently after what you have learned from this one?"

## Personal Self Assessment

*Parole Board Member 2*:

> "Mr./Ms. _____, please tell us why you believe you ought to be released from prison today."

## Acknowledging Hard-to-Hear Messages

*Parole Board Member 2*:

> "Now I have a hard message to share. The family of the person harmed talked about their great suffering and loss. We have to take these factors into account. What do you have to say about their feelings and needs toward your release from prison?"

*[This series of questions aims to achieve the program goals of insight, empathy, and accountability during a mock parole hearing. The questions assist the participant in self-reflection, taking responsibility for their actions, adopting an anticipatory standpoint, and looking at how others and a community are affected.]*

## Practice NVC in Responding to Challenging Inquiries

*[In responding to challenging inquiries using Nonviolent Communication (NVC) principles, the person who created the harm reflects on their feelings and needs while acknowledging the impact on others. This practice aims to foster understanding, empathy, and accountability within the mock parole hearing structure, aligning with the rehabilitative goals of the program.]*

<u>Parole Board Member 1</u>:

> "From what I can see, your actions had a devastating impact on this person [the person(s) harmed] and their family. Can you speak on how it feels to have caused pain like this? What need/needs were driving this behavior."

<u>Person Who Created the Harm</u>:

> "I feel so regretful for what I did. I needed support, but nobody seemed there for me. I want more integrity and honesty than I showed then. I understand that whatever one does affects other people's lives."

<u>Parole Board Member 2</u>:

> "Some might say that there is no excuse for your actions. What was happening in your life that led up to this crisis, and what was missing for you."

<u>Person Who Created the Harm</u>:

> "I am aware that what I did is very serious. At that time, I was overwhelmed by a lot of pressure and unmet needs for validation. This doesn't justify my actions, but it helps me to understand the underlying issues that need to be addressed for me to grow as an individual and to rehabilitate myself."

## Deliver Hard-to-Hear Messages with Empathy and Compassion

*[The parole board members deliver difficult truths with sensitivity when*

*giving these hard-to-hear messages using empathy and compassion. The approach recognizes the impact on those harmed and the community while allowing the person who committed the crime to respond from a place of empathy and show they are ready to make amends.]*

<u>Parole Board Member 1</u>:

"We have talked about how your action affects others; such a difficult message must be conveyed. The family(s) of those harmed expressed deep, long-lasting pain. What are you doing about this ongoing impact."

<u>Person Who Created the Harm</u>:

"First, I wish to extend my deepest sympathy to the bereaved family. I recognize that my actions caused them enduring pain and assure them they will engage in restorative practices (e.g., mention specific actions) if provided with a chance. This means finding paths towards healing."

<u>Parole Board Member 2</u>:

"Another hard-to-hear message is coming from community members afraid of reintegrating you into society. What are you doing or can you do to build trust again so that people know you want positive change."

<u>Person Who Created the Harm</u>:

"I have noted concerns raised by the community, and I will maintain transparency and be held accountable for my actions. For instance, I intend on joining community activities; sharing my journey of recovery; and undertaking programs that contribute positively, among other steps. Trust will take some time in rebuilding, and thus, I am ready to act instead of talking."

## Harm Impact Statements

*[The following messages are intended to promote transparency, accountability, personal growth, and rehabilitation. They are meant to challenge the parole candidate with difficult questions so that they can*

*respond thoughtfully and meaningfully.]*

## Impact on the Harmed

"Those harmed have submitted an impact statement that details the trauma they have undergone. What are your responses to their experiences, and how does it contribute to their healing."

## Rehabilitation Progress

"Efficiency doubts hover over the efforts of rehabilitation you made. What tangible proof can be made available by yourself as a person that shows personal growth and a commitment to change from the time of the crime?"

## Concerns About Accountability

"Your story seems to lack accountability, according to some people. How do you intend to show true remorse for your actions and their effects."

## Community Reintegration Plan

"The community is doubtful of your reintegration plan. Which specific actions and initiatives are in place for a smooth transition with minimal potential negative effects on the community?"

"Who is going to support your transition upon release? Do you have housing, transportation, a job, etc?"

## Potential for Repeat Offense

"There is concern about the possibility of repeating it given the nature of the offense you committed. What steps have you taken to address root causes and reduce the risk of similar behavior in the future."

## Addressing Stigma and Prejudice

"When you created this harm, you set up a stigma against yourself which exists till today. How will you address these issues, enable others to understand, and fight against barriers that can limit your successful integration back into society."

## Reflection and Accountability
*Person Who Created the Harm Reflects on Insights Gained*

*Facilitator*:

"I now would like to ask you as someone who committed this crime to reflect on what has been learned from those who've created harm. Now we go over here; tell me how this hearing affected your perception about that time events occurred or even feelings about yourself back then."

*Person Who Created the Harm*:

"This hearing has made me face my actual deeds and the pain caused to others. I'vee learned just how much pain my actions caused to the person(s) ahd society. It also came to me that I wish I would have addressed my needs in ways that did not harm others."

### Facilitate a Discussion on Accountability and Responsibility

*[From this part of the course, the candidate for parole gives his/her opinion about the parole hearing and what he/she has learned from it. The interviewer then brings up the subject of accountability and responsibility so that the candidate for parole can describe specific things he/she will do to show that he/she wants to change and rehabilitate himself.]*

*Facilitator*:

"Now, let us refocus on accountability and responsibility. What steps will you take to show that you accept responsibility for the harm done, and what actions will you take to meet your obligations?

*Person Who Created the Harm*:

"I realize how heavy my obligations are. I aim to rectify my wrongs, actively participate in restorative justice programs, continue working on my rehabilitation, and be useful to society. To me, it means that I choose to make visible steps towards mending what I ruined."

## Closing

*Thank you for your openness and engagement*

*Facilitator*:

> "Finally, let me say a sincere thank you to each participant here today for being open to us and engaging with us on this topic throughout this case study parole hearing. Without it, our journey towards knowledge would be impossible."

### Explain That This Is Intended to Be Rehabilitative Exercise

*Facilitator*:

> "We must understand that what we do today is not judgment but providing space for realization, compassion, and accountability. Ours has been a long process of returning to society, which has been made possible by each contribution helping us to know more about how intricate life can become."

### Keep Reflecting and Growing

*Facilitator*:

> "Lastly, I urge all, including the candidate for parole and parole board members and everyone else present here today, to reflect on the stories shared during this session as we conclude. It is just one step along a long corridor leading toward maturation and recovery in the community. Continue deeply about your experiences in life because this will make you grow personally."

*[Summarize key points from the mock parole hearing experience by acknowledging participants' involvement, focusing on rehabilitation, promoting continuous self-reflection, and urging growth beyond.]*

✔ Provide resources for continued support.

✔ Arrange follow-up sessions to explore and discuss further.

## RPP Participant's Questionnaire

Throughout the mock parole hearing, the facilitator will seek to balance emotional depth and maintain a safe environment for participants. Adjust the pace and intensity based on the group's dynamics and individual needs.

*This questionnaire is meant to gather comprehensive information for the mock parole hearing. Everything written here will remain confidential within this program. If you need more space you may use additional paper indicating the question referenced.*

**See form at the end section of this book.**

\*\*\*

*a trauma-informed approach to rebuilding the web of relationships harmed by crime*

*"A just future envisions walls not as barriers but as canvases for the art of understanding, empathy, and restoration."*

~Desmond Tutu

# Facilitation Guidelines for Restorative Dialogues

The following guidelines are intended to help orient participants to the process of Restorative Dialogue (RD). Participants may better understand how the activity works by reading through what follows.

Each practice must be tailored to the unique needs of the participants undergoing the process. For best results, participants may use this example to practice before undergoing their own RD.

*Note: This outline is a general guide and may be adapted based on the specific context and needs of the participants.*

# Introductions

## Setting the Tone
*For the Facilitator*

### Facilitator's Role

✔ Occupy a secure, confidential space.

✔ Show that this dialogue aims to understand each other, heal, and move forward.

✔ Make it clear that participation is voluntary and requires mutual respect.

### Participants' Dialogue

<u>*Facilitator*</u>:

> "Welcome to both of you and thank you for coming. Before we start, let's agree that this conversation will occur in a safe and confidential space. Everything shared here will remain between us.
>
> Our dialogue aims to bring understanding and healing and find a way forward. You can join in or not; it is your choice. But all of us aim to be respectful during our talk. Let's proceed now with that in mind. Share as you are comfortable, and please remember that this space is meant for openness and respect."

## Mutual Agreements
*For all participants*

### Participants' Engagement

✔ Give a brief self-introduction.

✔ Agree on the reason for engaging and accept ground rules for it.

## Participants' Dialogue

*Participant 1*:

"Hi! My name is *Alex*. I am ready to begin our dialogue, which I hope helps us to move forward with greater clarity, understanding, and respect."

*Participant 2*:

"Hello! My name is *Jordan*. I also want to approach this with a peaceful heart. I hope to be heard for the pain I have experienced and understand what was going on with you when all of this took place."

*Facilitator*:

"Thank you for introducing yourselves. Before we delve into our conversation, let us ensure we are on the same page regarding why we are here today. We want to know each other better and heal from our past experiences. This will help us move forward positively.

Do you two agree with me on these goals? Will you participate respectfully?"

*[Participants respond]*

# Building Connections

## Opening Circle
*For Facilitator and Participants*

### Facilitator's Role

- ✔ Encourage mindfulness to achieve presence.
- ✔ Recognize emotions and create an atmosphere of empathy.
- ✔ Introduce the concept of Nonviolent Communication (NVC) Consciousness.

## Participants' Dialogue

*Facilitator*:

> "Let's take a moment to center ourselves and be present in this dialogue. You can comfortably close your eyes, breathe deeply, and exhale slowly. Then, let us acknowledge how we are feeling now. All feelings are welcome; know that your experiences matter."

*Participant 1*:

> [*Pause. After a moment...*]""I am grateful for this opportunity to ground myself."

*Participant 2*:

> [nodding]""It feels good to admit our feelings before beginning."

*Facilitator*:

> "Before we begin our conversation, I want to introduce defining principles that will shape our discussion today. This is nonviolent communication consciousness or NVC consciousness. It is a communication strategy meant to foster understanding and empathy.
>
> In NVC, we learn to express our feelings and needs and listen empathically to others. This awareness helps create space for open conversations without judgment or blame. As we go further, we must remember how compassionate communication can bridge gaps and cultivate relationships.
>
> Also, we will approach this activity being considerate of each other's adverse experiences and needs surrounding safety, connection, and learning. Therefore, keep in mind the KISS framework as well as your R.O.L.E.S. as we move through this process.

## Participants' Engagement

✔ Share what participants can expect or any emotions they might have from the session.

✔ Indicate readiness to engage in candid, constructive talk openly.

**Participants' Dialogue**

*Participant 1:*

"Before we start, I feel nervous and hopeful about this dialogue. I hope that through this discussion, we will manage to get along better with each other."

*Participant 2:*

"Thanks for sharing that with us. I'mm also somewhat nervous, but I'mm here to find something in common with you that will make things easier for us to connect."

## Exploring Feelings and Needs
*For Facilitator & Participants*

**Facilitator's Role**

✔ To help participants discover their feelings and needs through NVC consciousness.

✔ Encourage consideration about how the offense made each party feel.

**Participants' Dialogue**

*Facilitator:*

"Let's take a moment to look at the feelings we had during that incident, which we are discussing. So, I invite you all to think about your feelings when you were there. Just give me some words that can describe the way you felt"

*Participant 1:*

"When I did what I did (*express using clear observations of events*), I felt hurt and betrayed."

*Participant 2*:

> "When he did what he did (*express using clear observations of events*), I was angry and frustrated with him.."

*Facilitator*:

> "Thank you both for sharing."
>
> [*If any evaluations need translating, reflect these to participants.*]
>
> "Now, let's dive deeper. What needs of yours were not met then, contributing to these emotions."

[*Have NVC feelings/needs handouts available for participants before posing this query. Where available, use Grokit decks.*]

*Participant 1*:

> "My need for trust and understanding was unmet."

*Participant 2*:

> "I think my need for respect and cooperation was not fulfilled."

*Facilitator*:

> "Thanks for being frank.""

[*Reflect on each participant after they offer their response. Provide an opportunity for the listening party to reflect the needs/values of the speaker. This helps each speaker trust that they are being heard. For example: "Participant 2, would you reflect the need/value that Participant 1 has expressed" Allow this for both sides. Once acknowledged or clarified, continue as follows. Understanding these emotions or needs is necessary to help us resolve this issue by empathizing with others with different needs but similar feelings.*]

## Participants' Engagement

✔ Prioritize sharing feelings and needs regarding the offense.

✔ Connect with the other person while listening actively to them.

## Participants' Dialogue

*Participant 1*:

"I felt hurt and frustrated when the incident happened because I value respect, and I thought that my need for respect wasn't honored."

*Participant 2*:

"Yeah, I hear you. Respect is important to you. Can you tell me why it's so important to you."

*Participant 1*:

"Absolutely. Respect creates a positive environment, and I believe it's crucial for healthy relationships."

*Participant 2*:

"I understand that. Healthy relationships are important. During the incident, my feelings were confused and concerned because my need for clear communication wasn't met."

*Participant 1*:

"Clear communication is important to you. I get that. It seems we both have needs that weren't met during that situation."

*Facilitator*:

"Your willingness to express and listen to each other's feelings and needs is a valuable step in the resolution process. Keep this open communication as we move forward."

## Understanding the Impact
*For Facilitator & Participants*

**Facilitator's Role**

✔ Let everyone share how the offense affected them.

✔ Use restorative questions that deepen understanding without blame.

**Participants' Dialogue**

*Facilitator:*

"Let's take a moment and explore the impact of the incident on each of you in turn. Participant 1: Could you share how this situation has affected you."

*Participant 1:*

"Well, it left me feeling anxious and frustrated. I could not concentrate on my work for some time, and I was unable to sleep for months."

*Facilitator:*

"Thank you for sharing that. Participant 2: Can you inform us what impact this incident had on you?

*Participant 2:*

"Now it makes me feel sad and shameful since I had no idea it affected you. No, indeed, Iwasn'tt trying to give you anxiety or lose so much sleep."

*Facilitator:*

"These impacts must be understood too. Participant 1: What things led to your frustration."

*Participant 1:*

"Well, it is the tone we used when we talked, which seemed lacking the consideration and respect I wanted."

*Facilitator*:

"I appreciate you clarifying that. Participant 2:How does this new information strike you."

*Participant 2*:

"If it was a tone, I didn't mean it to appear that way. I was preoccupied with trying to rid myself of a stressful situation in my life."

*Facilitator*:

"We're here not to blame but to understand. These insights will help us reach a more holistic resolution."

**Participants' Engagement**

✔ Share personal experiences and feelings about the impact.

✔ Acknowledge the other party's perspective with empathy.

**Participants' Dialogue**

*Participant 1*:

"The moment such an event occurs, in my mind, it reminds me of an episode I have gone through before. This made me angry and exposed me emotionally. That left me a bit scared as well. My sense of security was threatened."

*Participant 2*:

"I never thought about your past experiences. I can now see that my actions triggered these feelings, and I regret the harm I caused you."

*Participant 1*:

"Thanks for admitting it. I need you to know how much hurt I suffered because of this incident."

*Participant 2*:

> "Would you be willing to share more about how you were impacted so I can learn from it and avoid causing similar trouble."

*Participant 1*:

> "Thank you for being open-minded in listening. Trust was destroyed as in my previous situation, which I don't want to happen again."

*Participant 2*:

> "Indeed, trust is critical! To solve this, I am ready for everything, including trying to rebuild trust between us."

## Taking Responsibility
*For Facilitator & Participants*

### Facilitator's Role

✔ Sharing the understanding of making the wrongs right on the path of importance. It is crucial for participants to accept their mistakes and take responsibility to make amends.

✔ Getting participants to do this is to be accomplished without guilt, shame, or blame being imposed on them.

### Participants' Dialogue

*Facilitator*:

> "Alright, our next topic will be taking responsibility. [Participant 1], please tell us how you view what happened and its impact."

*Participant 1*:

> "I acknowledge that I affected [Participant 2] a lot. I sometimes interrupted them while they spoke or dismissed what they said, making them annoyed."

*Facilitator:*

> "Thanks for accepting that. Taking responsibility is an important milestone. So now, let's think about how to repair this harm and move forward. What steps are you prepared to take to fix the damage caused."

*Participant 1:*

> "I am willing to express ownership for what I did right now and take responsibility for the harm I caused [Participant 2] while ensuring that I listen to and validate their emotions in future times, too. Additionally, I would like to learn more about effective communication so I am more aware when it matters."

*Facilitator:*

> "This is a very nice way forward. We must emphasize learning and growing from the situation. Participants, does this commitment sound good to anyone."

*Participant 2:*

> "I appreciate [Participant 1's commitment, demonstrating his willingness to change and make amends."

*Facilitator:*

> "Great. Now let us talk about how we can continue this process."

## Participants' Engagement

✔ The perpetrator acknowledges their actions and apologizes.

✔ The survivor talks about how acknowledgment helps with healing.

## Participants' Dialogue

*Person Who Created Harm:*

> "I want to acknowledge my responsibility in this situation by recognizing my fault in this situation. Now, I realize what actions led me to harm you

[person harmed], for whose unintended harm I caused. I deeply regret it."

*Person Harmed:*

"Thank you for that. It means a lot hearing you say you truly mourn what you did. Healing can begin with just acknowledgement itself."

*Person Who Created Harm:*

"I know the negative influence of my actions, and I am ready to make things right with this relationship. Can you share more about how you experience this acknowledgment in your healing."

*Person Harmed:*

"It's empowering to hear you own up to what happened. When it comes to my need to have someone see it, this feels like a validation of the pain I felt. Moving forward, I hope we can work together to rebuild trust."

*Person Who Created Harm:*

"What do you believe we can do to bring restoration? If there's anything that needs to be done, just tell me. Your view matters greatly, and I would like things to be right."

## Empathy and Forgiveness
*For Facilitator & Participants*

**Facilitator's Role**

✔ Foster empathy by encouraging participants to see the humanity in each other.

✔ Discuss the potential for forgiveness as a step towards healing.

## Participants' Dialogue

*Facilitator:*

> "Now that we have covered impact and acknowledgment, let's discuss empathy. Both of you may acknowledge each other's humanity throughout the process. [person who created harm], what have you learned from [person harmed]'s experience."

*Person Who Created Harm:*

> "My activities deeply influenced the well-being of [person harmed]. It is enlightening to know their feelings."

*Facilitator:*

> "Thanks [person who created harm]. [Person harmed], how does it feel knowing that [person who created harm] is admitting what they did and the harmful impact they had on your life."

*Person Harmed:*

> "Emotionally speaking, this is a mix-up. On the one hand, I don't want to go through it again; on the other hand, I appreciate the person's admission of guilt. It helps me to humanize them."

*Facilitator:*

> "Okay. What about forgiveness? [Person harmed], what do you think about forgiveness given the acknowledgment."

*Person Harmed:*

> "Forgiveness is not automatic; appreciating that [person who created harm] admitted, however, goes a long way towards forgiveness. This is an opening although I am not ready to forgive."

*Facilitator:*

> "That's a reasonable point of view, [person harmed].
>
> [Person who created harm], do you think forgiveness is possible?"

*Person Who Created Harm:*

> "I know it won't happen overnight. I am committed to demonstrating change and working on deeper reconciliation over time. I want to be part of [person harmed]'s healing journey."

*Facilitator:*

> "Thank you both for sharing your stories with us today. Empathy and forgiveness are processes that never end, and this conversation is a step ahead in this process."

## Moving Beyond

### Agreement of Future Steps
*For Facilitator & Participants*

**Facilitator's Role**

✔ Facilitate a discussion on potential agreements for restitution or future actions.

✔ Emphasize the commitment to move forward positively.

**Participants' Dialogue**

*Facilitator:*

> "So, we have talked about acknowledgment, impact, and empathy; let us now deliberate upon potential agreements for moving forward. [Person harmed], [Person created harm], what are some of the steps or actions that can help to bring about positive changes in people's lives and bring them back."

*Person Harmed:*

> "I think it is important for [person who created harm] to fully commit to seeking therapy as he tries to grow personally. Moreover, a formal

apology and a plan for restitution would be appropriate."

*Person Who Created Harm:*

"I concur with these steps. I am going to therapy and engaging in personal growth activities. I sincerely apologize for my wrongdoings, too. And yes, we can discuss tangible restitution plans together."

*Facilitator:*

"Perfect. It is nice to have something in common we can work on together. What else may we talk about? [Person harmed], what would be meaningful to you regarding specific actions or reparations."

*Person Harmed:*

"Apart from the emotional toll, there were other expenses incurred too... paying these costs would be part of restitutions."

*Facilitator:*

"Thank you [person harmed] for sharing that with us. And yourself, [person who created harm], do you think financial restitution needs to be included in this agreement."

*Person Who Created Harm:*

"That is clear and fair to me. However, I wish to make amends whether money is involved or not. But if it must happen that way, then I will stick to it."

*Facilitator:*

"Fantastic! This is an excellent step towards building a new and moving forward. Let's document these agreements so they reflect our expectations correctly."

## Participants' Engagement

✔ Collaboratively develop a written agreement.

✔ Agree on practical steps for the future, if appropriate.

## Participants' Dialogue

*Facilitator:*

"Since we have discussed these points, let us develop a written agreement that reflects our shared understanding. I will draft it, and we can improve it as a group."

*[Facilitator starts drafting the agreement using a shared document listing the agreed-upon actions like counseling attendance, personal growth, formal apology, and financial restitution.]*

*Facilitator:*

"Kindly share your feedback on this draft agreement. [Person harmed], [person who created harm], are these statements consistent with your commitments."

*Person Harmed:*

"Yes, this is what we said earlier."

*Person Who Created Harm:*

"I agree with any of those steps."

*Facilitator:*

"Good. Now, we need to set a time frame for these activities. What is an adequate period for assessing progress according to you."

*Person Harmed:*

"Let's take this all back in three months to see how things go."

*Person Who Created Harm:*

"That's cool."

*[Participants settle for three months and finalize the written agreement. The facilitator ensures both parties receive copies and comprehend remaining parts.]*

*Facilitator:*

> "On that note, let us examine some practical steps for the future since we have come up with an agreement; so, are there any specific actions or behaviors that you think could lead to a positive relationship between both of you going forward?"

*[Both parties discuss together and determine practical steps for future interactions, ensuring mutual respect and understanding.]*

*Facilitator:*

> "This is an important part of the process by which we positively define the way forward. These practical steps will be part of our larger agreement."

*[Finally, the facilitator adds practical steps to be followed along through future periods in his drafted version of this document. The final copy is produced after incorporating these details and is given out to both participants.]*

## Reflection and Gratitude

*For Facilitator & Participants*

### Facilitator's Role

✔ Guide participants in reflecting on the dialogue's impact.

✔ Thank them for their bravery and commitment.

### Participants' Engagement

✔ Share thoughts of personal progress or experiences.

✔ Thank you for the opportunity to talk and understand each other better.

## Participants' Dialogue

*Facilitator:*

"Finally, before we go, I want you to speak briefly about what we've discussed. What impact has this conversation had on you? Do you have any insights? Or are there any moments of personal growth that you might want to share."

*Person Harmed:*

"I'm grateful that I got an opportunity to share my feelings, which were validated. It's a step towards healing on my part."

*Person Who Created Harm:*

"This has been an eye-opening dialogue for me. I am willing to make things right and become a changed and different person."

*Facilitator:*

"Before we finish, thank you both for being open and honest. We'lll take another minute to show our gratitude before we close. [Person harmed], is there anything you would like to express gratitude for."

*Person Harmed:*

"I appreciate being listened to as well as [person who created harm]'s willingness to engage in this process."

*Facilitator:*

"Thank you. And [person who created harm], is there something you'd like to express gratitude for."

*Person Who Created Harm:*

"I appreciate knowing how my actions affect others and also [person harmed] trying to resolve it with me in this manner."

*Facilitator:*

"Your courage and commitment through this process thus far have been commendable.""Thanking you sincerely – these are the words that come into my mind when I think about your contributions to the dialogue today. We will conclude our circle if no one else wants to say something."

*[Participants express that they'vee shared what they needed and are ready to conclude.]*

<u>*Facilitator*</u>:

"Thanks, both of you, for sharing these parts with us today. There is nothing more from me than this. If you change your mind about something later, it's okay to contact me. May the path be well."

# Closing Remarks
*For Facilitator*

## Facilitator's Role

✔ Reinforce confidentiality and ongoing support.

✔ Provide resources for additional assistance, if needed.

✔ Conclude the dialogue with a message of hope and healing.

## Participants' Dialogue

<u>*Facilitator*</u>:

"I want to underline that our conversation is confidential before we leave. What has been shared here stays here; you both have demonstrated courage in opening up.

If you require further help or support along the way, please ask for my assistance. The community has services you can access, and I can give you some information on this in case you need it.

I thank both of you for being open and willing to do what it takes for this to be successful. We are healing – do not forget it!

Change is possible for good. So, if there are no other comments or questions, we say goodbye and wish you good luck on your journey."

\*\*\*

*a trauma-informed approach to rebuilding the web of relationships harmed by crime*

*"Restorative Justice is respect. Respect for all, even those who are different from us; even those who seem to be our enemies. Respect reminds us of our interconnectedness, but also of our differences. Respect insists we balance concerns for all parties. If we pursue justice as respect, we will do justice restoratively."*

~Howard Zehr

# Resilience Prison Project Participant Questionnaire

*This questionnaire is meant to gather comprehensive information for the mock parole hearing and/or the Restorative Dialogue. Everything written here will remain confidential within this program.*

## 1. Personal Information

*Full Name:*_____

*Date of Birth:*_____

*Gender:*_____

*Ethnicity:*_____

## 2. Crime Details

*Date of the Incident:*_____

*Description of the Harm Created (detailed account):*

*Location of the Incident:*

*Were there any witnesses?* ____YES ____NO

*If yes, provide their names (can be alias) and relationship to incident:*

## 3. Background Information

*Educational Background:*

*Employment History:*

*Family Background (living situation, relationships):*




*History of Adverse Childhood Experiences (ACEs) if comfortable sharing:*




## 4. Personal Feelings and Needs

*Reflect on the incident. What were your feelings at the time?*




*What needs of yours were unmet during the events leading to the events creating harm?*

## 5. Rehabilitation Efforts

*Describe any programs, therapies, or activities you have engaged in since the incident to address the underlying issues.*

*How have these rehabilitation efforts influenced your perspective and actions?*

## 6. Personal Growth and Insights

*What insights have you gained through the mock parole hearing and other rehabilitation processes?*

*Reflect on any personal growth or changes in self-awareness since the incident.*

## 7. Harm Impact and Acknowledgment

*How do you perceive the impact of your actions on the person(s) harmed and their family?*

*How do you plan to acknowledge and address this impact?*

## 8. Community Reintegration Plan

*Outline your plan for reintegrating into the community if granted parole.*

*What steps will you take to rebuild trust within the community?*

## 9. Accountability and Responsibility

*How do you plan to be accountable for the harm caused?*

*What concrete steps will you take to fulfill your responsibility towards those affected?*

## 10. Hard-to-Hear Messages

*Anticipate and describe potential hard-to-hear messages that the parole board members may deliver. How do you plan to respond empathetically?*

## 11. Additional Information

*Is there any other information or context you believe is crucial for the parole board members and facilitators to understand?*

## Declaration

*I understand that the information provided in this questionnaire is solely to be used for the mock parole hearing within the rehabilitation program.*

*I acknowledge the importance of honesty and openness in this process.*

_____

*Signature*                                             *Date*

*a trauma-informed approach to rebuilding the web of relationships harmed by crime*

"Adulthood is an attempt to become the antithesis of the wounded child within us."

~Stewart Stafford

# ACEs Quiz

**#1.** Did a parent or other adult in your household often or very often swear at you, insult you, or put you down? __ YES __ NO

*Exposure to verbal abuse can have lasting effects on mental and emotional well-being. It may contribute to low self-esteem, anxiety, and difficulties in forming healthy relationships.*

**#2.** Did a parent or other adult in your household often or very often push, grab, slap, or throw something at you? __ YES __ NO

*Physical abuse during childhood is a traumatic experience that can lead to physical injuries, emotional scars, and increased vulnerability to mental health challenges in adulthood.*

*a trauma-informed approach to rebuilding the web of relationships harmed by crime*

**#3.** Did an adult or person at least 5 years older than you ever touch or fondle you, or have you touch their body in a sexual way? __ YES __ NO

*Childhood sexual abuse is a severe form of trauma with profound implications for mental health, often resulting in long-term emotional distress, relationship difficulties, and increased risk of mental health disorders.*

**#4.** Did you often or very often feel that no one in your family loved you or thought you were important or special? __ YES __ NO

*Emotional neglect can impact the development of a child's sense of self-worth and belonging, leading to challenges in forming healthy relationships and coping with stress in adulthood.*

**#5.** Did you often or very often feel that you didn't have enough to eat, had to wear dirty clothes, and had no one to protect you? __ YES __ NO

*Experiencing neglect in terms of basic needs such as food, clothing, and safety can contribute to issues such as anxiety, trust issues, and challenges in developing a sense of security.*

**#6.** Was a biological parent ever lost to you through divorce, abandonment, or other reasons? __ YES __ NO

*Losing a parent through divorce or abandonment can be emotionally distressing for a child and may contribute to feelings of rejection, insecurity, and difficulties in forming stable relationships.*

**#7.** Was your mother or stepmother often or very often pushed, grabbed, slapped, or had something thrown at her? __ YES __ NO

*Witnessing domestic violence can have a significant impact on a child's mental and emotional well-being, potentially leading to increased stress, anxiety, and challenges in forming healthy relationships.*

**#8.** Did you live with anyone who was a problem drinker or alcoholic, or who used street drugs? ___ YES ___ NO

*Living with someone who struggled with alcohol or drug use can deeply affect a child's sense of safety and well-being, adding to their adverse childhood experiences.*

**#9.** Was a household member depressed or mentally ill, or did a household member attempt suicide? ___ YES ___ NO

*Living in an environment where a family member struggles with mental health issues can create a challenging and sometimes traumatic upbringing, influencing an individual's own mental health in adulthood.*

**#10.** Did a household member go to prison? ___ YES ___ NO

*Having a family member incarcerated can lead to a range of adverse experiences, including social stigma, financial strain, and emotional distress, potentially affecting an individual's mental health and well-being.*

*Change is the echo of voices, and advocacy is the chorus that invites a transformative melody in the halls of justice.*

- Malala Yousafzai

# 42 Resilience Building Blocks

I am currently developing a second small book called *Playing with a Full Deck* where I explore the *42 Resilience Building Blocks* with greater depth.

For now, however, I wanted to at least provide the following list so that you might find ways to implement your own resilience building practice on your own - something that, yes, you guessed it, builds resilience.

By starting with one of these per day and seeing how often you can include it is a healthy way to begin. Once you have gone through the complete 42 day cycle, you can increase the challenge and depth by taking a week for each building block and working harder to incorporate them into your life and relationships.

*a trauma-informed approach to rebuilding the web of relationships harmed by crime*

## 42 Resilience Building Blocks

#1 Learning to Ask for Help

#2 Learning to Accept Help

#3 Modeling Appropriate Behavior

#4 Learning to Show Appreciation

#5 Allowing the Experience of Success or Failure

#6 Following Through on Tasks

#7 Mastering a Skill

#8 Developing Hope

#9 Verbally Saying I Love You

#10 Developing Trust

#11 Practicing Self-Discipline

#12 Learning to Self-Advocate

#13 Developing the Ability to Calm Oneself

#14 Creating a Sense of Control

#15 Setting Clear Expectations & Boundaries

#16 Respecting the Ability to Make Decisions

#17 Developing Self-Esteem

#18 Accepting Ownership for My Behavior

#19 Expressing Feelings

#20 Giving Back to the Community

#21 Showing Empathy

#22 Creating a Sense of Belonging

#23 Learning Responsibility

#24 Developing Friendships

#25 Helping a Friend

#26 Making Thoughtful Choices

#27 Modeling Problem-Solving Skills

#28 Appreciation of Cultural & Ethnic Heritage

#29 Experiencing Success

#30 Learning to Solve Problems & Make Decisions

#31 Sensing Triggers that Create Negative Behaviors

#32 Thinking Ahead About Consequence Before Acting

#33 Feeling Empowered to Ask Questions & Share My Ideas

#34 Letting Others Know I'm Available to Help

#35 Developing a Growth Perspective

#36 Acknowledging When I Am Wrong

#37 Sharing Something Important

#38 Developing Communication Skills

#39 Working as a Team

#40 Developing Critical Thinking Skills

#41 Connecting with Others" Feelings

#42 Developing Positive Relationshi

## Acknowledgements

This book could not have been written without all of the brilliant authors, speakers, influencers, and friends that have helped inspire my path toward wholeness and service.

One thing I know from my own and others experiences with trauma and shame is that we never move through either one of them by ourselves in isolation. It truly takes a village to help heal hurts and restore human beings back to their true nature. So many have been here for me in this way. I am truly grateful for their giving me a chance to be fully human.

Eric, I couldn't have done any of this without you. You have been my right hand man in all of this from the very beginning. I'm so grateful for your friendship and commitment to what matters.

Ellen, you, have labored tirelessly to make this book what it is today. Without you doing all that I couldn't from the inside, *Restorative Justice Recalibrated* would remain composition notebooks filled with handwritten words, scattered notes, and the unrealized dreams of an invisible man behind bars.

I am ever thankful for all that you both have done to see this project through and for helping fulfill a key milestone in the mission and vision of the *Resilience Prison Project*.

And of course to Dr Fred Sly, Ellen Rohr, Rick Griffin, and Fritzi Horstman - your inspirations to my everyday work have been saving graces in my journey. I honestly do not know what my past 15 years or next 15 years in the future would be without people like you all. Your impact and influence on my life is forever indelible. Thank you.

Finally, for countless others, some acquainted personally, others professionally - you know who you are! For your support, your belief, your time, and your heart to help me never give up in this journey, I am forever thankful.

*a trauma-informed approach to rebuilding the web of relationships harmed by crime*

# Glossary

**ACE studies** - Risk factors identified in research as contributing to trauma and toxic stress.

**Adverse Childhood Experiences** - The landmark study that correlated early negative childhood experiences with later adult health outcomes.

**Adverse Community Environments** - Risk factors in the community domain, such as poverty.

**Adverse Cultural Exposures** - Risk factors from mistreatment based on culture, such as racism.

**Adverse Circuitry Expressions** - Risk factors from mistreatment based on brain diversity, such as Autism.

**beneath behavior** - Process of looking to neurodevelopment at the root of behavior.

**body budget** - a metaphor for how your brain allocates energy resources within your body. The scientific term is allostasis.

**brain states** - Generalized model of how the vertebrate brain evolved based on an "essential" view that the rational brain "manage" the more primitive emotional brain. Advances in psychology and neuroscience now tell us this model is outdated and does not accurately represent the brain's development of concepts, generalizations and predictions of pleasurable or unpleasurable states that shape our patterns of response utilizing the 100 billion neurons and their extensive networks. Variation is the theme.

**brain networks** - Networks of neurons consisting of several discrete brain regions that are said to be "functionally connected" due to tightly coupled activity.

**categorization** - The process by which the brain uses a concept to make sensory input meaningful.

**community capacity building** - The "process of developing and strengthening the skills, instincts, abilities, processes and resources that organizations and communities need to survive, adapt, and thrive in the fast-changing world" (Wikipedia contributors. Retrieved January 15, 2020 from https://en.wikipedia.org/wiki/Capacity_building.)

**constructed emotion** - How we each shape our understanding of emotion based on experience, culture and mental concepts. When the concepts involved are emotion concepts, your brain constructs instances of emotion.

**contextual community resilience** - Using social domains and culture to build opportunities for mutual help, collective efficacy, shared norms and values, in order to promote, model and teach resilience and protective factors to youth and children.

**cortisol** - Hormone released by the adrenal glands when the body needs a burst of energy as when stressed. It floods the bloodstream with glucose to provide energy to cells.

**CRI** - *Community Resilience Initiative*, a non-profit entity dedicated to community capacity building and mobilization. CRI's goal is to build communities by expanding minds on the NEAR sciences and the power of resilience to buffer the negative health outcomes predicted by the ACE Study. CRI offers training, conferences, consulting, curriculum and product development in order to help move emerging best practices into community systems.

**C+U+R=E** - mutual clarity means both parties making clear observations instead of evaluations, mutual understanding means both parties getting at the true feelings instead of thought and universal needs instead of strategies, and mutual respect means both parties making clear doable real time requests instead of demands. When we combine these three elements, empathy is present.

**empathy** - The capacity to clearly understand the feelings and needs of other people. To know what it's like to "walk a mile in someone else's shoes."

**epigenetics** - Emerging research that explains how our genes are always adapting based on our environment and our experience.

**Golem Effect** - a psychological phenomenon where low expectations placed on individuals lead to poorer performance. It's a self-fulfilling prophecy where negative beliefs about someone's potential hinder their actual achievement.

**H.O.P.E.** - Three acronyms the author created to correspond with the three components of C.R. Snyder's Psychology of Hope 1. Having Only Positive Expectations (Goals) 2. Helping Opportunities Progress Effectively (Pathways) 3. Habitually Offering Persistent Effort (Agency)

**K.I.S.S.** - Community Resilience Initiative's (CRI's) framework for community capacity building for resilience. The acronym represents **K**nowledge, **I**nsight, **S**trategies, and **S**tructure.

**mirror neurons** - Neurons that "mirror" the behavior of the other, as though the observer was itself acting.""Serve and return"' is another way to describe this interaction between an adult caregiver and a child.

**N.E.A.R.** - Cluster of sciences (**N**euroscience, **E**pigenetics, **A**CE Studies, **R**esilience) on which CRI bases a portion of its curriculum.

**nervous system** - Divided into central (brain, spinal cord and nerves) and peripheral (somatic and autonomic). The somatic is voluntary, conscious, and with muscle control (sensory and motor nerves). The autonomic is involuntary, unconscious, and with gland/organ control.

**neuro-lens** - a way we can perceive and interpret the world from knowledge of the NEAR sciences so as to gain insight into the uniqueness of each individual's experiences.

**neuroplasticity** - Also known as brain plasticity, or neural plasticity, is the ability of the brain to change continuously throughout the lifespan.

**neuroscience** - Study of the structure and function of the nervous system and brain.

**NVC (nonviolent communication)** - An approach to enhanced communication, understanding, and connection based on the principles of nonviolence and humanistic psychology. It is not an attempt to end disagreements, but rather a way that aims to increase empathy and understanding to improve the overall quality of life.

**prediction** - Neural "conversation" within the brain trying to anticipate every fragment of sight, sound, smell, taste and touch that is experienced. Predictions are the brain's best guesses of what is going on in the world around you, and how to deal with it to keep you alive and well.

**prediction error** - The brain is structured as billions of predictions creating intrinsic brain activity. A brain works like a scientist. It's always making a slew of predictions, just as a scientist makes competing hypotheses. Sometimes, based on past experience, the prediction may be incorrect, and a prediction adjustment is then made.

**Pygmalion Effect** - refers to a psychological phenomenon where higher expectations lead to improved performance in others.

**Q.T.I.P.** - An acronym for **Q**uit **T**aking **I**t **P**ersonally. In short, it refers to emotional triggers where people take far too much personally when simply, it often is not about you. It is about the individual being triggered and reacting according to their default patterns.

**resilience** - The ability to adapt positively to an adverse event and emerge strengthened, with more life skills and strategies, confidence, and hope. See "mirror neurons."

**Resilience Prison Project** - An organization created in Oklahoma to transform lives, restore relationships, and create peaceful thriving communities by offering an integrated framework of Transformative Learning to adults in custody. This framework includes Trauma Informed, supportive and practitioner courses, nonviolent communication, restorative justice, and mindfulness. See also **RPP**.

**restorative justice** - An approach to justice that aims to repair the harm done to victims. In doing so, practitioners work to ensure that those who have created harm take responsibility for their actions, to understand the harm they have caused, to give them an opportunity to redeem themselves, and to discourage them from causing further harm. For those harmed, the goal is to give them an active role in the process, and to reduce feelings of anxiety and powerlessness. See also **RJ**.

**restorative justice recalibrated** - Refers to justice adapted to include: trauma-informed approach to all crime participants - those harmed and those who have created harm; restoring those who have created harm back to society by applying restorative practices with or without the participation or involvement of those harmed. See also **RJR**.

**RJ** - An acronym for **r**estorative **j**ustice.

**RJR** - An acronym for **r**estorative **j**ustice **r**ecalibrated,

**R.O.L.E.S.** - An acronym that helps us become trauma-informed agents: **R**ecognize, **O**bserve, **L**abel, **E**lect, **S**olve.

**RPP** - An acronym for **R**esilience **P**rison **P**roject.

**social reality** - Agreement by a group of people that something is real, which they share by way of language.

**spurters** - A person or thing that spurts. We call the period when children grow the most a growth spurt. It indicates an accelerated level of growth.

**statistical learning** - Inborn ability of the brain to learn patterns by observation, computing probabilities of what is similar and what is not.

**threat response** - Our body's response to the perception of danger and the release of certain hormones to prepare our response to the threat.

**trauma** - Deeply distressing or disturbing experience which sets our threat response system into high alert to protect us from potential danger.

**trauma-informed** - Understanding the impact of stress on our individual and community health so that we can interrupt the cycle of punishment, shame, blame and humiliation, shifting instead to positive intent, insight, empathy, compassion and love.

**triggers** - How we respond to our personalized histories based on concepts and culture and how we shape our predictions of actively constructing our experiences.

**triune brain model** - Theory constructed in 1952 by Dr. Paul MacLean that described the evolution of the vertebrate forebrain and behavior. Recent advances in neuroscience and psychology help us understand that brain regions are not compartmentalized, and that construction of concepts relative to prediction, culture, environment and interpretation affects our social reality.

\*\*\*

*"Good company on a journey makes the way seem shorter."*

~Izaak Walton

# References

A Tünde Barabás. *Responsibility-Taking, Relationship-Building and Restoration in Prisons: Mediation and Restorative Justice in Prison Settings.* Budapest, National Inst. Of Criminology, 2012.

Amstutz, Lorraine S. *The Little Book of Victim Offender Conferencing.* Simon and Schuster, December 1, 2009.

Arden, John B. *Rewire Your Brain: Think Your Way to a Better Life.* Hoboken, N.J., Wiley, 2013.

Armour, Marilyn, and Mark S. Umbreit. *Violence, Restorative Justice and Forgiveness: Dyadic Forgiveness and Energy Shifts in Restorative Justice Dialogue.* London, UK, Jessica Kingsley Publishers, 2018.

Badshah, Akhtar, and Brad Smith. *Purpose Mindset: How Microsoft Inspires Employees and Alumni to Change the World.* Nashville, TN, HarperCollins Leadership, 2021.

Baron-Cohen, Simon. *Zero Degrees of Empathy: A New Theory of Human Cruelty and Kindness.* London, UK, Penguin, 2012.

Barrett, Lisa Feldman, et al. *Handbook of Emotions.* NY/London, The Guilford Press, 2018.

Barrett, Lisa Feldman. *Seven and a Half Lessons about the Brain*. S.L., Houghton Mifflin Harcourt, 2020.

Barrett, Lisa Feldman. *How Emotions Are Made the Secret Life of the Brain*. Boston, MA, Mariner Books, 2018.

Brown, Brené. *The Gifts of Imperfection: Let Go of Who You Think You're Supposed to Be and Embrace Who You Are*. Charleston, Sc, Instaread Summaries, 2014.

Buber, Martin. *I and Thou*. London, Continuum, Reprint, 2008.

Carnegie, Dale. *How to Win Friends & Influence People*. NY, NY, Pocket Books, 1990.

Conte, Christian. *Mastering What You Practice*. CreateSpace Independent Publishing Platform, October 17, 2018.

Conte, Christian. *Walking through Anger: A New Design for Confronting Conflict in an Emotionally Charged World*. Boulder, CO, Sounds True, 2019.

Conte, Christian, and Christian Conte. *Life Lessons*. CreateSpace, November 1, 2013.

Csikszentmihalyi, Mihaly. *Finding Flow*. Basic Books, March 3, 2020.

Csikszentmihalyi, Mihaly. *Flow: The Psychology of Happiness*. London, Rider, 2002.

Csikszentmihalyi, Mihaly. *The Evolving Self: A Psychology for the Third Millennium*. NY, NY, Harper Perennial Modern Classics, 2018.

Dingle, Jonathan, and Judith Kelbie. *The Mediation Handbook 2014/15*. 2014.

Dyer, Wayne W. *The Power of Intention*. Hay House Publishing, 2010.

Eagleman, David. *Incognito: The Hidden Life of the Brain*. Edinburgh, Canongate, 2011.

Eagleman, David. *Livewired*. Doubleday Canada, August 25, 2020.

Eagleman, David. *The Brain: The Story of You*. NY, NY, Vintage Books, 2017.

Eckert, Holly Michelle. *Graduating from Guilt*. PuddleDancer Press, April 1, 2010.

For, Foundation. *A Course in Miracles*. Glen Elen, CA, Foundation For Inner Peace, 1992.

Forbes, Heather T. *Help for Billy : A Beyond Consequences Approach to Helping Challenging Children in the Classroom.* Boulder, Co., Beyond Consequences Institute, 2012.

Goleman, Daniel. *Emotional Intelligence: Why It Can Matter More than IQ.* NY, NY, Bantam Books, 1995.

Goleman, David J. *Rewire Your Brain.* Charlie Creative Lab, October 24, 2020.

Goyer, Mary Ellen. *Healing Power of Empathy.* PuddleDancer Press, May 1, 2019.

Grosmaire, Kate. *Forgiving My Daughter's Killer.* Thomas Nelson, March 15, 2016.

Gwinn, Casey, and Chan Hellman. *Hope Rising.* Morgan James Publishing, May 15, 2018.

Hari, Johann. *Chasing the Scream: The First and Last Days of the War on Drugs.* NY, NY, Bloomsbury Publishing, 2016.

Hari, Johann. *Lost Connections.* Bloomsbury, 2018.

Hart, Sura, and Victoria Kindle Hodson. *Respectful Parents, Respectful Kids.* PuddleDancer Press, October 28, 2006.

Henepola Gunaratana. *The Mindfulness in Plain English Collection.* Somerville, MA, Wisdom Publications, 2017.

Johansen, B. E. (1995). *Dating the Iroquois Confederacy. Akswesane Notes New Series*, 1, 62-63. November 30, 2018. https://ratical.org/many_worlds/6Nations/DatingIC.html

Kabat-Zinn, Jon. *Mindfulness for Beginners.* Boulder, CO, Sound True, 2016.

Kabat-Zinn, Jon. *Wherever You Go, There You Are.* Hachette Go, December 5, 2023.

Kellermann, Peter Felix, and Kate Hudgins. *Psychodrama with Trauma Survivors: Acting out Your Pain.* London; Philadelphia, Jessica Kingsley Publishers, 2000.

King, Christine, and Jean Morrison. *GROKit!* July 1, 2009.

Kinyon, John, and Ike Lasater. *Mediate Your Life Training Manual.* December 13, 2014.

Klein, Shari, and Neill Gibson. *What's Making You Angry?* PuddleDancer Press, Sept. 1, 2004.

Kohler, Brad. *Board Preparation: With New Perspectives Comes New Insight.* Dorrance Publishing, February 7, 2020.

Kohn, Alfie. *Punished by Rewards: The Trouble with Gold Stars, Incentive Plans A's, Praise, and Other Bribes.* Boston, MA; NY, NY, Mariner Books/Houghton Mifflin Harcourt, 1993.

Kohut, Heinz. *The Search for the Self: Selected Writings of Heinz Kohut 1978-1981.* Boca Raton, FL, Routledge, 2018.

Kornfield, Jack. *The Art of Forgiveness, Lovingkindness, and Peace.* NY, NY, Bantam Books, 2008.

Larsson, Liv. *Anger, Guilt & Shame: Reclaiming Power and Choice.* Svensbyn, Friare Liv, 2012.

Larsson, Liv. *Human Connection at Work; How to Use the Principles of Nonviolent Communication in a Professional Way.* Lulu.com, August 13, 2017.

Larsson, Liv. *The Power of Gratitude.* Svensbyn, Friare Liv, 2014.

Larsson, Liv, and Johan Rinman. *A Helping Hand: Mediation with Nonviolent Communication.* Sweden, Friare Liv, 2010.

Lipton, Bruce H. *The Biology of Belief : Unleashing the Power of Consciousness, Matter & Miracles.* Carlsbad, California, Hay House, Inc, 2016.

Lipton, Bruce H. *The Wisdom of Your Cells : How Your Beliefs Control Your Biology.* Boulder, Sounds True, 2006.

MacRae, Allan. *Little Book of Family Group Conferences New Zealand Style.* Simon and Schuster, January 1, 2004.

Marantz Connor, Jane, and Dian Killian. *Connecting across Differences.* PuddleDancer Press, March 1, 2012.

Maslow, Abraham H. *Maslow's Hierarchy of Needs.* 1943. Norderstedt Grin, 2011.

Mauer, Marc, and Ashley Nellis. *The Meaning of Life.* The New Press, December 11, 2018.

Mbiti, John S. *African Religions & Philosophy.* Jordan Hill, Heinemann, 2010.

Mezirow, Jack. *Learning as Transformation.* Jossey-Bass, October 5, 2000.

Mezirow, Jack. *Transformative Dimensions of Adult Learning*. San Francisco, Jossey-Bass, 1991.

Moreno, J L. *Psychodrama*. Mclean, VA, American Society For Group Psychotherapy & Psychodrama, 1994.

Morin, Judi, et al. *Nonviolent Communication Toolkit for Facilitators*. PuddleDancer Press, December 1, 2022.

Morrison, Jean. *Communication Fundamentals*. 2007.

Nellis, Ashley, and Sentencing Project (U.S. *Life Goes On*. The Sentencing Project, 2013.

Nevzlin, Irina. *The Impact of Identity: The Power of Knowing Who You Are*, USA, Irina Nevzlin, 2019.

Nguyen, Joseph. *Don't Believe Everything You Think*. April 24, 2023.

Oxford University Press. *New Oxford Annotated Bible: New Revised Standard Version with the Apocrypha*. Oxford University Press, 2010.

Peale, Norman Vincent. *The Power of Positive Thinking for Young People*. London, UK. Vermilion, 1998.

Petroski, Henry. *The Pencil: A History of Design and Circumstance*. Knopf Doubleday Publishing Group, 2011.

Pranis, Kay. *Little Book of Circle Processes: A New/Old Approach to Peacemaking*. NY, NY, Skyhorse Publishing Company, Inc., 2015.

Prieto, Jaime L. *The Joy of Compassionate Connecting*. CreateSpace, November 1, 2010.

Redekop, Paul. *Changing Paradigms*. Herald Press (VA), 2007.

Reivich, Karen, and Andrew Shatte. *The Resilience Factor*. Harmony, October 14, 2003.

Rogers, Carl. *A Way of Being*. Boston, MA, Houghton Mifflin Co, 1980.

Rosenberg, Marshall B. *Getting Past the Pain between Us: Healing and Reconciliation without Compromise*. Encinitas, CA, PuddleDancer Press, 2005.

Rosenberg, Marshall B. *Nonviolent Communication*. PuddleDancer Press, 2003.

Rosenberg, Marshall B. *Speak Peace in a World of Conflict: What You Say Next Will Change Your World*. Encinitas, CA, PuddleDancer Press, 2005.

Rosenberg, Marshall B. *Teaching Children Compassionately: How Students and Teachers Can Succeed with Mutual Understanding*. Encinitas, CA, PuddleDancer Press, 2005.

Rosenberg, Marshall B. *The Surprising Purpose of Anger: Beyond Anger Management: Finding the Gift*. Encinitas, CA, PuddleDancer Press, 2005.

Rosenberg, Marshall B. *We Can Work It Out: Resolving Conflicts Peacefully and Powerfully: A Presentation of Nonviolent Communication Ideas and Their Use*. Encinitas, CA, PuddleDancer Press, 2005.

Rosenberg, Marshall B, and Center For Nonviolent Communication (CNVC *Being Me, Loving You: A Practical Guide to Extraordinary Relationships: A Nonviolent Communication Presentation and Workshop Transcription by Marshall B. Rosenberg*. Encinitas, CA, PuddleDancer Press, 2005.

Rosenthal, Robert, and Lenore Jacobson. *Pygmalion in the Classroom Teacher Expectation and Pupils' Intellectual Development*. New York Irvington, 1992.

Ruiz, Don Miguel. *The Four Agreements*. Hay House Inc, 2008.

Sampson, Robert J, and John H Laub. *Crime in the Making: Pathways and Turning Points through Life*. Cambridge, MA, Harvard University Press, 1993.

Sasser, Charles. At Large: The Life and Crimes of Randolph Dial. New York, New York. St. Martin's Paperback. 1998.

Schiraldi, Glenn R. *The Adverse Childhood Experiences Recovery Workbook: Heal the Hidden Wounds from Childhood Affecting Your Adult Mental and Physical Health*. Oakland, CA, New Harbinger Publications, Inc., 2021.

Schiraldi, Glenn R. *The Resilience Workbook*. New Harbinger Publications, November 1, 2017.

Seligman, Martin E P. *Flourish: A Visionary New Understanding of Happiness and Well-Being*. NY, NY, Atria Paperback, 2011.

Shanker, Stuart, and Teresa Barker. *Self-Reg : How to Help Your Child (and You) Break the Stress Cycle and Successfully Engage with Life*. New York, New York, Penguin Books, 2017.

Siegel, Ronald D. *The Mindfulness Solution: Everyday Practices for Everyday Problems*. New York, Guilford Press, 2010.

Sinek, Simon, et al. *Find Your Why: A Practical Guide for Discovering Purpose for You and Your Team*. NY, NY, Portfolio / Penguin, 2017.

Sinek, Simon. *Infinite Game*. S.L., Portfolio Penguin, 2020.

Sinek, Simon. *Start with Why: How Great Leaders Inspire Everyone to Take Action*. NY, NY, Penguin Audio, 2010.

Snyder, C.R. *The Psychology of Hope : You Can Get There from Here*. New York, Free Press, 1994.

Southwick, Steven M, and Dennis Charney. *Resilience : The Science of Mastering Life's Greatest Challenges*. 2nd ed., Cambridge, Cambridge University Press, 2018.

Stanier, Michael Bungay. *The Advice Trap*. 2020.

Szasz, Thomas S. *The Myth of Mental Illness*. 1988.

Tate, Marcia L. *Sit and Get Won't Grow Dendrites*. Corwin Press, June 20, 2012.

Thích-Nhất-Hạnh. *The Miracle of Mindfulness: An Introduction to the Practice of Meditation*. Boston, Mass., Beacon Press, 2013.

Toews, Barb. *Little Book of Restorative Justice for People in Prison*. Simon and Schuster, August 1, 2006.

Umbreit, Alexa W, and Mark S Umbreit. *Pathways to Spirituality and Healing*. 2002.

Umbreit, Mark. *Victim Meets Offender*. Wipf and Stock Publishers, September 14, 2023.

Umbreit, Mark S. *Dancing with the Energy of Conflict and Trauma*. CreateSpace Independent Publishing Platform, June 12, 2013.

Umbreit, Mark S. *The Energy of Forgiveness: Lessons from Those in Restorative Dialogue*. Eugene, Oregon, Cascade Books, 2015.

Umbreit, Mark S. *The Handbook of Victim Offender Mediation*. John Wiley & Sons, February 28, 2002.

United States. Select Committee on Indian Affairs. (1988). H. Con. Res. 331. Retrieved on November 20, 2018, *https://www.senate.gov/reference/resources/pdf/hconres331.pdf*

Van Der Kolk, Bessel. *The Body Keeps the Score: Brain, Mind, and Body in the Healing of Trauma.* NY, NY, Penguin Books, 2015.

Wiens, Kristin. Illustrations of Stressors for the *Five Domains of Self Reg.*

Williamson, Marianne. *A Return to Love :Reflections on the Principles of a Course in Miracles.* London, Thorsons Classics, 2015.

Winfrey, Oprah, and Dr Bruce Perry. *What Happened to You?* Boxtree, April 27, 2021.

Wink, Walter. *Jesus and Nonviolence.* Fortress Press, April 1, 2003.

Wink, Walter. *The Powers That Be.* Harmony, 24 February 24, 2010.

Yoder, Carolyn. *The Little Book of Trauma Healing: When Violence Strikes and Community Security Is Threatened.* NY, NY, Good Books, 2020.

Zehr, Howard. *Changing Lenses: A New Focus for Crime and Justice.* Scottdale, PA, Herald Press, 1990.

Zehr, Howard. *The Little Book of Restorative Justice.* NY, NY, Good Books, 2002.

Zehr, Howard. *Transcending.* Simon and Schuster, October 1, 2001.

a trauma-informed approach to rebuilding the web of relationships harmed by crime

*"If we don't learn to start thinking for ourselves in a way that promotes what is helpful, there's generally someone right around the corner who will try to do it for us in a way that promotes what is harmful."*

~Alexis Franklin Osborn

## About the Author

Alexis Osborn, 46, has spent almost all of his adult life seeking to understand human nature and help human beings shift from disconnection and harm to the true and authentic self. Surrounded by trauma and pain, his research and practice led to the creation of Pathways for LIFE (Living in Full Empathy), the organization behind the Resilience Prison Project.

The Resilience Framework supports Transformative Learning inside correctional environments, offering Hope for true and lasting change for those in custody.

www.ingramcontent.com/pod-product-compliance
Lightning Source LLC
Chambersburg PA
CBHW080433110426
42743CB00016B/3148